Racing

THE TIME-LIFE LIBRARY OF BOATING
HUMAN BEHAVIOR
THE ART OF SEWING
THE OLD WEST
THE EMERGENCE OF MAN
THE AMERICAN WILDERNESS
THE TIME-LIFE ENCYCLOPEDIA OF GARDENING
LIFE LIBRARY OF PHOTOGRAPHY
THIS FABULOUS CENTURY
FOODS OF THE WORLD
TIME-LIFE LIBRARY OF AMERICA
TIME-LIFE LIBRARY OF ART
GREAT AGES OF MAN
LIFE SCIENCE LIBRARY
THE LIFE HISTORY OF THE UNITED STATES
TIME READING PROGRAM
LIFE NATURE LIBRARY
LIFE WORLD LIBRARY
FAMILY LIBRARY:
HOW THINGS WORK IN YOUR HOME
THE TIME-LIFE BOOK OF THE FAMILY CAR
THE TIME-LIFE FAMILY LEGAL GUIDE
THE TIME-LIFE BOOK OF FAMILY FINANCE

Racing

By the Editors of
TIME-LIFE BOOKS

The

TIME-LIFE Library of Boating

TIME-LIFE BOOKS, NEW YORK

First printing.
Published simultaneously in Canada.
Library of Congress catalogue card number 75-34791.

The Cover: Driving hard with all sails set, two 470-class high-performance planing boats churn downwind during a World Championship race at Association Island on Lake Ontario. These fast, tricky one-design craft provide a supreme test of small-boat racing. The numbers on the bows are issued by the race committee for easy identification.

The Consultants: Halsey Herreshoff, navigator for *Courageous* in her successful defense of the America's Cup in 1974, has piloted sailing craft as well as powerboats for 25 years.

Steve Colgate is an Olympic skipper and a well-known author of books on racing and cruising techniques; he also conducts racing seminars at his Offshore Sailing School.

John Rousmaniere, a small-boat sailor and veteran ocean racer, is the West Coast editor of *Yachting* magazine.

Owen C. Torrey Jr. is chief designer of Charles Ulmer, Inc., sailmakers.

Valuable assistance was given by the following departments and individuals of Time Inc.: Editorial Production, Norman Airey; Library, Benjamin Lightman, Lester Annenberg; Picture Collection, Doris O'Neil; Photographic Laboratory, George Karas; TIME-LIFE News Service, Murray J. Gart; Correspondent Maria Vincenza Aloisi (Paris); Tom Ettinger, SPORTS ILLUSTRATED Enterprises.

Contents

6
KC 20

The Special Zest of Racing

The Special Zest of Racing

by Bob Bavier

It wasn't a formal race that first made me aware of the enormous bonuses that racing can add to boating. It was a chance encounter that occurred when I was 10, during a summer cruise from Long Island Sound to Nova Scotia in my father's 66-foot ketch, *Dragoon*. For me the highlight of each day's sailing came when we finally reached port. Then we could launch the dinghy, a lovely 12-footer that normally functioned as a rowboat to take us ashore. But this summer, Dad had fitted her with a centerboard and a simple cat rig, and each afternoon as soon as *Dragoon's* anchor was down, my sister, Marge, and I would be off in the dinghy to explore the harbor. Dad never actually said that the dinghy was my own boat, but I always thought of her that way. When I was aboard her, I felt like a full-fledged sailor and I would not have traded the dinghy for *Dragoon*.

One day, in a spacious Maine harbor whose name escapes me, we encountered another kid in a dinghy of comparable size. "Let's race to that red nun over there and back to this mooring buoy," he shouted.

"Okay," I shouted back bravely, and only slightly less noisily told Marge to shut up when she whispered agitatedly, "But we don't know how to race!" Since the boats were now side by side, our start consisted of broad reaching off toward the buoy. To my dismay, the other boat eased out in front and rounded several lengths ahead of us—largely, I now know, because I had trimmed in our sail too far, reducing our speed significantly.

On the beat back, though I still didn't know what I was doing, we fared a bit better. He stayed ahead for half of this second leg of our informal course by repeatedly tacking just in front of us, keeping us from getting a steady flow of wind—what racers call clear air. But our sail was cut to a better shape for going to windward and we finally edged ahead, tacked for the finish at about the right time and had a two-length lead at the end. I didn't say much, but I felt as though I had won the America's Cup. Moreover, I was hooked for life on racing—and my real education as a sailor had begun.

During the rest of that cruise, Marge and I were constantly challenging other kids to race. Sometimes we won, at first mostly because our boat was inherently faster—which always makes a sailor seem smarter than he really is. Sometimes we lost. But we learned something from almost every race, and we learned the most by figuring out why we lost to kids who were better sailors than we were. We gradually improved at trimming our sails, distributing our weight in the boat and keeping the dinghy on her most efficient sailing lines. We also picked up a few basic—very basic—tactics: keeping between the mark and the other boat when we were ahead; maneuvering to keep our wind clear or to obstruct another boat's wind.

By the end of the summer we had become better racers and, perhaps more important, better boat handlers. Among other things, we had become better at maneuvering in close quarters, at tacking and jibing in difficult circumstances, not just when convenient. In addition, sailing had become a lot more fun. When we were actually engaged in a race, we got the thrill that comes from competing with worthy opponents—and from winning, if only once in a while. And as we sharpened our skills we became aware that increased efficiency is a large part of the joy of sailing. A boat *feels* better if the sails are trimmed correctly and the weight is properly distributed.

Imagine a 35-foot cruising boat on a 25-mile passage with a five-knot wind abaft the beam. A skipper with no racing background is apt to wallow along on a predetermined compass course at a bare one or two knots. But a racing man in the same circumstances will automatically apply the basic competitive rule of sailing into the wind slightly in light air, then bearing off in the puffs. When he sails more directly into the wind, he increases the velocity of the air moving over the boat—the apparent wind. This makes his sails draw

Author Bob Bavier squints up to check the sails on the 54-foot sloop Salty Goose as he eases her to windward during a Southern Ocean Racing Circuit contest. A champion in several one-design classes in his home waters of Long Island Sound, Bavier served as helmsman of the America's Cup victor, Constellation, in 1964. He is the president and publisher of Yachting magazine.

better, raising his speed to three or four knots. His extra speed offsets the added distance and he enjoys a cool breeze in his face. If the wind increases, as it may well do, he can bear off toward his original course while maintaining speed. And if the wind drops, there's always the engine.

In the same way, certain powerboat racing skills translate into expert boat handling. I used to assume that little skill was involved in driving powerboats and that the boat with the best-tuned engine and consequent highest top speed would reach its destination first. Not so. In the dawn of offshore powerboat racing in the early '60s, I had the pleasure of navigating for master helmsman Sam Griffith in the Around Long Island Marathon. Maybe ours was the best-tuned of the several identically powered 31-footers competing. But I soon saw that our speed depended also on the way Sam drove.

In a sizable ocean swell and a 15-knot following wind, Sam kept one hand on the wheel and the other on the throttles of the twin engines. As we went over a sea and started down its back side, he eased off on the throttles briefly, causing the stern to squat while the bow lifted correspondingly, thus preventing us from plowing into the face of the sea ahead. Then he jammed the throttles full ahead, and we surged over the oncoming sea. Meanwhile, our rivals were rooting into these same seas, rattling the teeth of their crews, throwing far more spray than we were and needing more steering to keep from broaching. Our ride was amazingly comfortable, the engines suffered less strain and we kept easing out ahead. Yes, we won—and in the process I learned a lot about powerboat handling.

Unfortunately, the kind of racing I enjoyed with Sam Griffith has evolved to the point where only factory teams or the very well-heeled and very rugged can compete. Unfortunately, too, most other types of formal powerboat races are no place for weekend boatmen. For example, hydroplanes of the type that race in Seattle for the Gold Cup thunder along the straights at 180 miles an hour, demanding consummate nerve and skill—not to mention huge bankrolls—to keep them going.

For the owners of powered pleasure craft in the 24-foot-and-up class, however, there is a challenging and a far more instructive kind of sport called predicted-log competition. In this test of piloting skills, a skipper and a navigator take their boat around a designated course at any speed they choose, and attempt to forecast the exact times at which they will pass each checkpoint on the course. All ship's clocks, speedometers and other time-related instruments must be covered during competition. An official observer, the only person aboard permitted a watch, records their actual times. The winner is the boat with the lowest margin of error, and in a good fleet that margin can be a matter of seconds. Nothing hones a pilot's abilities more effectively than having to calculate his boat's exact speed while underway, using only his engine's rpm's, and at the same time making proper allowances for wind, sea and current—so as to round, say, a specified bell buoy in fog, dark or storm at exactly 17 and one half minutes past four. Most boatmen who have tried it find it both a humbling and an instructive experience.

Virtually all my other racing experience, however, has been in sailboats. There, I have found, racing comes more easily if you begin in a class or a fleet whose boats and level of competition are suited to your abilities. Age has little to do with it. It helps to start young, as I did, but some of today's top sailors started late. Philadelphia lawyer Don Cohan, for example, began in his late thirties and five years later won a medal aboard a Dragon in the 1972 Olympics. And though you must be tough and agile to race some of the smaller, high-performance boats, racing is, in general, a sport that puts more emphasis on mental than on physical abilities. Skills stored up over the years can keep you competitive for a lifetime. Another Olympic competitor, Switzerland's Louis Noverraz, at age 67 won a silver medal in the 5.5-meter class. Any keen, observant sailor can make himself a winner—though perhaps not an Olympic medalist—by starting in one of the less demanding classes and learning in proportion to the losses he is certain to suffer in his first season.

And when he starts winning consistently, he should move up to a class offering more competition and learning opportunities.

The year after my first taste of scrub racing in *Dragoon's* dinghy, I graduated to a Herreshoff Bullseye—a comfortable, seaworthy 15-foot keel sloop, and a fine craft both for acquiring racing skills and for boning up on basic boatmanship. She was unusually sensitive on the helm for a keel boat, maneuvered nicely, and taught me the advantages of delicate, precise steering—especially on windward legs, when you try to head as close to the wind as possible without losing headway. I raced every weekend against five other Bullseyes, skippered by juniors a year or two older than I was. To my initial surprise, I almost always won. It was a good class to start in because it gave me confidence, not to say a certain cockiness. I know now that we did well partly because all the others were inexperienced, but mostly because Dad bought us good sails and introduced Marge and me to the vital concept of maintenance. He made us scrub and wet-sand the Bullseye's bottom regularly to keep it slick and clean, and taught us to keep the boat in good shape generally—absolute musts for racing and excellent training for boating of any kind.

After a couple of years, Dad bought an Atlantic-class sloop and I soon learned I wasn't all that hot. Our first season we were usually well down in the fleet as a result of some typical novice's mistake: being in the wrong place to take advantage of obvious wind shifts; being buried among other boats at the start; heeling too much in heavy air. We watched the better sailors, however, and noticed that they headed toward shifts, maneuvered to ensure clear air at the start and feathered their boats—luffing the mainsail in heavy air when going to windward to keep from burying the leeward rail. I also had to learn how to get a spinnaker up properly and how to trim it to take best advantage of the wind. But by copying our conquerors, we started moving up in the standings and finally—to my great elation—we won a race in this good class. In our third year we took the season championship and Dad concluded that it was time for us to move on.

Our next class, the 33′5″ International One Design, marked the end of any possibility of going stale by winning too often. I've never had that problem since. It was a class crammed with hotshot skippers against whom I was never consistent enough to win the season championship, though in our third season we did manage to win more races than anyone else. Sailing in such keen competition was not only tremendous fun but enormously educational. Bill Luders, a noted yacht designer who is equally adept at sailing everything from small boats to ocean racers, gave me a valuable lesson one day on sailing in light and fluky airs. He seemed to smell where the wind was coming from, kept working into headers—wind shifts—which allowed him to come about and head higher on the other tack. He won going away. Following him on a similar course, I did poorly, not realizing until later that by blindly following someone else in fluky air you take a double risk. By the time you reach the spot where he got his advantage, conditions will have changed. Moreover, by not patterning your course on what you yourself see, and failing to tack into your own headers, you miss vital chances to gain advantages—a lesson in alert and self-confident analysis that applies to both racers and day sailors.

Each one of these discoveries brings with it a special satisfaction. In the learning process there is no substitute for honest, objective appraisal. Here, too, my father provided superb guidance. Most helpful was his habit of asking me to tell him after a race I had skippered why we had won or lost. Bad luck was the one excuse for losing that he never accepted. And I came to learn that, in racing, one's own actions usually contribute heavily to luck, good or bad. For example, he would suggest that I could have foreseen that "bad luck" wind shift by noting a darker line of wind on the water ahead, by watching the angle of other boats in a class ahead or by the direction of smoke from a stack on shore. Years later when I was sailing *Constellation* in the 1964 America's Cup trials and in the subsequent, successful challenge match against Britain's *Sovereign,* skippered by Peter Scott, we held a postmortem on each day's racing. Despite sailing at the highest level of competition, we were still making mistakes; but our ability to recognize those mistakes and to learn from them finally reduced them to a minimum.

Along with the sense of fulfillment that comes from mastering his boat, a competing skipper can also savor the spicy pleasure that comes with a mastery of racing tactics. This knowledge, too, is often best learned from an opponent. That grand old master of Long Island Sound, Cornelius Shields, is a wizard in anything from frostbite dinghies to 12-meters, and he taught me a lot about starting tactics the year I entered the International class. Good starts were vital because of the difficulty of trying to work up through a keen fleet that is making few mistakes. Corny's daring and his fine sense of timing made him murderously effective at the start, especially as he wasn't above using intimidation. And trying to beat him was marvelous practice.

One day Corny was abeam of us approaching the starting line, and it appeared that one of us would get a perfect start. He was to weather, closest to the committee boat that marked one end of the line; we were slightly to leeward, and there was no room for both of us to squeeze past at the same time. Corny shouted to me for room. I was a novice of 18 and he was a distinguished sailor more than twice my age, but he knew as well as I did that, under the rules, he was in a so-called barging situation and therefore was not entitled to room to cross the starting line.

"Corny," I shouted back, "I'm going to take you right through the committee boat!" Corny immediately killed way and fell in astern of us; I got my first top start in that hot class and Corny never tried that bluff on me again. He did continue for years to get better starts than I did, but by copying him I eventually became nearly as good.

There are two other aspects of racing that I feel are especially critical. One is that, although practice may be beneficial in such areas as sail changing, nothing increases proficiency like live competition—as has been shown by the effects of competition on the defenders of the America's Cup. The Cup is defended by an American boat, in response to a challenge from a foreign vessel. Until recently, the challenger has had only a few preparatory brushes with trial-horse boats before facing the defender—which has had to survive three months of eliminations involving four boats and more than 30 races. Under the spur of their more intensive intramural competition, Americans have learned far more than their challengers about the design and structural materials of boats, sails and fittings, have become expert in interpreting local winds and currents, and have mastered the best ways to sail their boats in various conditions. Crew coordination has been brought to concert pitch—along with the skipper's ability to anticipate and to choose the right moment and method for taking an educated risk. The result has been superior boats sailed by better-prepared crews, and 22 straight United States victories in a series extending well over a century.

The second key factor I always try to keep in mind is that to do well in racing and to learn the most about boat handling from it, you must enjoy yourself. The skipper and crew who are having fun will do better than those who are so uptight that they can no longer think straight. Throughout the 1964 America's Cup trials to select a defender, despite extremely close races against *American Eagle,* I kept having fun, kept loose, sailed *Constellation* to the best of my ability, and won. Ten years later when I was skipper of *Courageous,* we started the summer slower than our leading rival, *Intrepid,* but we were relaxed and aggressive, and won as many races as she did. By the time of the final trials in August, *Courageous* was as fast as *Intrepid,* perhaps faster, but by then I was as tight as a jib sheet in a gale and sailing less well in consequence. With the score tied 4-4 in the final trials, Ted Hood took over and skippered *Courageous* to the deciding victory. Perhaps I could have won that race, perhaps not. In any case, I relearned a lesson I thought I had mastered in more than 40 years of racing: try hard, think hard, but to do your best in boat racing never forget to have fun.

2097

1

If there were to be such a thing as a perfect sailing race, all the boats would have to be of identical design so that victory would be achieved through the skill of the skipper, rather than the brilliance of the naval architect who designed the hull—or the bankroll of the yacht owner who ordered it built. Traditionally, this ideal has been all but unachievable in ocean racing, where almost every boat is either custom-built or custom-altered. But in the bustling, contentious world of one-design racing, which embraces an estimated 90 per cent of all regattas held in the United States, every contest goes off under conditions that are as fair and equal as meticulous craftsmanship and restrictive rules can make

ONE-DESIGN: A GREAT EQUALIZER

them. All the boats in a given race are of one design, virtually identical in length, weight and all other significant respects.

Though the boats in each race are the same, one-design skippers are under no lifetime sentence to sail forever in the same vessel. There are, in fact, over 200 different classes now active in local or regional competition around the country. While most of these boats are small, open-cockpit 10- to 25-footers, they vary enormously from class to class in hull type, rig, boat speed, handling qualities—and in the demands they place on the skill and energy of skipper and crew. The prospective racing captain can choose, for example, between an easy-to-sail but relatively slow-moving pram like the one described on page 16, or a tricky, high-performance planing boat like the Finn *(page 17)*, designed for international Olympic matches and requiring quick judgments, artful sail handling and constant hiking out. Between these two performance extremes lies a broad and variegated spectrum of racing craft —cat-rigged dinghies such as Penguins and Optimists, two- or three-man centerboard sloops like Thistles and Lightnings, fast-footing scows and catamarans, and trim keelboats such as the Rhodes 19, a stable and forgiving craft that can double as both a racer and a family picnic boat.

Competition among each type of boat is regulated by a national governing body, or class association, whose principal aim is to promote well-organized, fairly run racing, and to keep the design standardized. The association enforces rules detailing the weight, dimensions, construction material, sails, rig and other specifications of its particular boat; it also lists auxiliary equipment, such as hiking straps, that a skipper may or may not use. In some classes, such as Flying Juniors *(page 18)*, a minor variation in rig and cut of sails is permitted, while in others, like the Laser, the position and type of each fitting are rigidly prescribed.

When choosing between the various classes, a skipper should first find out what local boatmen race; there is little point in owning a racing vessel, no matter how lovely, if the nearest rival is 200 miles away. Races in any given area are generally organized by racing associations or yacht clubs, and membership in one of these groups provides the best entree into regularly scheduled competition. Before buying a boat of his own, a prospective skipper may want to spend a season crewing at the local yacht club for a friend—an approach that not only introduces him to the characteristics of a particular class, but also allows him to bone up on his own racing techniques.

When the boatman finally does make a purchase, he should register with the national association; the supervising body will issue his boat a sail number, and will frequently send him booklets and newsletters updating class regulations and reporting on regattas and other class events. Then he begins the challenging adventure of working his way through the competition along a route that can lead to a club championship, a regional or even a national title —and hundreds of afternoons of plain, good fun.

Passing one another in the course of three simultaneous but separate contests, Lasers, Sunfish and Ensigns compete against their own kind in a regatta on Lake Dillon, Colorado.

Board Boats

A tightly packed fleet sweeps downwind at the Sunfish Nationals in Biscayne Bay, Florida. With more than 150,000 craft in commission, the Sunfish is the world's largest one-design class. It is also the most popular of all board boats—so called because their hulls are basically oversized surfboards equipped with mast, sail and centerboard. The Sunfish also has a small cockpit well. Light, quick and simple to manage, it has a lateen-rigged sail on a demountable mast; at day's end the whole rig comes out for stowage. Though raced as a single-hander, it can carry a passenger for day sailing.

Sunfish

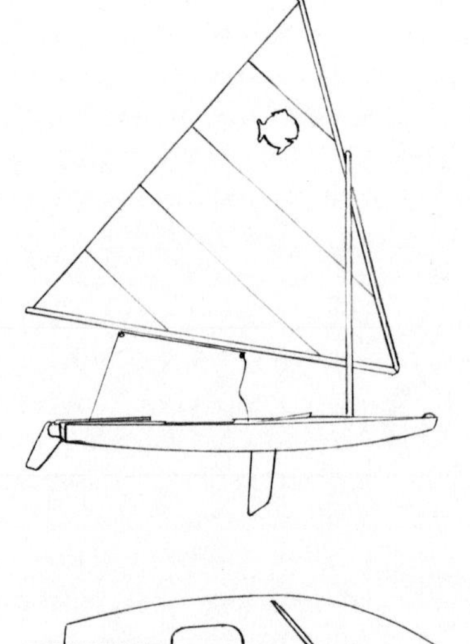

Length overall:	13'10"
Length waterline:	13'10"
Beam:	4'½"
Draft, board up:	3"
Draft, board down:	2'8"
Sail area:	75 sq. ft.
Spinnaker area:	none
Racing crew:	1
Hiking gear:	none
Construction material:	fiberglass
Hull weight:	139 lbs.
Year designed:	1952
Boats in commission:	150,000
Transportability:	cartop or trailer
Similar classes:	Minifish, Butterfly

Jockeying for position, a group of Lasers rounds the windward mark off Norwalk, Connecticut. A new and rapidly growing class in the U.S., Canada and Europe, the Laser is faster than the Sunfish and other board boats of comparable size. Its tall Marconi mainsail drives it to windward more efficiently than the Sunfish's lateen rig; but in a breeze the boat requires a 150-pound-plus skipper, hiked well out, to hold it down. For lighter sailors —and for easier handling in strong winds—a shorter mainsail is available. Like the Sunfish, the Laser's unstayed mast is demountable for trailering or cartopping at day's end.

Laser

Length overall:	13′10½″
Length waterline:	12′6″
Beam:	4′6″
Draft, board up:	6″
Draft, board down:	2′8″
Sail area:	76 sq. ft.
Spinnaker area:	none
Racing crew:	1
Hiking gear:	straps
Construction material:	fiberglass
Hull weight:	130 lbs.
Year designed:	1971
Boats in commission:	35,000
Transportability:	cartop or trailer
Similar classes:	Force 5, Banshee, Cyclone

Full-Hull Single-Handers

El Toro

Length overall:	14′9″
Length waterline:	14′
Beam:	4′10″
Draft, board up:	6″
Draft, board down:	2′3″
Sail area:	115 sq. ft.
Spinnaker area:	none
Racing crew:	1
Hiking gear:	straps
Construction material:	wood or fiberglass
Hull weight:	278 lbs.
Year designed:	1952
Boats in commission:	5,000
Transportability:	cartop or trailer
Similar classes:	OK Dinghy

The smallest of one-man displacement boats are sailing dinghies—like the pair of El Toros below, gliding along on Central Lake, California. Essentially a rowboat with rudder and centerboard added, the El Toro has a squared-off bow, a short, boxy hull and a tiny sail. Thus, despite its light weight, it seldom capsizes, making it an ideal craft for a youngster just starting out, or for an adult who wants to play at racing on the smallest scale. The El Toro's simple lines also lend themselves to home construction, and in fact, many El Toro owners have built their own boats and raced them to victory.

ERRATUM

Your volume of *Racing* includes photographs and line drawings on pages 16 and 17 for two craft called the El Toro and the Finn. The specification lists accompanying the drawings were inadvertently transposed. The correct statistics for the El Toro are found in the box at the bottom of page 17, and for the Finn at the top of page 16.

The Editors

A fleet of Finns crowds across the starting line at Lake Huntington, California. These high-performance craft represent perhaps the ultimate one-man racing-dinghy design. Developed as a new class for the 1952 Olympics in Finland, the boat carries a 115-square-foot mainsail on an unstayed mast that bends slightly with the wind, thus efficiently flattening the sail in heavy air. Like many other high-performance racers, the Finn needs a heavy, strong, athletic skipper who can hike out for as much as two thirds of the race to keep the boat upright and moving.

Finn

Length overall:	8′
Length waterline:	7′
Beam:	3′10″
Draft, board up:	3″
Draft, board down:	22″
Sail area:	40 sq. ft.
Spinnaker area:	none
Racing crew:	1
Hiking gear:	none
Construction material:	wood or fiberglass
Hull weight:	60 lbs.
Year designed:	1940
Boats in commission:	9,000
Transportability:	cartop
Similar classes:	Sabot, Optimist

Basic Crew Boats

With brightly patterned spinnakers trimmed for a beam reach, Flying Juniors move smartly along Lake Charlevoix, Michigan. Like most boats with headsails, these craft require a minimum crew of two: one person at the tiller and mainsheet, the other to tend the jib and spinnaker (in the diagram at right, the spinnaker pole, sheet and guy are not shown for simplicity). The Flying Junior is an ideal trainer in the teamwork necessary for a headsail rig. In addition, class rules permit enough flexibility in deck layout, mast position and sheet arrangements to give the skipper practice in fine-tuning his rig.

Flying Junior

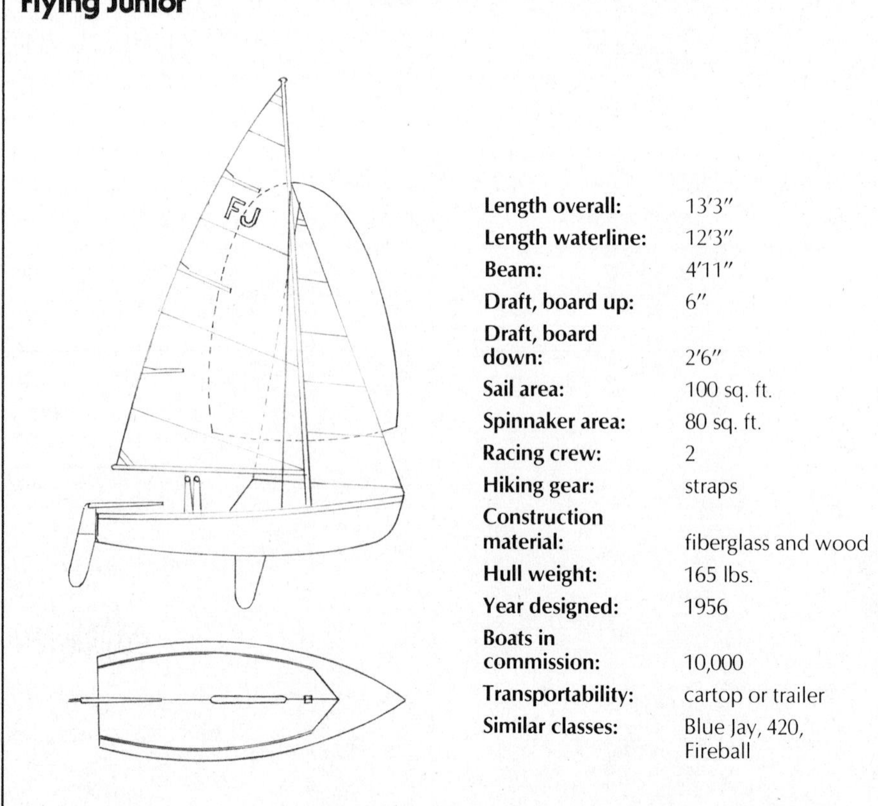

Length overall:	13'3"
Length waterline:	12'3"
Beam:	4'11"
Draft, board up:	6"
Draft, board down:	2'6"
Sail area:	100 sq. ft.
Spinnaker area:	80 sq. ft.
Racing crew:	2
Hiking gear:	straps
Construction material:	fiberglass and wood
Hull weight:	165 lbs.
Year designed:	1956
Boats in commission:	10,000
Transportability:	cartop or trailer
Similar classes:	Blue Jay, 420, Fireball

Thistle

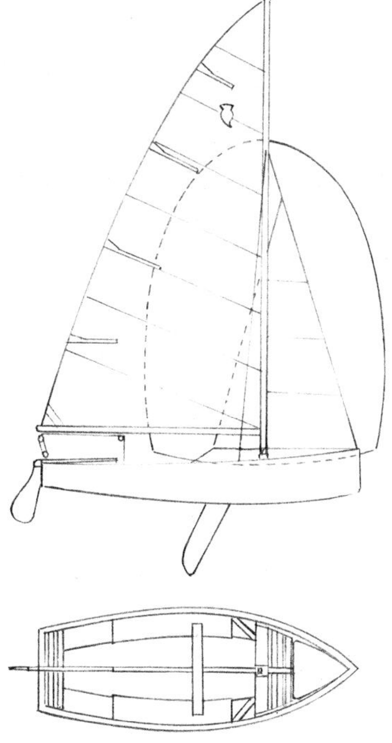

Length overall:	17′
Length waterline:	17′
Beam:	6′
Draft, board up:	9″
Draft, board down:	4′6″
Sail area:	75 sq. ft.
Spinnaker area:	125 sq. ft.
Racing crew:	3
Hiking gear:	straps
Construction material:	wood or fiberglass
Hull weight:	500 lbs.
Year designed:	1945
Boats in commission:	3,500
Transportability:	trailer
Similar classes:	Lightning, Flying Scot, Highlander, 470

Thistles with three-man racing crews round a windward mark on Lake Erie during a national championship regatta. A faster, trickier boat than the Flying Juniors on the opposite page, the Thistle needs the extra crew member to handle the 125-square-foot spinnaker, and to provide added ballast for efficient sailing on windward legs. Despite an old-fashioned hull design—plumb bow, full bilges and open cockpit—the Thistle's nearly flat stern lets it plane in winds of 12 knots or more.

High-Speed Hulls

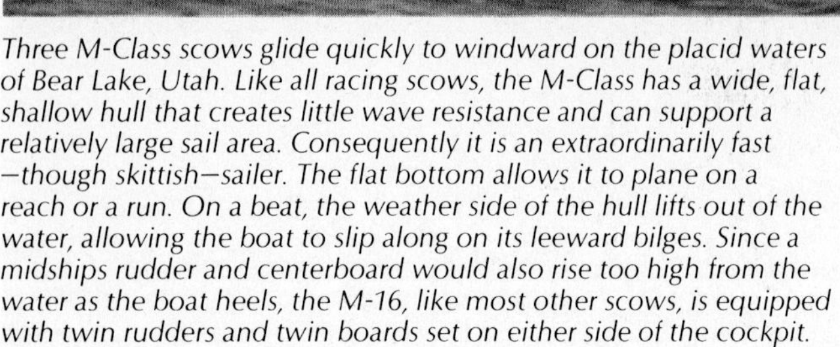

Three M-Class scows glide quickly to windward on the placid waters of Bear Lake, Utah. Like all racing scows, the M-Class has a wide, flat, shallow hull that creates little wave resistance and can support a relatively large sail area. Consequently it is an extraordinarily fast —though skittish—sailer. The flat bottom allows it to plane on a reach or a run. On a beat, the weather side of the hull lifts out of the water, allowing the boat to slip along on its leeward bilges. Since a midships rudder and centerboard would also rise too high from the water as the boat heels, the M-16, like most other scows, is equipped with twin rudders and twin boards set on either side of the cockpit.

M-Class Scow

Length overall:	16′
Length waterline:	10′
Beam:	5′8″
Draft, board up:	2″
Draft, board down:	3′
Sail area:	150 sq. ft.
Spinnaker area:	none
Racing crew:	2
Hiking gear:	straps
Construction material:	wood or fiberglass
Hull weight:	440 lbs.
Year designed:	1952
Boats in commission:	2,500
Transportability:	trailer
Similar classes:	C-Class Scow, M-20

Hobie 16

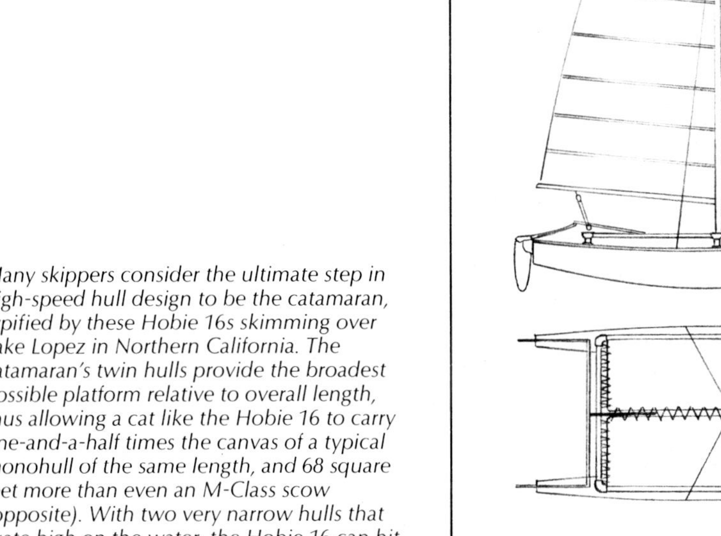

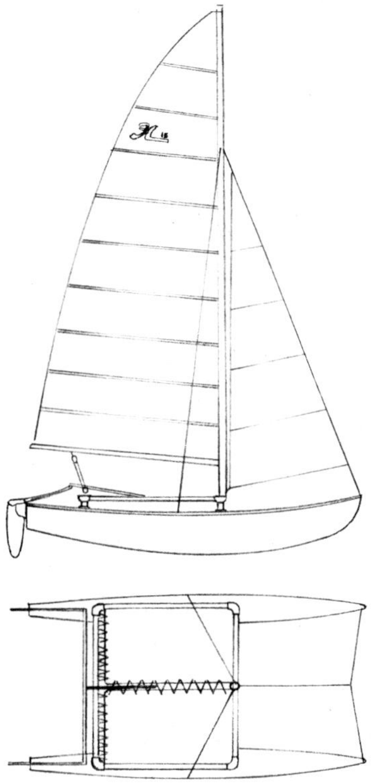

Length overall:	16′7″
Length waterline:	15′9″
Beam:	7′11″
Draft:	10″
Sail area:	218 sq. ft.
Spinnaker area:	none
Racing crew:	2
Hiking gear:	trapeze and straps
Construction material:	fiberglass
Hull weight:	350 lbs.
Year designed:	1970
Boats in commission:	18,000
Transportability:	trailer
Similar classes:	Sol Cat, Alpha Cat, Tornado

Many skippers consider the ultimate step in high-speed hull design to be the catamaran, typified by these Hobie 16s skimming over Lake Lopez in Northern California. The catamaran's twin hulls provide the broadest possible platform relative to overall length, thus allowing a cat like the Hobie 16 to carry one-and-a-half times the canvas of a typical monohull of the same length, and 68 square feet more than even an M-Class scow (opposite). With two very narrow hulls that skate high on the water, the Hobie 16 can hit speeds as high as 25 mph in a good breeze.

Keelboats

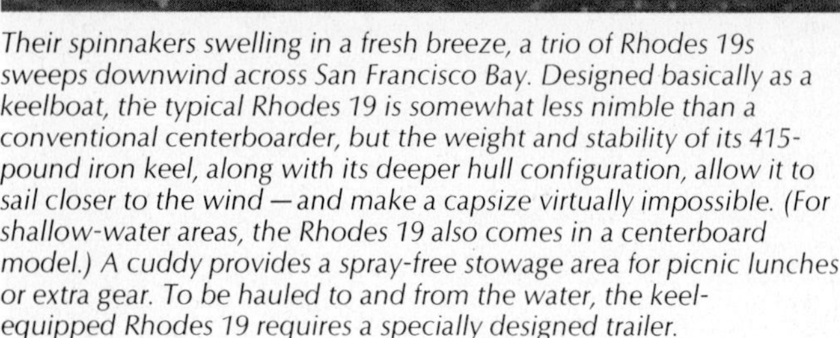

Their spinnakers swelling in a fresh breeze, a trio of Rhodes 19s sweeps downwind across San Francisco Bay. Designed basically as a keelboat, the typical Rhodes 19 is somewhat less nimble than a conventional centerboarder, but the weight and stability of its 415-pound iron keel, along with its deeper hull configuration, allow it to sail closer to the wind—and make a capsize virtually impossible. (For shallow-water areas, the Rhodes 19 also comes in a centerboard model.) A cuddy provides a spray-free stowage area for picnic lunches or extra gear. To be hauled to and from the water, the keel-equipped Rhodes 19 requires a specially designed trailer.

Rhodes 19

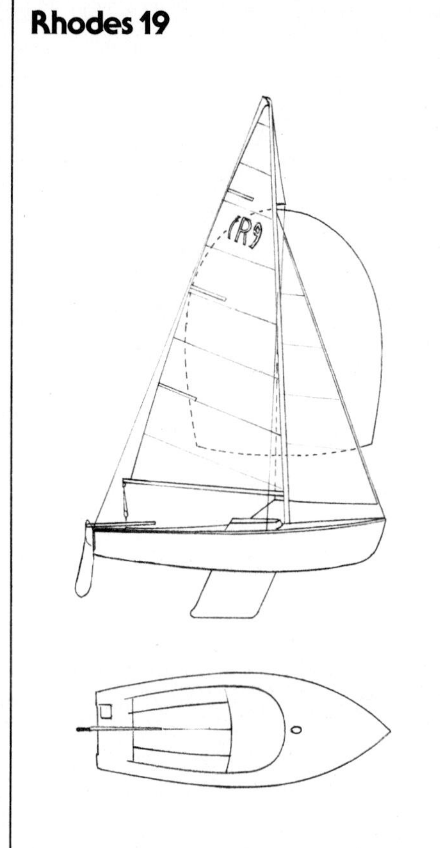

Length overall:	19′2″
Length waterline:	17′9″
Beam:	7′
Draft:	3′3″
Sail area:	175 sq. ft.
Spinnaker area:	155 sq. ft.
Racing crew:	2 or 3
Hiking gear:	none
Construction material:	fiberglass
Hull weight:	1,355 lbs.
Year designed:	1959
Boats in commission:	2,500
Transportability:	custom trailer
Similar classes:	Ensign, Soling, Yngling

Etchells 22

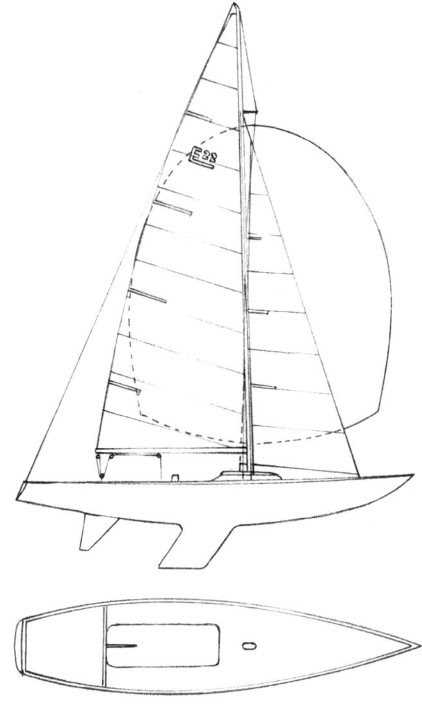

Length overall:	30′6″
Length waterline:	22′
Beam:	6′11½″
Draft:	4′6″
Sail area:	291 sq. ft.
Spinnaker area:	400 sq. ft.
Racing crew:	3
Hiking gear:	none
Construction material:	fiberglass
Hull weight:	3,400 lbs.
Year designed:	1966
Boats in commission:	250
Transportability:	custom trailer
Similar classes:	Shields, International One-Design, Herreshoff S Boat, Atlantic

A cluster of Etchells 22s noses toward the starting line in a race on Long Island Sound. The Etchells carries a thin, deep keel called a fin, which makes the boat very responsive going to windward and allows it to plane in a heavy blow. Because of the fin keel, this brisk performance requires no hiking out. In fact, class rules forbid trapezes or other hiking assists, enabling older skippers to stay competitive with athletic youngsters in a fast and lively class. Though it is a comparatively new design, the Etchells class is expected to expand rapidly and perhaps dominate the field of larger day-racing-class boats.

2

SECRETS OF FASTER SAILING

Sailboat races are not often thought of as spectacles of speed—for good reason. The fastest sailboat in the world can barely go as fast as a person can run; most racing sailboats proceed at a pace equivalent to a brisk walk. Given these limitations, the slightest increase in boat speed is enormously important to the outcome of a race. If, for example, two boats of identical design equipped with equally good sails and skippered by equally competent sailors raced for 10 miles, but one had two weeks' growth of algae on its bottom—enough to slow it a mere one eighth of a knot—the well-scrubbed boat would lead by a quarter of a mile at the finish. A host of other more subtle influences, such as improper sail shape and heeling angle, also cause fractional but important changes in performance—particularly in light air where even a slight adjustment in the luff of a mainsail can give one boat an edge over another. (In winds of 13 to 15 knots or more, in which a boat is likely to be already traveling near its top potential speed, the effect of these factors is reduced—though still significant.) Perhaps the least understood of all the elements affecting a boat's performance is stall—that is, the loss of smooth flow of wind over sails or of water over the hull. When this happens, the boat slows dramatically, and a skipper who wants to win must know not only how to prevent stall but also how to correct it. For even the best-designed racing machine must be coaxed and coddled like a purebred show horse if it is to take best advantage of wind and sea conditions.

Preparation begins even before a boat is put in the water for the opening of the season; while the vessel is still in the boatyard its bottom is scraped, sanded, painted and polished to ensure a smooth finish with minimal drag. Particular attention must be given to smoothing the leading edges of the keel or centerboard, where friction and turbulence can be especially costly. After launching, the mast must be stepped and adjusted with great care, and the rigging tuned *(page 34)* to provide the best aerodynamic shape for the sails.

On race day, the bottom of any class boat is almost invariably rechecked for smoothness. The skipper then judges the prevailing wind velocity, and as he bends on the sails he modifies their shape accordingly *(pages 36-39)*. He also inspects his lines and fittings to be sure none of them has become stretched, bent, weakened or frayed enough to influence the boat's performance—or to cause a breakdown during the race.

Even after the race has started, continual adjustments must be made—or at least considered. The most familiar, of course, is trimming the sails. But other changes, such as redistributing crew weight for different wind velocities and points of sail, and slight corrections in sail shape during a tack, can be equally important and almost as frequent.

The nature of these adjustments, particularly on sails, varies widely, not only from one moment of a race to another but also from one racing class to another. A Laser, for example, has no spinnaker and no jib, and its skipper would probably wind up in the water if he tried to reshape the mainsail while underway. On the other hand, the Etchells 22 at left has more than 18 sail-handling devices, and its crew can make as many as nine changes to compensate for an unexpected change in the strength of the wind. Yet ultimately these adjustments, however differently they may be made, influence the performance of all sailboats in basically similar ways. For example, proper sail shape and angle of heel affect a Sunfish exactly as they do an America's Cup contender. The basic physical principles that underlie these adjustments—as well as their applications—are provided on the following pages to illuminate a whole gallery of boat-speed improvements.

The constant challenge—and frustration—of adjusting to the elements is revealed in this picture of a well-tuned Etchells 22 whose mainsail is bellied too far out as the wind picks up.

True and Apparent Winds

Every sailor has noticed that a stiff breeze seems to die abruptly when a boat changes its heading from a beat to a run. This phenomenon is rooted in a subtle relationship between two sorts of wind—the natural, or true, wind that blows across the race course and the wind created by the boat's own motion (equivalent to the breeze felt by a bicyclist as he pedals along on a windless day). The two winds combine to form a third, known as the apparent wind because it is the only wind that can be sensed aboard a boat. But its role is far more than a matter of appearances. This third, blended breeze—usually either weaker or stronger than the true wind—is the force that drives the boat.

Just as the strength of the apparent wind can differ markedly from the true wind, so may its direction. And in this respect too it is only the apparent wind that matters. On any given point of sail—a beat, close reach, beam reach, broad reach, or run—a vessel's sails are always trimmed to meet the apparent wind rather than the true.

As shown by the diagrams at right, the speed and angle of the apparent wind vary according to the velocity and direction of its two component winds. For example, if the speed of the true wind picks up when a boat is going to windward, the speed of the apparent wind rises and its direction shifts as well, moving farther aft and permitting the boat to point higher *(page 105)*. Conversely, if the speed of the true wind stays constant but its angle to the boat moves aft—either because of a wind shift or because the skipper changes his heading—the apparent-wind speed will drop *(bottom right)*.

Due partly to the workings of the apparent wind and partly to the aerodynamic behavior of sails *(pages 28-31)*, a boat's performance is markedly affected by the heading it takes relative to the actual wind. The performances analyzed on these pages have been standardized for clarity and emphasis. Actual sailing conditions often produce varying figures.

All boats go much faster on a reach than on a beat or run. And planing boats or catamarans can far exceed the norm on certain sailing angles. When the true wind comes from an angle that would place most boats on a reach, these craft go so fast that the apparent wind swings well forward—and the sails must be trimmed for a beat. In addition, a catamaran generates such a hefty apparent breeze that its ultimate speed will often exceed that of the true wind across the race course.

Apparent wind is always stronger than the true wind when a boat sails close-hauled, a fact illustrated at right with vectors —directional arrows whose length indicates wind speed. On a heading 43° to the direction of a 10-knot true wind, a prototypical racing boat creates a 5.4-knot breeze by its motion, and the two winds combine to yield a 14.5-knot apparent wind, nearly the sum of the two speeds. The blending process also shifts the apparent wind forward of the true wind, so the boat sails within 28° of its actual power source.

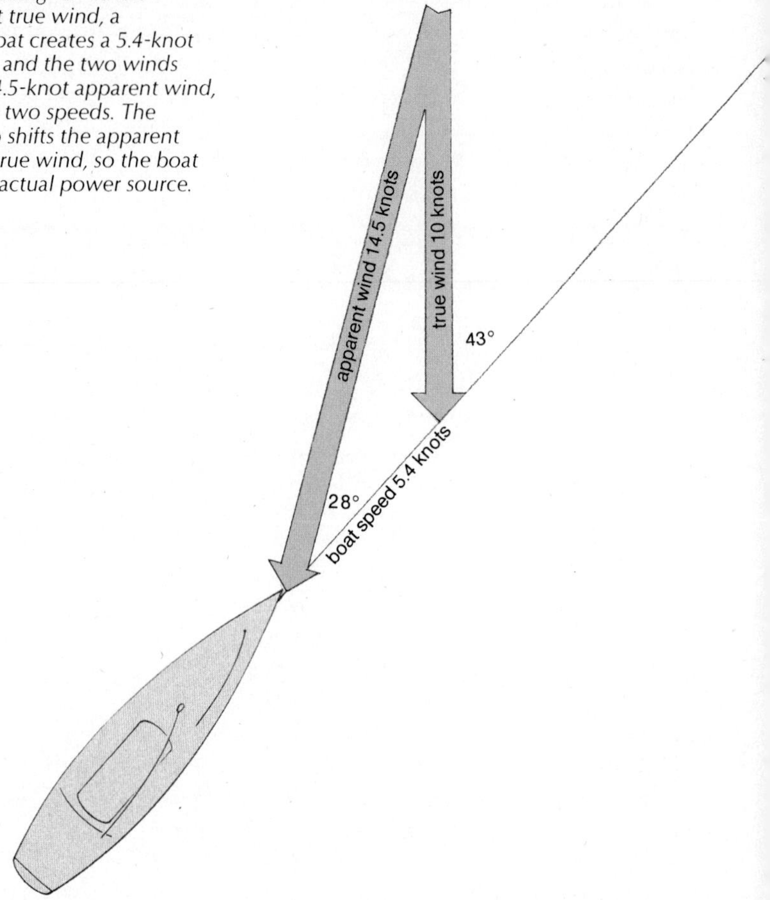

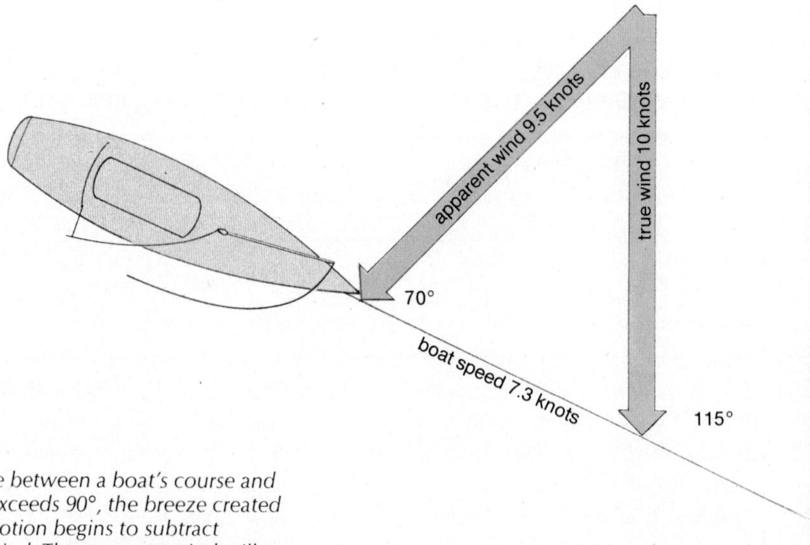

When the angle between a boat's course and the true wind exceeds 90°, the breeze created by the boat's motion begins to subtract from the true wind. The apparent wind will thus be weaker than the true—although only a half knot less in the case of the boat above, heading at 115° to the true wind. However, the boat goes faster than when sailing close-hauled in an equally strong breeze, since there is more propulsive force.

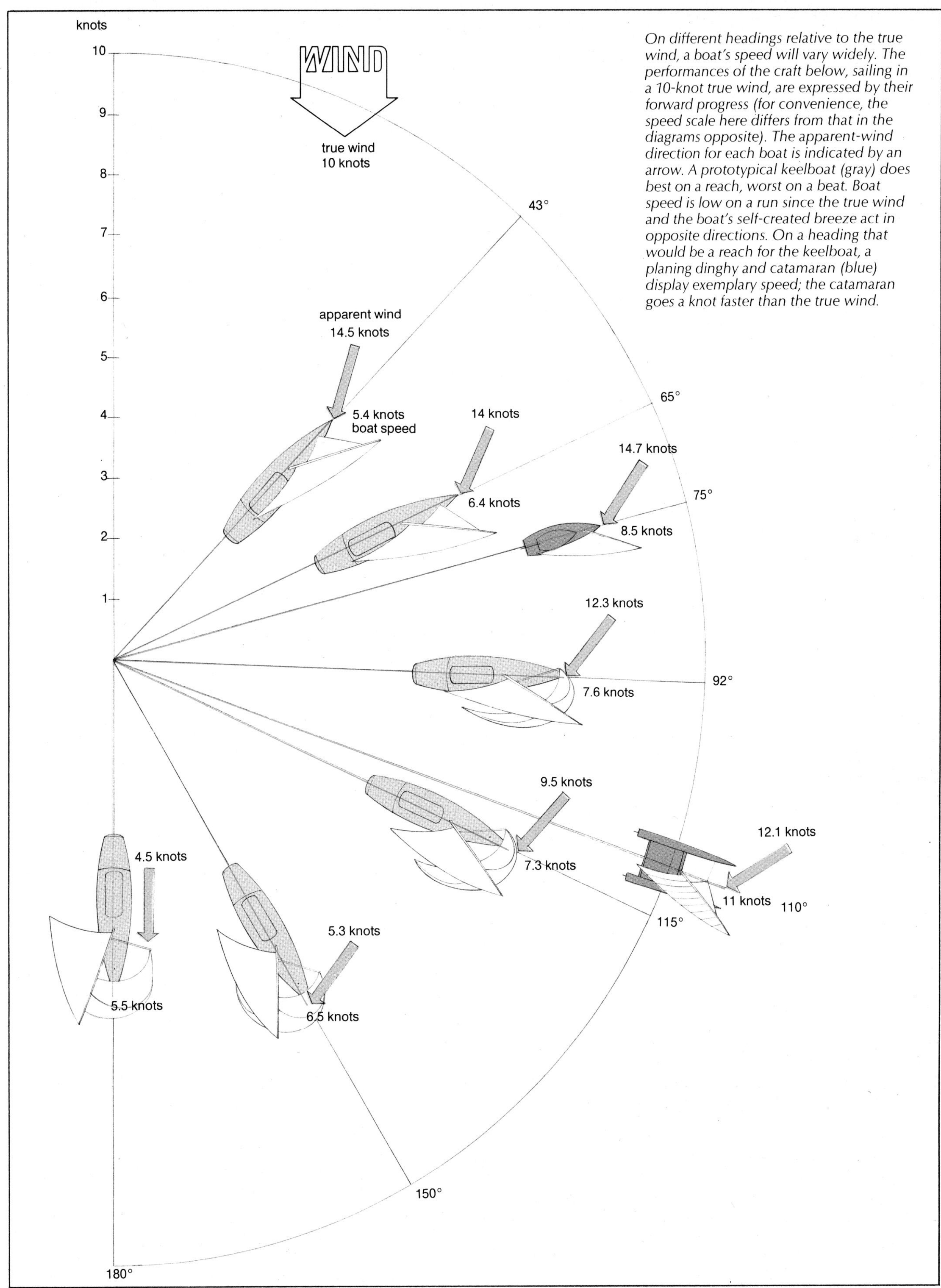

On different headings relative to the true wind, a boat's speed will vary widely. The performances of the craft below, sailing in a 10-knot true wind, are expressed by their forward progress (for convenience, the speed scale here differs from that in the diagrams opposite). The apparent-wind direction for each boat is indicated by an arrow. A prototypical keelboat (gray) does best on a reach, worst on a beat. Boat speed is low on a run since the true wind and the boat's self-created breeze act in opposite directions. On a heading that would be a reach for the keelboat, a planing dinghy and catamaran (blue) display exemplary speed; the catamaran goes a knot faster than the true wind.

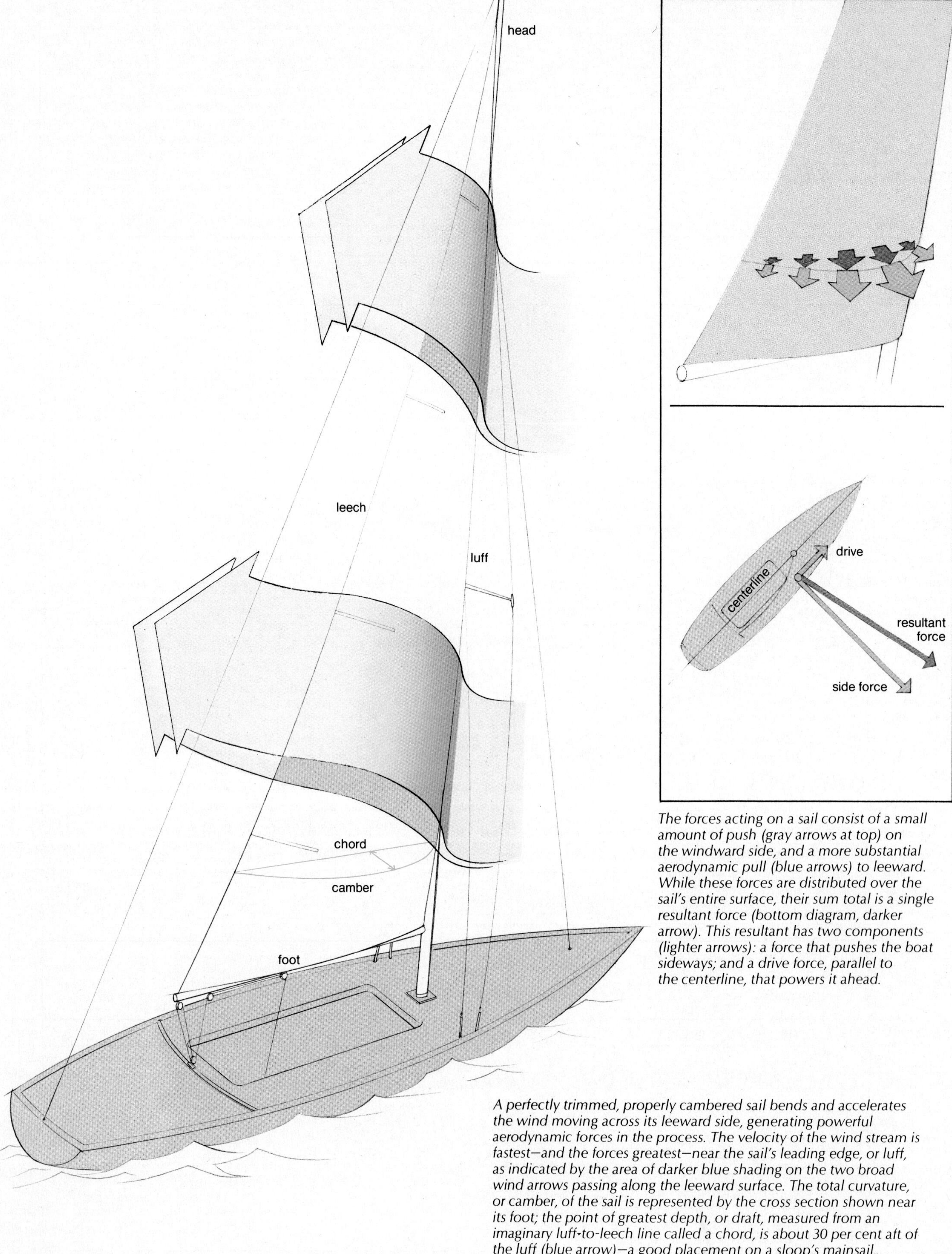

The forces acting on a sail consist of a small amount of push (gray arrows at top) on the windward side, and a more substantial aerodynamic pull (blue arrows) to leeward. While these forces are distributed over the sail's entire surface, their sum total is a single resultant force (bottom diagram, darker arrow). This resultant has two components (lighter arrows): a force that pushes the boat sideways; and a drive force, parallel to the centerline, that powers it ahead.

A perfectly trimmed, properly cambered sail bends and accelerates the wind moving across its leeward side, generating powerful aerodynamic forces in the process. The velocity of the wind stream is fastest—and the forces greatest—near the sail's leading edge, or luff, as indicated by the area of darker blue shading on the two broad wind arrows passing along the leeward surface. The total curvature, or camber, of the sail is represented by the cross section shown near its foot; the point of greatest depth, or draft, measured from an imaginary luff-to-leech line called a chord, is about 30 per cent aft of the luff (blue arrow)—a good placement on a sloop's mainsail.

Forces of Wind Flow

Of all the factors that affect a boat's speed, none is more basic than the efficiency with which its sails extract energy from the wind. For a boat headed downwind, most of this energy comes from a straightforward push against the sailcloth *(page 30)*. But on other headings, as illustrated on these two pages, a far greater proportion of the sail's drive comes from an aerodynamic pull on its leeward side.

A sail can generate this aerodynamic pull only if it meets two key criteria: it must be trimmed to the wind at the proper angle, or incidence; and it must have the correct shape, technically known as camber, and the right amount of fullness, called draft. These two considerations work together to bend the wind stream so that it flows past the sail in a smooth, curvilinear path *(opposite, left)*. As the wind stream changes direction, the portion traveling along the sail's leeward side speeds up. As its velocity increases, pressure drops—creating a pulling effect that even on a small boat amounts to hundreds of pounds of force.

For maximum aerodynamic force, the ideal sail angle is about 30° to the apparent wind, no matter what the boat's heading; thus, if a skipper changes course, he must alter the trim of his sails to maintain a correct angle. The function of the sail's camber is more complex. A sail must be given a fullness that bends the wind as much as possible, but not so much that the airstream breaks away, wasting power and slowing the boat. Since the proper degree of camber depends on the strength of the wind *(pages 36-37)*, there are a number of devices for altering a sail's shape as wind conditions change *(pages 32-33)*.

While some of the most efficient racing boats carry a single sail, the aerodynamic pulling power of any one sail increases when it is coupled with another. A jib improves the mainsail's performance by smoothing the airflow on its lee side. Also, because the wind must go a greater distance to pass around the added sail —picking up more speed en route—the jib contributes even more pull per square foot than does the main.

On a beat, a boat's main and jib are close-hauled at the proper angle to the apparent wind to extract a maximum amount of aerodynamic power. The jib channels air along the lee surface of the main while receiving a plentiful airflow of its own. But as the setting on this heading angles the sails in close to the boat's centerline, their combined resultant force (below) acts predominantly to the side, making the boat heel and leaving only a small proportion of the force as drive to urge it forward.

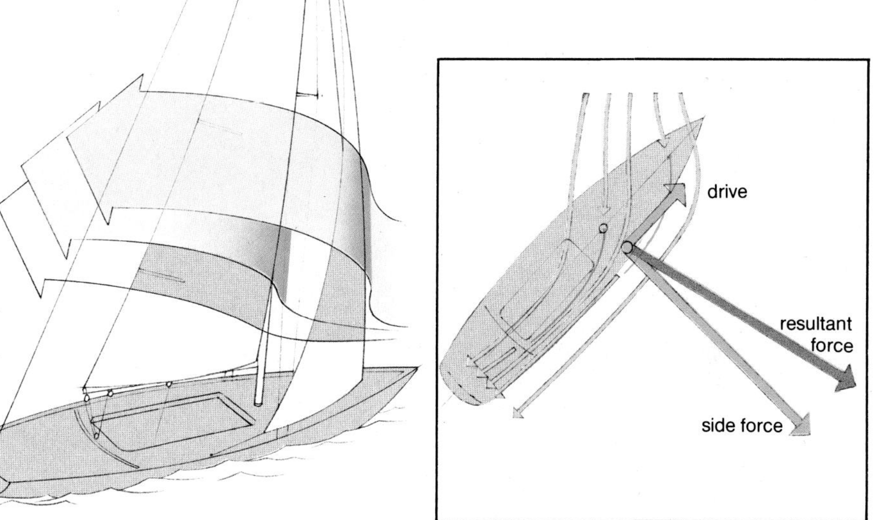

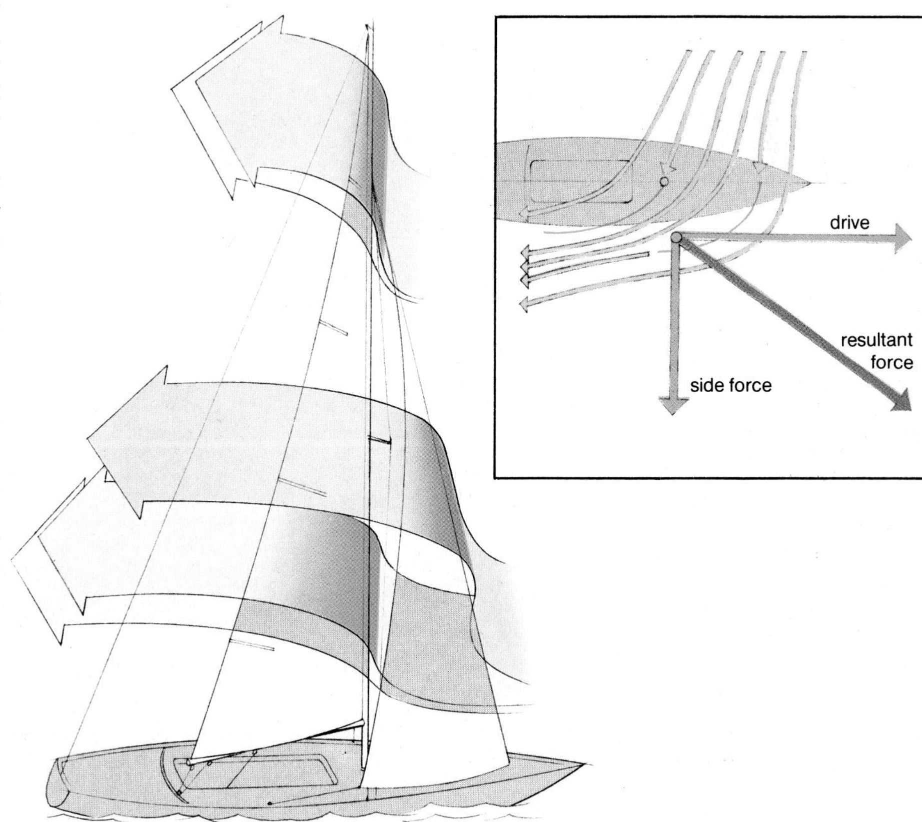

On a close reach, a boat's main and jib are trimmed to maintain the proper aerodynamic wind flow for this heading. While still set at an optimum angle to the wind (far right), they are angled away from the centerline, giving more drive and less side force.

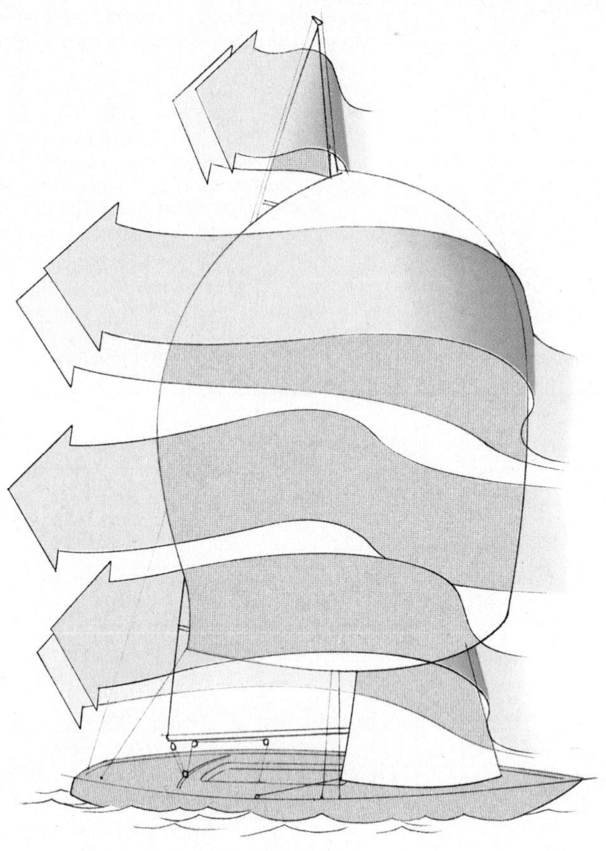

On a beam reach, a racing skipper may elect to carry both a jib and a spinnaker—a very efficient double-headsail rig that extracts the greatest practicable aerodynamic pull from the wind. The spinnaker, itself an enormous airfoil when trimmed for this point of sail (left), adds a second slot to channel the wind, while the jib makes use of any air that would pass beneath the spinnaker. Though on this heading the apparent wind is less strong than on close-hauled courses (page 29), the sails are set at a greater angle to the boat's centerline (below). Side force decreases, with a corresponding boost in drive.

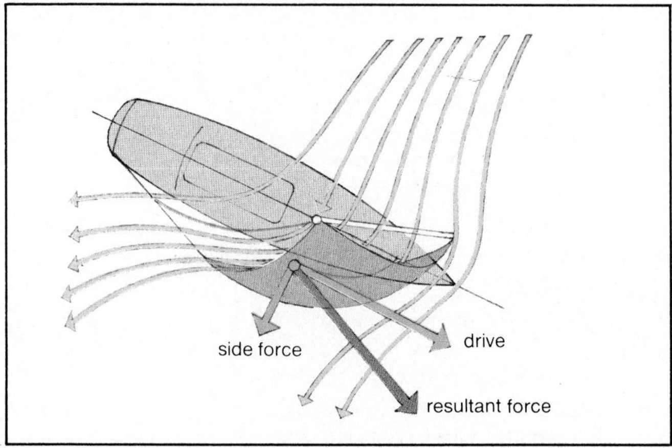

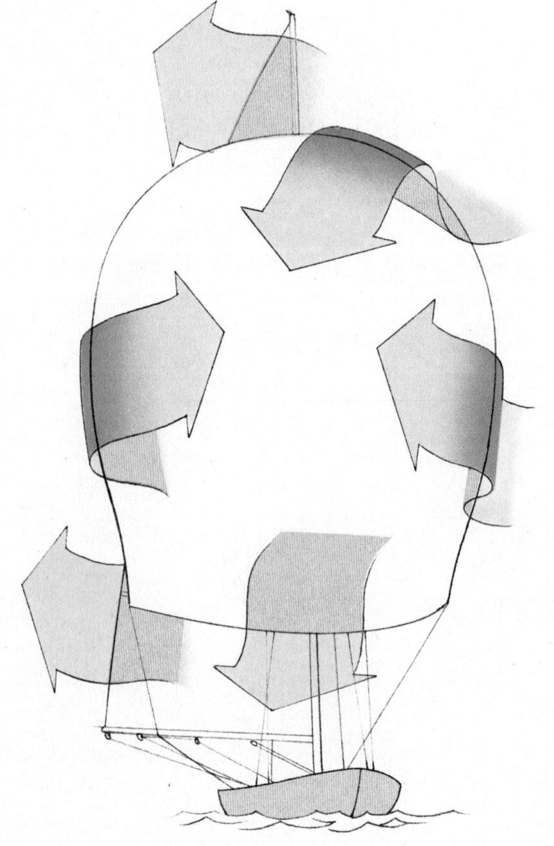

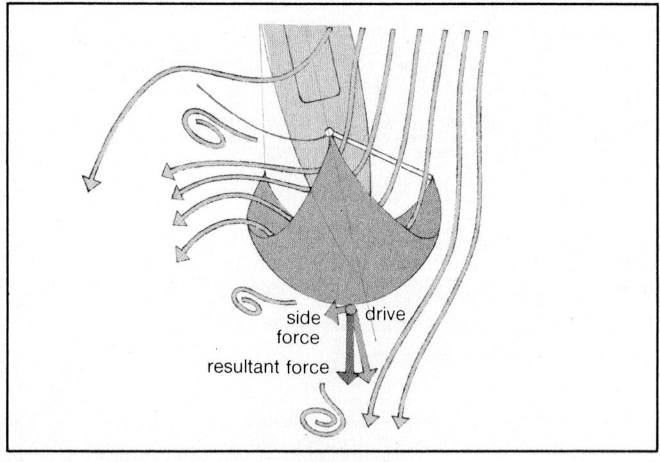

Before the wind under main and spinnaker, a greater percentage of the wind's force is exerted as a straightforward push against the sailcloth, but the spinnaker still generates a significant aerodynamic pull. Wind curling around the edges of the spinnaker creates an aerodynamic lift (left) that helps keep the chute full and suspended high in front of the boat. While the aerodynamic pull is weaker than on other points of sail, it operates at a more effective angle (above) to the boat's heading: most of the wind's energy is converted into useful drive, and very little of it is expended as side force.

A NECESSARY TWIST

To derive the most aerodynamic energy from the wind, the upper and lower portions of a sail must be trimmed at different angles—a feature of sail adjustment known as twist. This vertical variation in trim is necessary because the apparent wind comes from a progressively more forward direction near the foot, due to the slowing of the true wind by friction as it blows over the water: at a height of four feet, the wind may be three knots slower than at a height of 30 feet, causing a 12° shift in the apparent wind. One way to tell whether twist is correct for a given wind strength is to head up; if the sail luffs from head to foot simultaneously, the twist is correct.

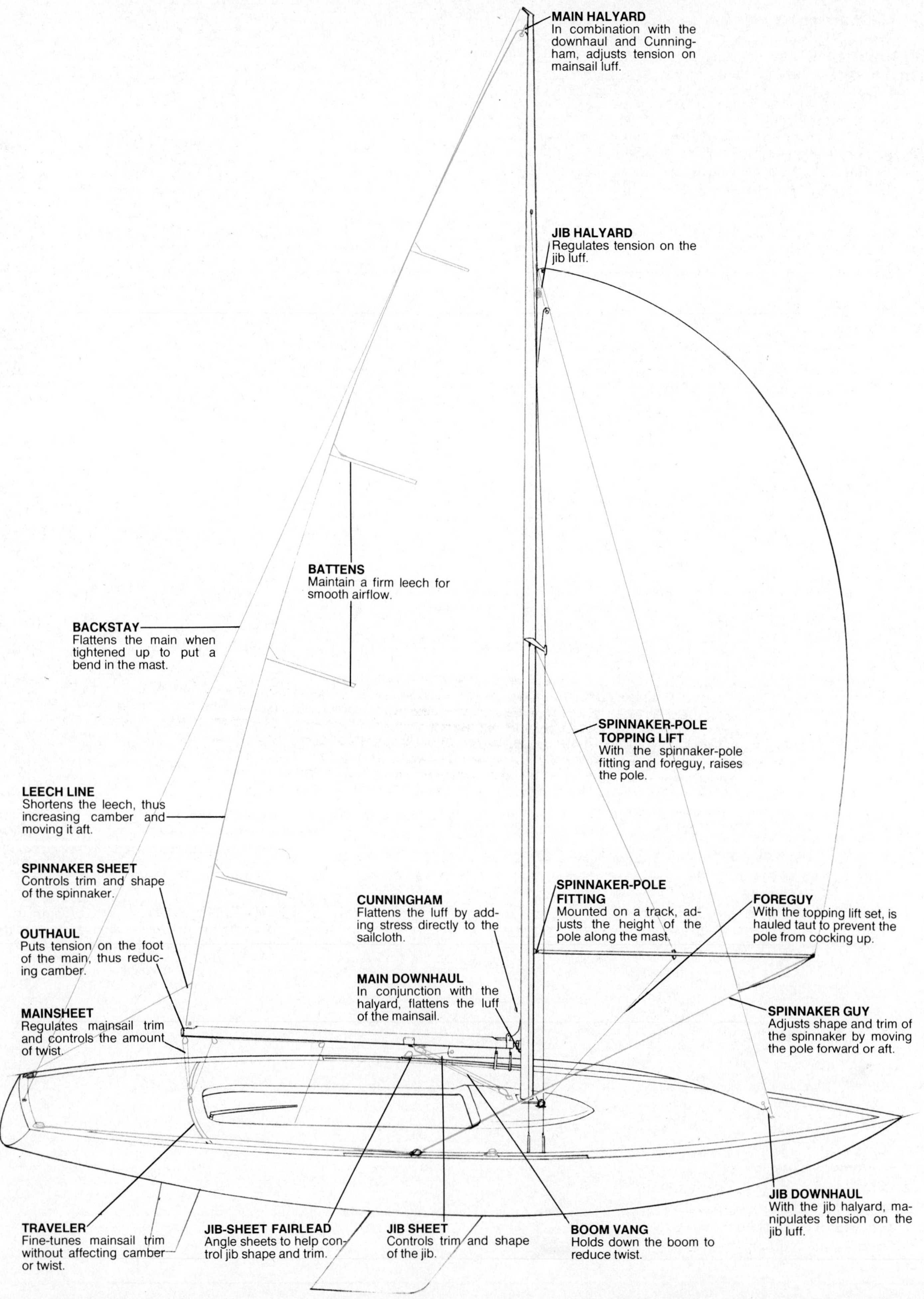
MAIN HALYARD
In combination with the downhaul and Cunningham, adjusts tension on mainsail luff.
JIB HALYARD
Regulates tension on the jib luff.
BATTENS
Maintain a firm leech for smooth airflow.
BACKSTAY
Flattens the main when tightened up to put a bend in the mast.
SPINNAKER-POLE TOPPING LIFT
With the spinnaker-pole fitting and foreguy, raises the pole.
LEECH LINE
Shortens the leech, thus increasing camber and moving it aft.
SPINNAKER SHEET
Controls trim and shape of the spinnaker.
CUNNINGHAM
Flattens the luff by adding stress directly to the sailcloth.
SPINNAKER-POLE FITTING
Mounted on a track, adjusts the height of the pole along the mast.
FOREGUY
With the topping lift set, is hauled taut to prevent the pole from cocking up.
OUTHAUL
Puts tension on the foot of the main, thus reducing camber.
MAIN DOWNHAUL
In conjunction with the halyard, flattens the luff of the mainsail.
MAINSHEET
Regulates mainsail trim and controls the amount of twist.
SPINNAKER GUY
Adjusts shape and trim of the spinnaker by moving the pole forward or aft.
JIB DOWNHAUL
With the jib halyard, manipulates tension on the jib luff.
TRAVELER
Fine-tunes mainsail trim without affecting camber or twist.
JIB-SHEET FAIRLEAD
Angle sheets to help control jib shape and trim.
JIB SHEET
Controls trim and shape of the jib.
BOOM VANG
Holds down the boom to reduce twist.

Sail-Control Catalogue

The process of trimming and shaping a sail is a little like stretching the canvas for a painting. When one edge of the sail has been adjusted, the opposite side may either bag or crease out of shape. The solution is to exert controlled tension upon the fabric simultaneously from as many directions as possible. Most modern racing craft are equipped with sophisticated sail-control devices designed to do just that; a typical selection is shown at left.

The principal mechanisms for trimming a boat's sails are, of course, the sheets —but not on all headings. When a boat is close-hauled, the trim of the mainsail can be fine-tuned more effectively by means of the traveler, a metal track and sliding block that allows the boom to be moved athwartships without changing the tension on the sheet. The sheet then takes on an important secondary function: trimming it in will pull the boom downward, and thus reduce the amount of sail twist *(page 31)*. When sailing downwind, on the other hand, since the sheet must be slacked off to give the sail its proper trim, twist is controlled by putting tension on the boom vang *(page 37)*.

Almost any other line on the boat will alter the shape of the sails. Tightening the backstay, for example, will reduce the draft in the center of the mainsail; increased tension on the halyard will flatten the luff, thus diminishing camber in the forward part of the sail. On some boats, a downhaul *(top, near right)* will perform the same job. Some lines serve no other purpose than fine-tuning a main's camber. Tightening the outhaul flattens the foot. A Cunningham *(top, far right)* augments the downhaul by further flattening the luff. A line sewn into the leech, or after edge, of some mainsails, when pulled taut, will put in more belly *(page 37)*.

A similar array of tuning mechanisms can be brought to bear on a boat's headsails. But the basic adjustment in the shape of any jib is accomplished by trimming the leeward sheet and by shifting the sheet fairlead. A variety of sophisticated arrangements have been contrived for positioning the fairleads—either fore and aft, or athwartships, or both; the H-track and Barber haul at right are two examples.

The spinnaker, too, can be shaped by manipulating the sheet and guy, and the height of the pole. Lowering the pole flattens the chute, while raising it gives the sail more belly. The proper shape and trim for the chute under various wind conditions—and for the jib and mainsail as well —are demonstrated on pages 42-43.

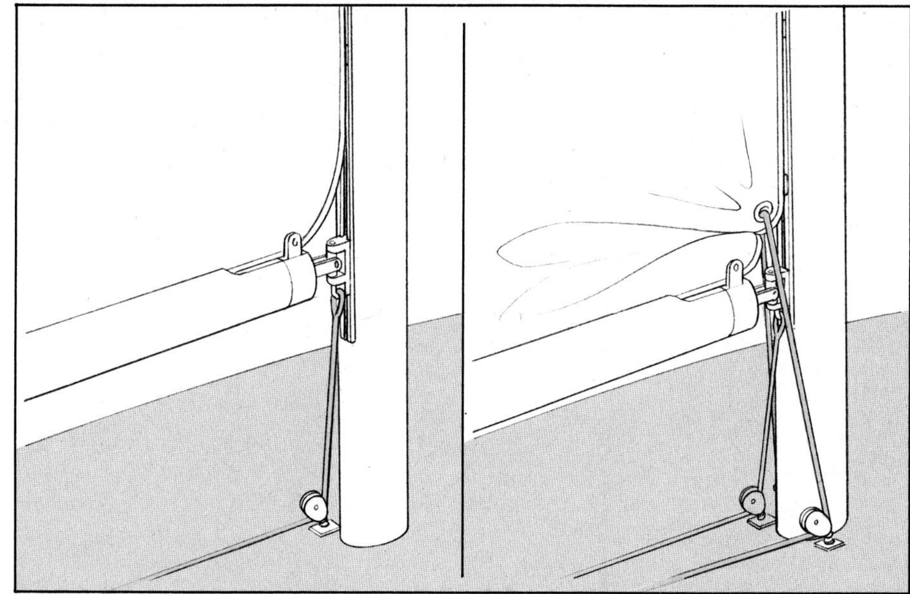

The mainsail downhaul consists of a line running from the fitting that connects the boom to the mast—typically the slide and track arrangement shown above. From the slide, the line leads through a block near the base of the mast to a cleat. After the sail has been raised and the halyard made fast, the downhaul is drawn tight, lowering the boom along the track. The resulting tension flattens the luff, reducing the sail's camber.

A Cunningham looks very much like a downhaul and in fact is used to further flatten the luff. In this case, a line runs through a cringle at the tack of the sail. When the line is drawn downward, it pulls the sailcloth near the tack into a pleat, further reducing draft and holding it forward.

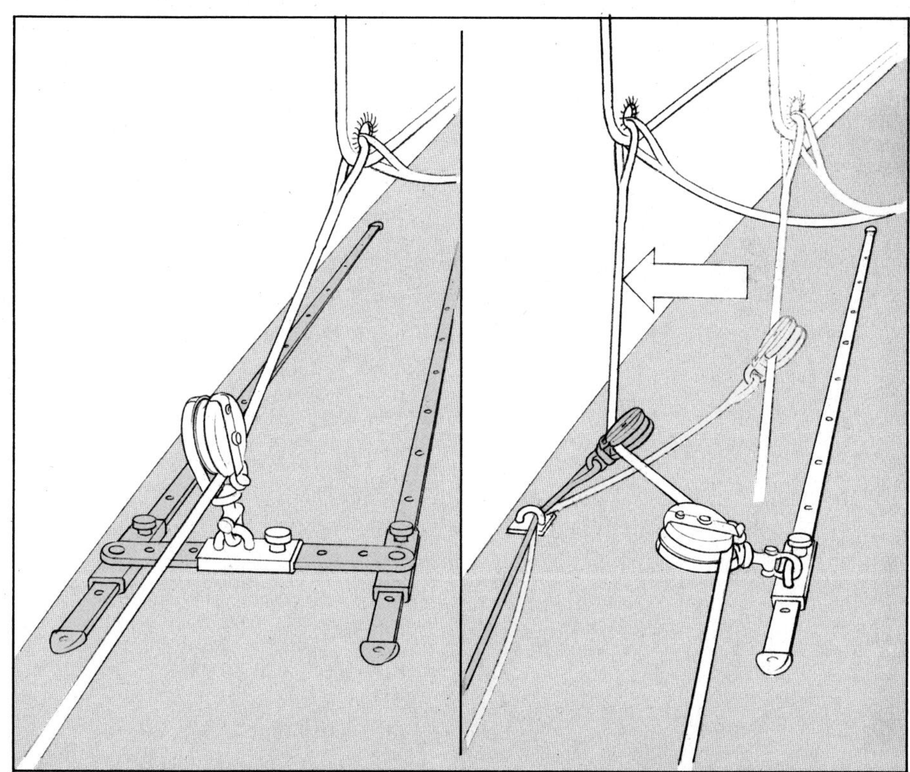

Two handy rigs for controlling the lead of the jib sheet—and thus the shape of the sail itself—are the H-track (left) and the Barber haul (right). With both, the jib-sheet fairlead can be slid forward on a track arrangement to put tension on the sail's leech, reducing twist; or it can be moved aft to ease the leech and flatten the foot. Athwartships movement along the H-track trims the jib without changing the tension in the sheet; the sheet is then used to adjust the sail's fullness. The Barber haul provides the same athwartships control by means of a block rigged to the sheet between the fairlead and the clew of the jib; tension on the block hauls the clew outboard.

Tuning the Rig

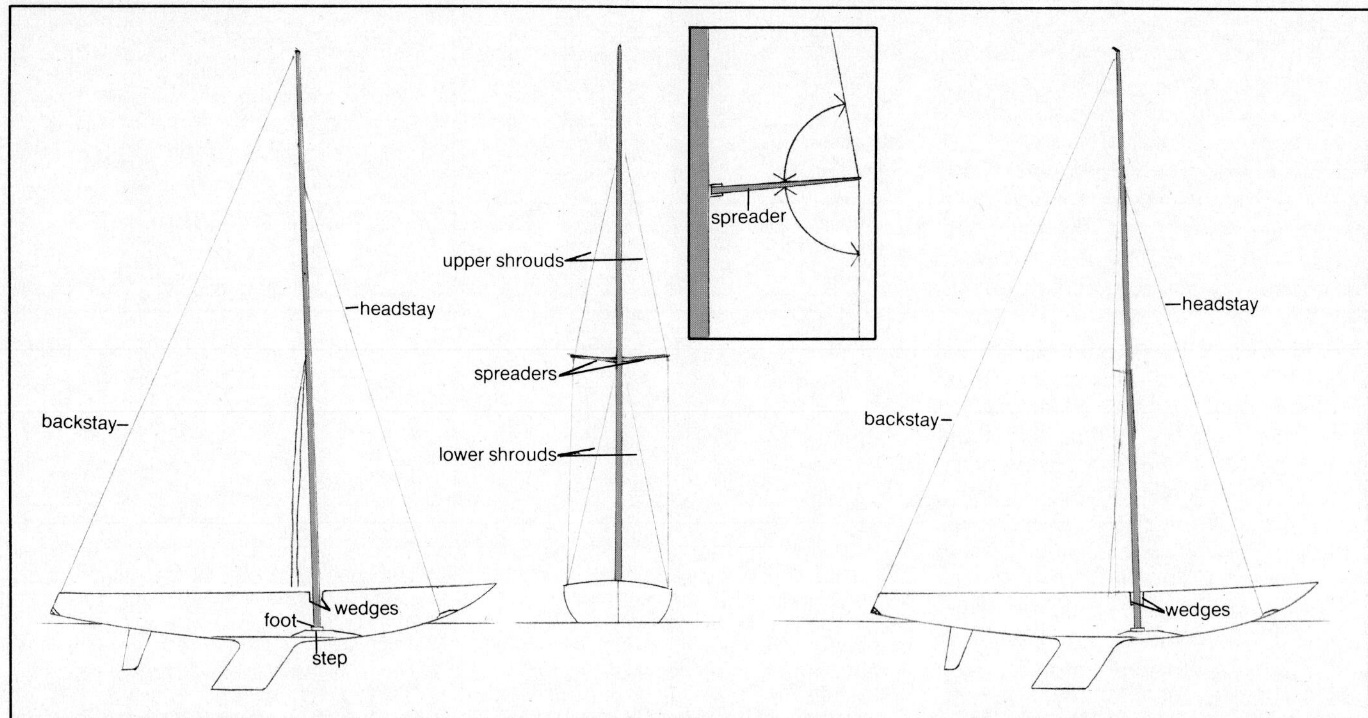

To perform up to its potential, a sailboat must have a mast with no unintended lean or bend; and a racing skipper should exercise great care when putting the mast in place during fitting out. After seating the foot of the mast firmly in its step, connect the headstay and backstay to hold the mast upright. Then tie a small weight to the end of the main halyard to use as a plumb. With the boat level in the water, the mast is vertical if the weight does not swing forward or aft. If the sail plan indicates that the mast should be raked, slack the headstay and adjust the wedges to produce the proper angle.

Next, connect the upper and lower shrouds to their chain-plate terminals on the hull and remove slack in the wires by tightening the turnbuckles. The spreaders must be set so that they bisect the angle created where the wires are rigged over their tips (inset); otherwise, uneven tension in the shrouds will force them to slip out of alignment. Then, using the halyard as a yardstick, compare the distances from the masthead to the chain plates on either side. Equalize the distances by slackening the turnbuckles on the short side and taking up a corresponding amount on the turnbuckles on the opposite side.

After the shrouds and stays have been set temporarily, they must have the proper tension. Tighten each turnbuckle as much as possible by hand, then lever it around two full turns with the shaft of a screwdriver. Even for a nonraked mast, apply a slight additional pressure to the backstay to bend the mast back by an amount equal to the spar's diameter. The bend will compensate for the forward force of the sails when the boat is underway, making the mast perpendicular. Fit the mast wedges firmly at the partners where the spar passes through the deck.

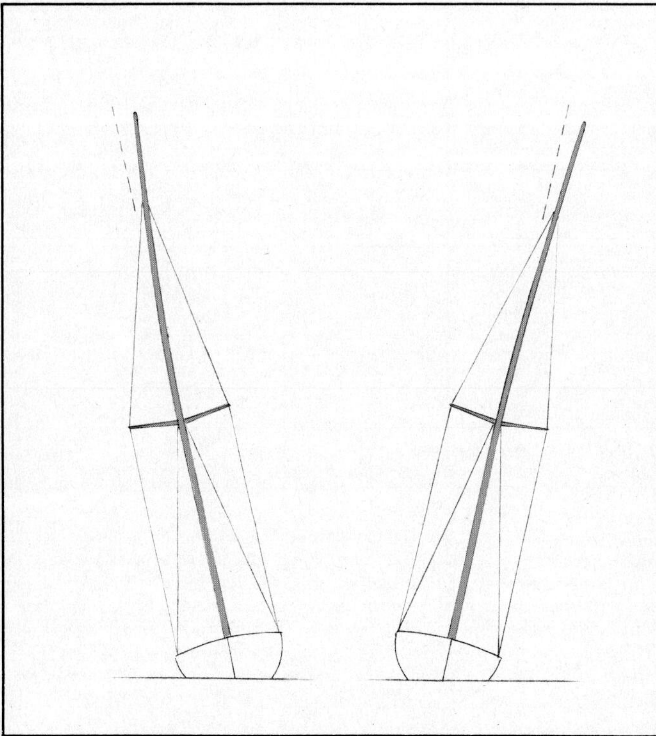

The final touches to a tuning job are done while the vessel is underway. Sight up the mast, first on one tack, then the other; if the mast appears to bend to either side, adjust the upper shrouds so that they remain equally tight but eliminate the bend. Only by comparing the tightness of the two shrouds is it possible to determine whether, for example, a bend to windward (left) should be removed by tightening the leeward shrouds or by loosening the windward ones.

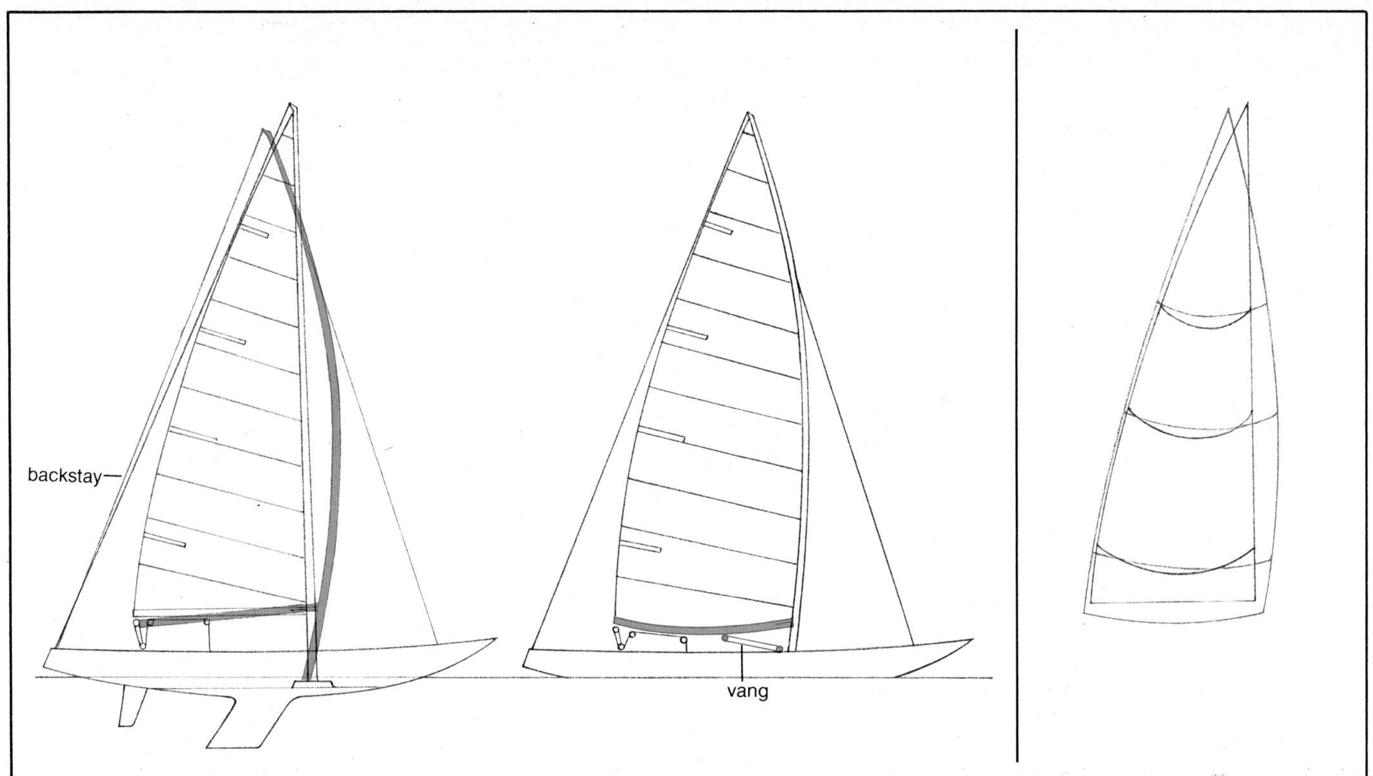

Stays and spars do not necessarily remain in a fixed position after the initial tuning: on some boats they may be readjusted whenever a flatter-than-usual mainsail is desired (pages 36-37). To reduce camber in the main, haul down on the backstay. The middle part of the mast will bow forward as the top moves aft; this forward bulge stretches the sail. Some stiff-masted boats are equipped with mechanical aids such as a block and tackle to haul on the backstay. And racing boats like the Finn have flexible masts—lacking stays or shrouds—that automatically flex and produce a flatter sail when it is needed.

The boom can also be enlisted in the sail-flattening procedure. To reduce unwanted fullness along the sail's foot, rig a vang at the center of the boom, as above. Tension on the vang will produce a bow in the boom and pull the foot of the sail downward.

The outline of a stretched sail (blue) superimposed upon a regular sail shape (gray) indicates the complementary effects of bending the mast and bowing the boom. The mast bend flattens the middle of the sail, while the bowed boom accounts for reduced camber in the sail's lower region.

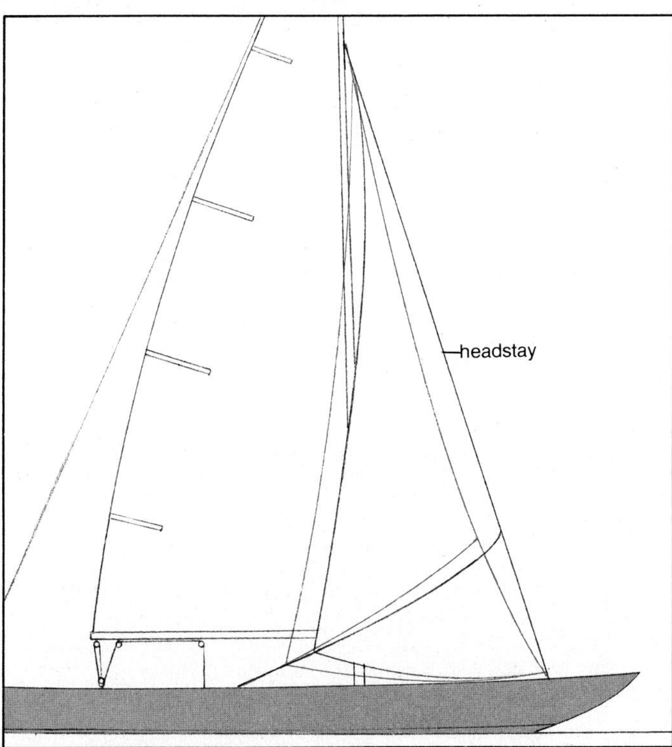

A flaw that afflicts all sailboats going to windward is headstay sag (blue). Due to the tremendous pressures exerted on the leading edge of the sail, the headstay on most boats simply cannot be tightened enough to keep it absolutely straight. Therefore, sailmakers cut jibs with a built-in allowance for a little headstay sag. However, the headstay should be tightened to the maximum allowable specifications of the rig. And if the jib has a wire luff line, increasing the tension on the halyard and downhaul will also help to straighten out its leading edge.

With the wind under six knots, a close-hauled boat moves fastest with its sails bellied—a shape achieved by reducing the tension on the luff and foot. First ease the outhaul (1) until small wrinkles appear along the sail's foot. Next, ease the halyard (2) and the downhaul (3) to create a slight bag at the luff. If the vessel is equipped with a Cunningham (4), free it. Finally, take up the leech line (opposite) if there is one.

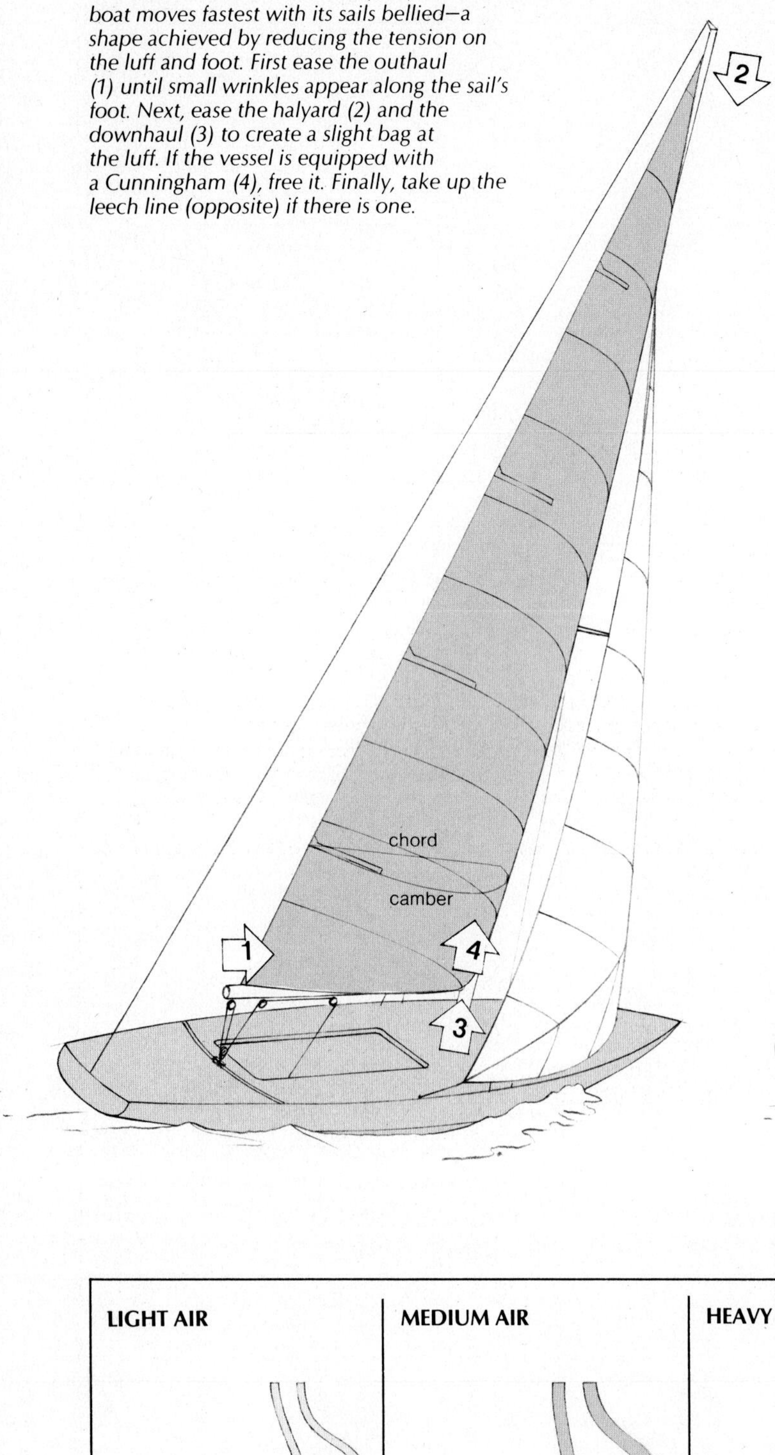

When the wind pipes up to 10 knots or more, the camber of a boat's sails should be reduced. First, if the leech line has been tightened, slack it off. Then take up on the halyard (1) and downhaul (2), increasing tension in the luff of the sail. Stretch out the foot of the sail by taking up on the outhaul (3). Finally, tighten the Cunningham (4). Flattening the mainsail is most easily done during a tack, when stress is off the sail.

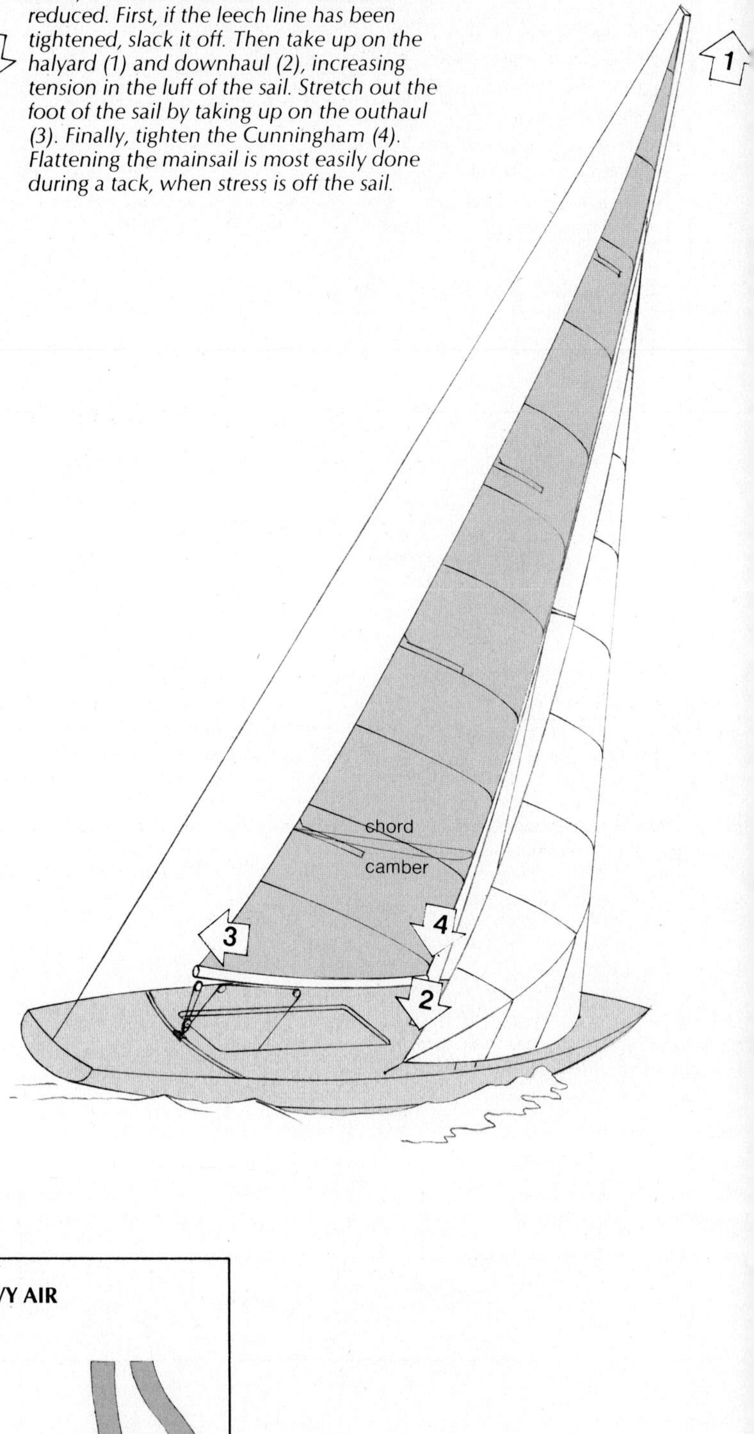

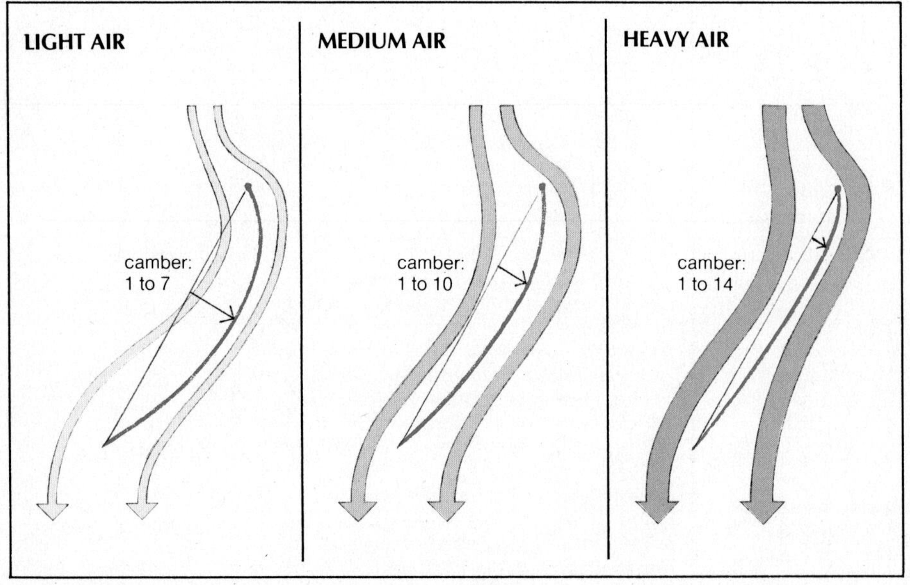

To achieve maximum aerodynamic force in different wind strengths, a sail requires differing degrees of camber because the ability of an airstream to cling to a curve decreases as its speed increases. Camber is measured as a ratio between the depth (black arrows) of the sail's curve and the length of a chord (black lines) from the luff to the leech. In light air, a good ratio is one foot of depth for every seven feet of chord. In medium air—for which most sails are designed—the sail has a natural camber of 1 to 10. And in heavy air, the ratio is 1 to 14.

Shaping the Main

The fuller a sail is, the more it bends the wind flow on its leeward surface and the greater its output of power—up to a limit. Beyond a certain point, the air has a tendency to break away from the convex leeward curve before completing its journey around the sail. The result is a condition called stall—a mass of turbulent air that produces no drive.

Most one-design mainsails are cut to provide a camber best suited to six to 10 knots of wind when close-hauled. But by employing the various devices explained on pages 32-33, the curvature of the mainsail can be changed to render it efficient in wind strengths outside this range.

In light air, a particularly useful aid is the leech line, with its ability to control the tension of a sail's after edge. Tightening the leech line not only increases the sail's fullness *(top right)* and boosts the drive, but it also can enable the boat to point several degrees higher in light air. For off-wind headings the single most important sail-shaping device is the boom vang, which serves to reduce unwanted twist and also to stretch out the main so that the sail gets every bit of potential power from the wind.

LIGHT AIR | MEDIUM AIR | HEAVY AIR

Some racing mainsails can be shaped for best performance in various wind conditions by means of a leech line—a line that runs the length of the sail's leech (after edge) under the hem and acts like a drawstring to belly the sail. In light air, the leech line should be tightened, cupping the after edge of the main and bending the wind as much as possible. In medium air, it is eased a bit to keep the wind from breaking away from the sail prematurely, or stalling. And in very heavy air, when the boat has more wind than it needs, the leech line should be slack so that the after edge of the main falls away to leeward, thus spilling wind out of the sail to reduce heeling.

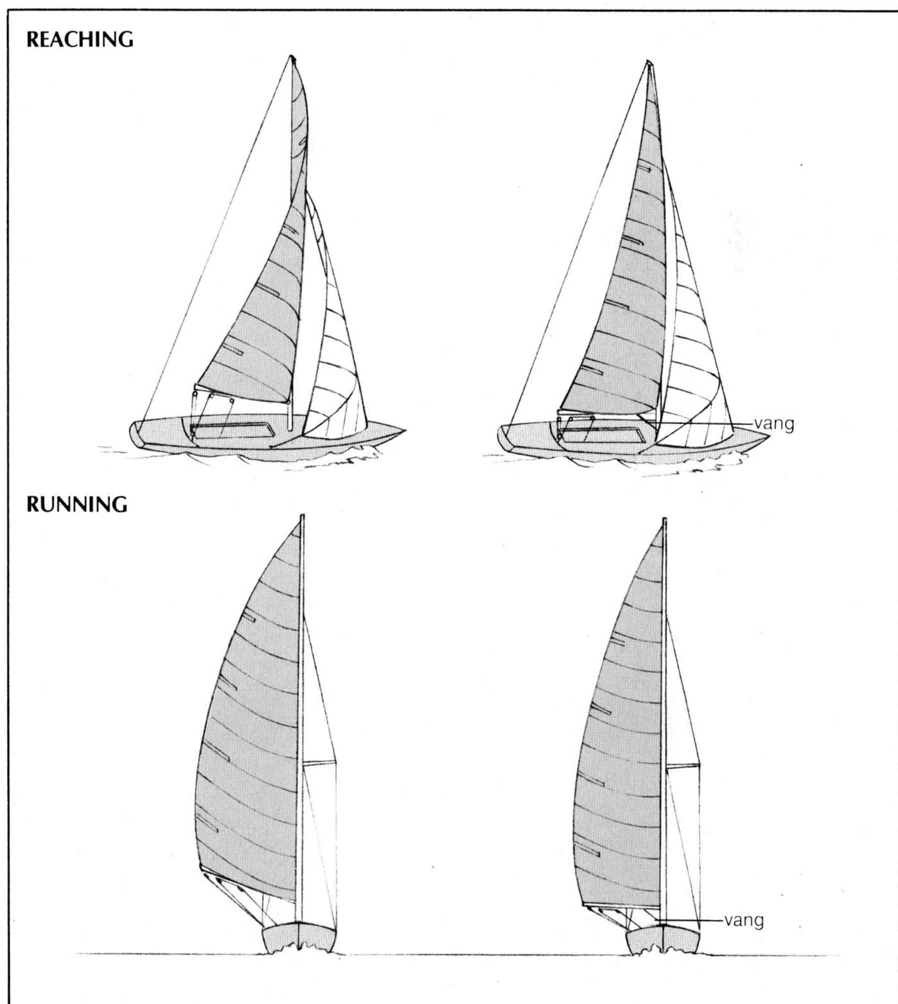

When a boat is reaching, the upper part of the mainsail tends to twist forward (top left), spilling wind from the sail. To prevent this power loss, the boom should be pulled down with a vang (top right), rather than by trimming the sheet, which would stall the foot. The same phenomenon occurs when a boat is heading straight downwind (bottom), and the solution is the same. Vanging the boom on a run pays another, equally significant, dividend: it stretches the main to its fullest, thus presenting the greatest possible sail area to the push of the wind.

SHAPING THE JIB

Beating, full

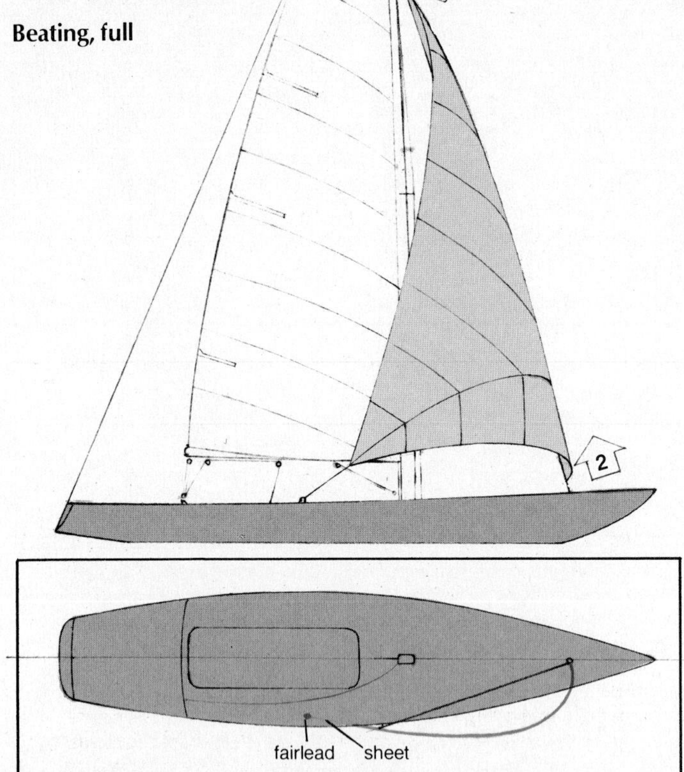

A full jib—like a full main—gives a much better aerodynamic performance when going to windward in light air. Jib camber can be increased by the adjustments indicated in the side and top views above. To add body to the sail's luff, the halyard (1) or downhaul (2) should be slacked. The fairlead should be set aft to prevent the weight of the sheet and sail from pulling down the leech; if the fairlead can be moved athwartships (page 33), it should be set inboard. Finally, the sheet is slacked until the sail verges on a luff.

Beating, flat

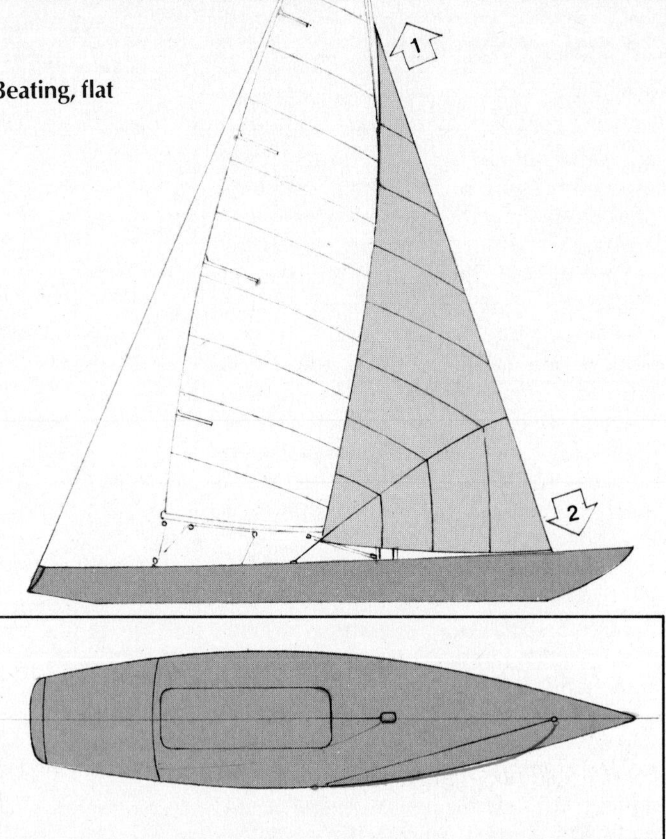

To flatten the jib for sailing close-hauled in a breeze, first tighten the halyard (1) and downhaul (2). Position the fairlead forward to equally distribute the tension on the leech and the foot of the sail. To tell if the tension is properly equalized, head up into the wind momentarily; the jib should luff evenly along the headstay. If there is a device such as an H-track or Barber haul for lateral adjustment of the fairlead, set it outboard to maintain a proper slot between the jib and main.

SHAPING THE SPINNAKER

Running

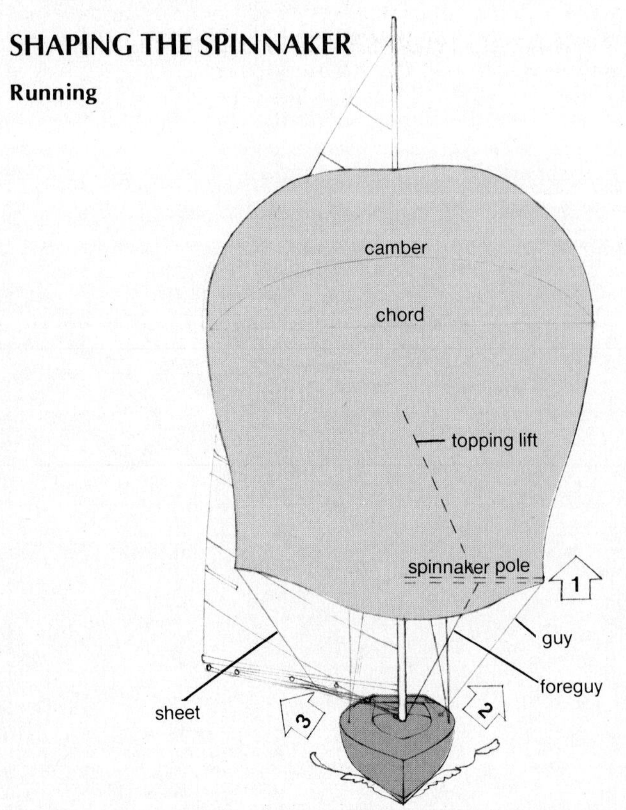

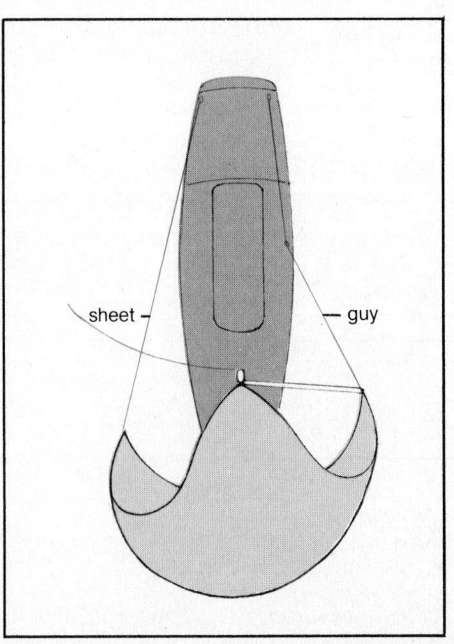

A spinnaker should be high and full on a run (left). Set the pole well up on the mast track but perpendicular to the mast (1). Then slack the guy (2) to move the pole about 10° forward of athwartships (top view, above). Slack the sheet (3) to float the spinnaker up to windward and clear of the mainsail. In heavier weather, some skippers ease the spinnaker halyard about six inches and let the sail billow out to windward to keep it from being obstructed by the main (page 40).

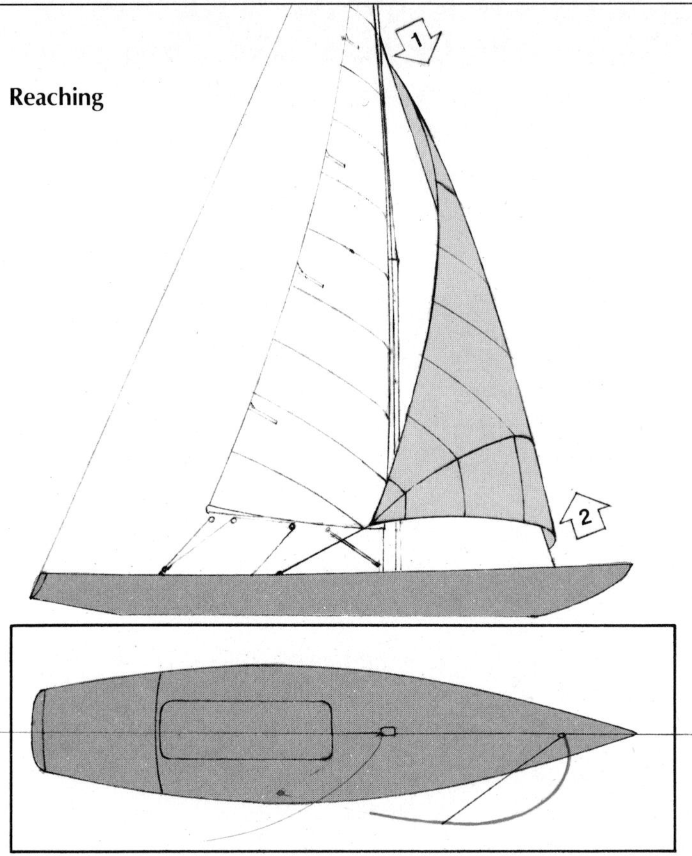

When a jib is trimmed for a reach, the slackened sheet automatically gives some fullness to the sail; this fullness can be increased by slacking the halyard (1) and downhaul (2). Position the fairlead outboard to open the slot between the two sails. The fairlead should also be moved aft to add twist to the sail, because the shift of the apparent wind at different heights (page 31) is more pronounced on this heading. But if the boat heads onto a broader reach, the fairlead will have to be moved forward again to prevent excess twist.

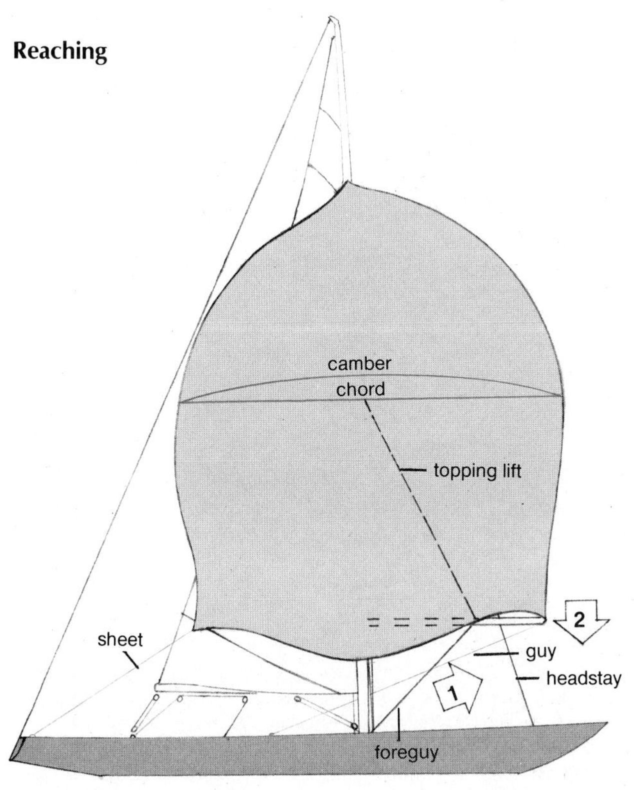

Shaping Headsails

As with the main, the aerodynamic contours of a jib or spinnaker are determined by the tension on the three edges of the sail. But there is one important difference. Since these headsails are largely free-flying—that is, held in place only by a stay or a spinnaker pole—they rely heavily upon their sheets for stability. As a result, sheets inherit the major role in shaping jibs and spinnakers as well as in determining their trim.

Owing to this dual function of the sheets, the camber of a headsail is greatly influenced by the angle of the wind. Headsails automatically get fuller when a boat heads off and the sheet is eased *(near left)*. Fortunately, the greater forces developed by this fuller sail can be utilized more easily on a reach than on a beat because they act in a more forward direction and cause less heeling.

On any heading, a crewman can also use the sheets to make a headsail flatter or fuller for different wind strengths. He simply trims or eases the sheet and at the same time repositions the fairlead to maintain the proper sail angle. If these steps prove inadequate, he can amplify the change in camber with the aid of the halyard or downhaul, as shown at left.

Trimming and shaping both headsails and the main must be done within fine tolerances to avoid problems of luffing or stall. And because headsails and the main affect each other, they must be adjusted in tandem—always starting with a jib, since it meets the wind first.

On a reach, a spinnaker should be kept as flat as possible. Ease the guy (1) to position the pole forward, almost touching the headstay. Set the pole high at first to keep the sail drawing. Then ease the topping lift and lower the pole on its mast track (2); secure the topping lift and tighten the foreguy to hold the pole firmly in place. In this lower position, the pole will stretch the spinnaker's foot downward, reducing camber. With a very flat spinnaker, some boats can head as high as 70° to the true wind.

Common Problems of Shape and Trim

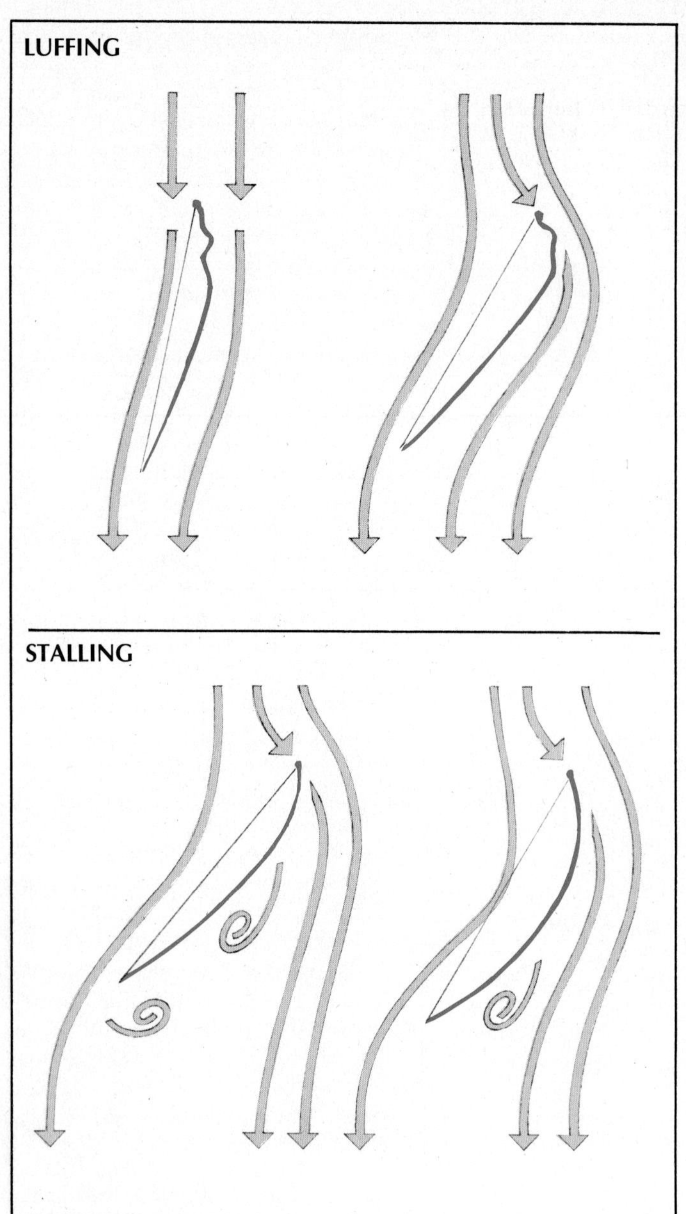

A sail may luff—that is, cease to bend the airstream—for one of two reasons. If it is undertrimmed—at an angle to the wind that is too small—it will not fill and the airstream will cause it to flap like a flag (far left). Alternatively, a properly angled sail may still luff, due to excess camber near the leading edge; the wind will cave in this bulge instead of flowing around it (left). To remedy the latter sort of luffing in the main, the point of greatest camber in the sail must be positioned aft, either by slacking the halyard or by taking up on the outhaul. In a jib, either luffing problem can usually be solved by increasing tension on the halyard or by trimming the sheet.

A stall condition in a sail is harder to detect than a luff—particularly without the aid of the tuft devices shown at opposite bottom. A sail stalls if it is either overtrimmed (far left) or overcambered (left) so that wind flowing along the lee side breaks away prematurely from the sailcloth arc, leaving eddies that produce no power. Stall can often be eliminated by easing the sheet until the sail begins to luff, then trimming in slightly. If the sail still stalls, it must be flattened.

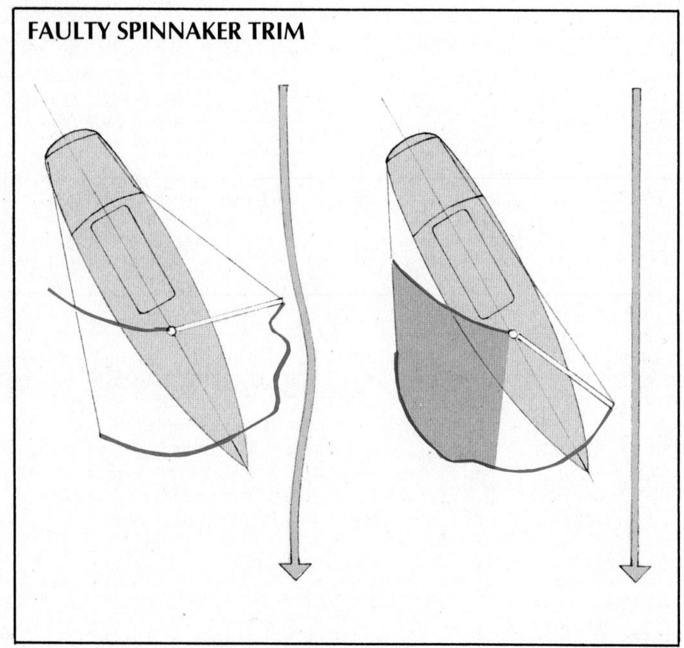

A spinnaker luffs if its windward edge is pulled so far aft that the wind approaching from astern curls the sail inward rather than filling it (far left). This problem can be solved by slacking the guy and trimming the sheet. Conversely, if the windward edge is too far forward and the leeward edge too far aft, the mainsail will block the flow of air to the spinnaker (gray area, left). To get the spinnaker drawing again, trim the guy to bring the pole aft, and ease the sheet.

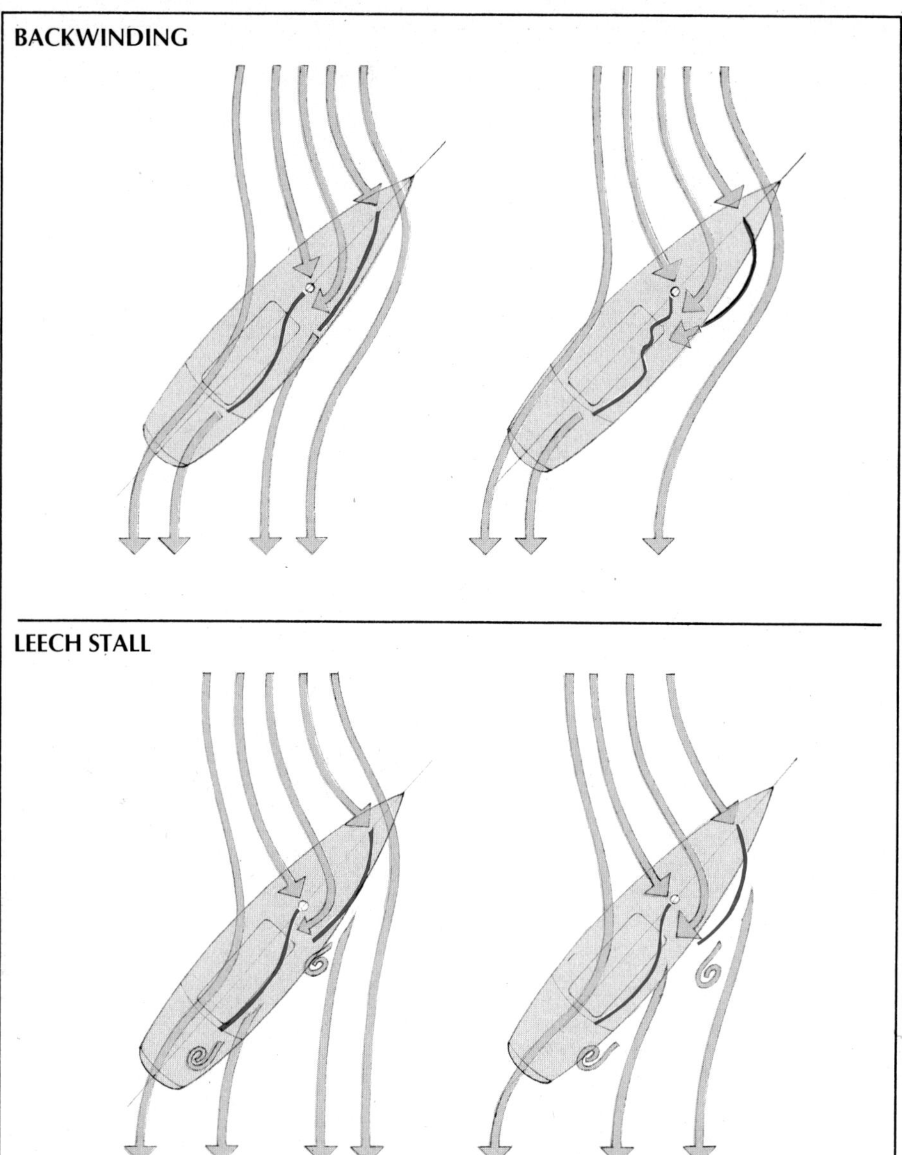

If a headsail either is trimmed in too tight (far left) or is too full (left), it will cause turbulence around the lee curve of the mainsail, spoiling the aerodynamic flow just where the flow should be most productive. This condition is called backwinding. If trim is the cause, it can be remedied by easing the jib sheet and setting the fairlead outboard. If the backwinding is caused by excess camber in the headsail, flatten the sail by increasing the tension of the halyard and move the fairlead further aft.

When the leeches of the main and jib are too far to windward—due to either overtrimming (far left) or overshaping (left)—the sails will stall along their after edges, and a jib thus stalled will also backwind the main. If leech stall is caused by trimming the sails in too tight, ease the sheets. If excess camber is causing the problem, the solution, in the case of the mainsail, is to take up on the outhaul, halyard and downhaul. In the case of the jib, move the fairlead aft. If the sails are equipped with leech lines, slack them off.

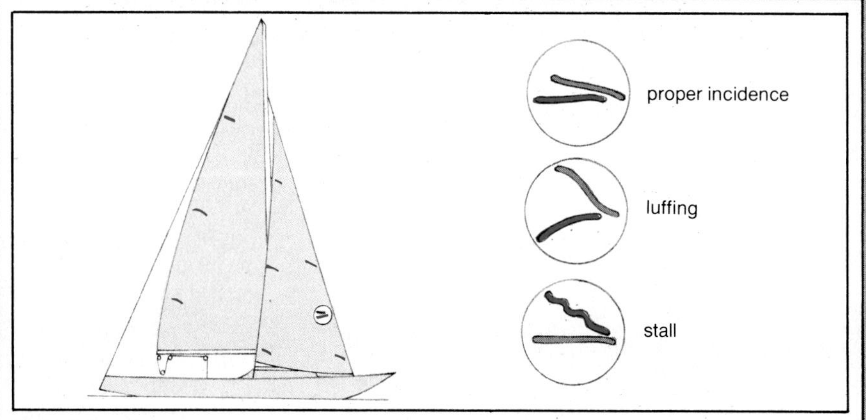

Telltale Yarns

A skipper can devise a warning system for faulty wind flow by attaching tufts of yarn to both sides of his sails at various heights along the leeches of main and jib, and along the jib's luff (some jibs have a window for viewing the leeward tuft). If sail incidence is perfect, the tufts blow back evenly *(top)*. If luffing is incipient, the windward tuft on the jib's leading edge flutters upward *(middle)*; if stall is imminent, the lee tuft flutters *(bottom)*.

Adjustments for Changing Winds

BEATING

REACHING

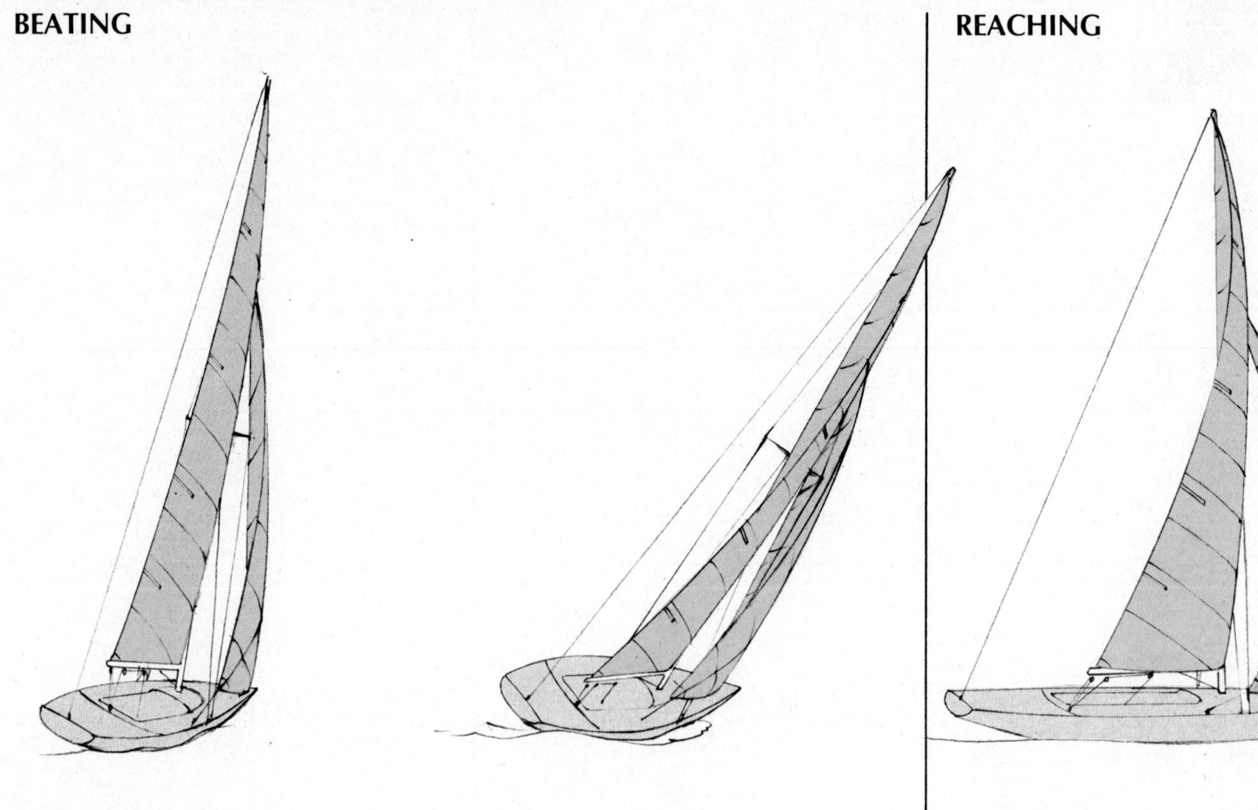

LIGHT AIR

When beating in winds of five knots or less—or under any of the other special conditions of light or heavy air shown on these pages—a racer's competitive edge depends on close coordination between the shapes of the two sails, their trim and the boat's heading. First, adjust both main and jib for maximum fullness (pages 36-39) to bend the slight wind as much as possible (below). Head off to get the boat moving; as it gathers way, gradually head up (above), trim the jib, and trim the main amidships by moving the traveler block to weather. Then sail on the verge of a luff, pointing as high as possible.

HEAVY AIR

Going to windward in a breeze of 14 knots or more, flatten both main and jib, using the downhaul and Cunningham (page 33) to hold the draft forward. Move the traveler block outboard to reduce twist and prevent excess heeling; having thus reduced the main's incidence, head off slightly to keep the sail full (below). As the breeze freshens, heeling will increase (above), and the boat may develop severe weather helm—a tendency to turn to windward. To combat this, ease the mainsheet to increase twist and spill wind; if necessary, slack the sheet to luff the main. Sheet the jib in to keep the boat driving.

LIGHT AIR

On a reach in light-wind conditions, adjust the sail controls on both jib and main for full camber and maximum bending of the airflow (below). Slack the jib sheet and move the fairlead outboard, if possible, for proper shape and incidence. Ease the mainsail by moving the traveler to leeward, and slack the sheet; vang down the boom to prevent too much twist (above). With both sails set for the boat's general heading, they should be fine-tuned for minor fluctuations in wind direction by means of slight alterations in course—a quicker and more precise method than attempting to retrim the sheets.

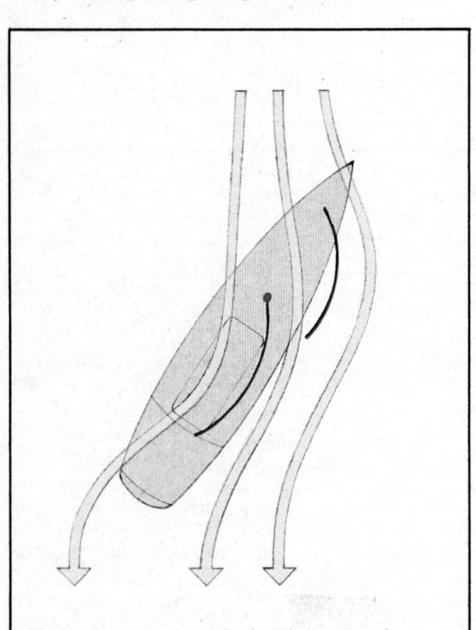

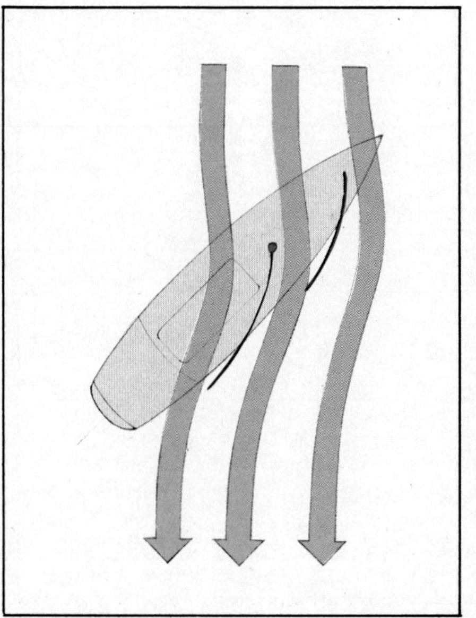

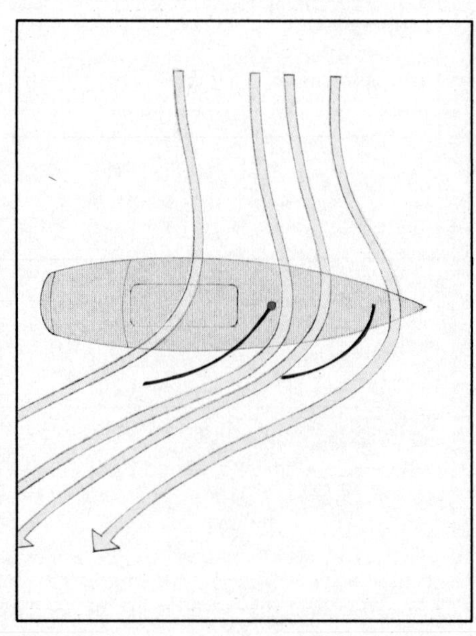

RUNNING

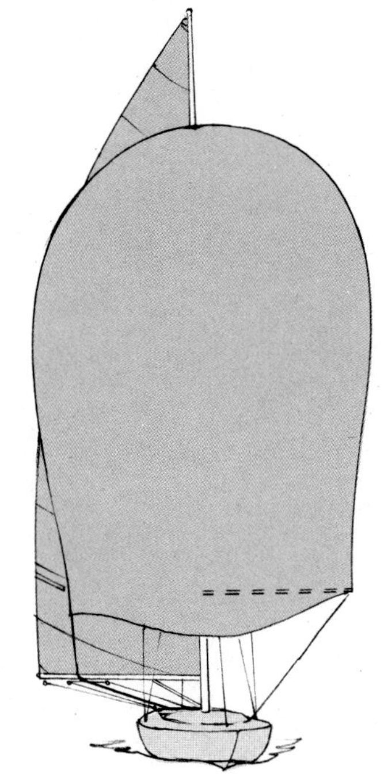

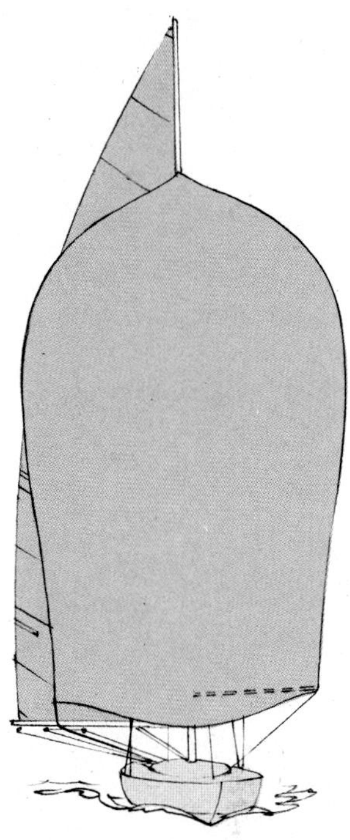

HEAVY AIR

Reaching in winds that are strong enough—usually 14 knots or more—to push a boat up to its top speed, the skipper steers a straight course while the crew plays the sheets for variations in apparent wind (below). Tighten the luffs of both sails to flatten them and keep the draft forward; these adjustments diminish the aerodynamic side force that causes heeling. Reduce twist in the jib by moving the fairlead forward, and in the main by vanging down the boom (above). If excessive heeling continues or too much weather helm develops, ease the mainsheet to luff the main.

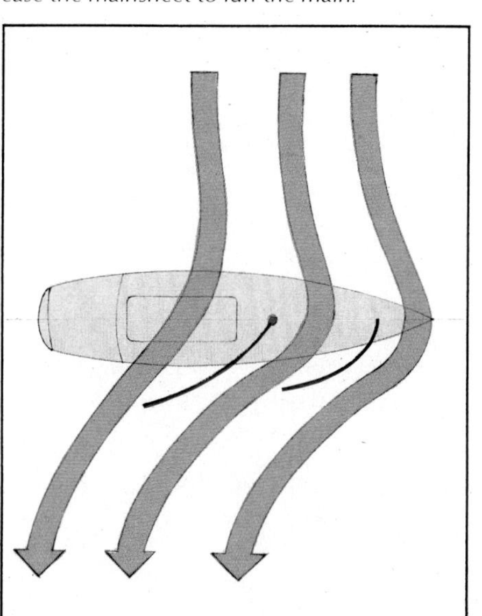

LIGHT AIR

The principal driving sail on a run is the spinnaker; in light air adroit handling is needed to keep it full and drawing. First, with the pole low on the mast and the spinnaker sheet trimmed, head up to increase the apparent wind. When the sail catches the wind and fills (below), head off and slowly raise the pole (page 39), easing both the guy and the sheet. This allows the chute to belly out high in front of the boat (above). While the crew plays the sheet, the helmsman steers to help keep the sail full—heading up in lulls and down in puffs (page 121). The main is full—eased out to the shrouds and vanged down.

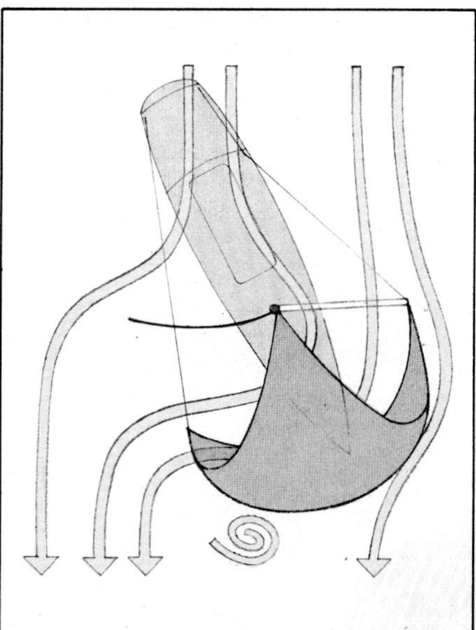

HEAVY AIR

In winds above 20 knots, the spinnaker may swing uncontrollably from side to side, alternately heeling the boat dangerously to windward, then pulling it broadside to the wind and waves—a condition called broaching. To tame the chute for consistent wind flow (below), the spinnaker should be flat. Lower the pole, move the sheet fairlead forward and trim both guy and sheet. If the boat still heels to windward, trim the sheet and ease the guy, bringing the sail to leeward and its power more forward (above). If a broach threatens, trim the sail to windward and head off—being careful not to jibe.

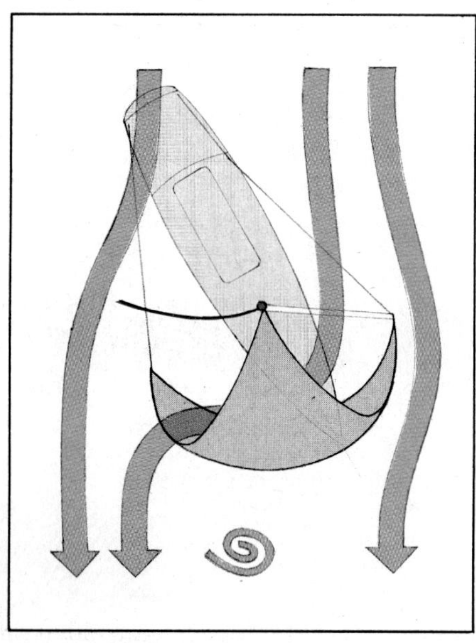

A boat's streamlined hull and keel split and bend the water moving past, thus generating hydrodynamic forces that hold the boat on its intended course. Because the boat travels at a slight angle to its course, water is forced away from a high-pressure area on the downwind side toward a section of low pressure on the upwind side. The pressure differential is greatest along the keel's leading edge, where both the bending and acceleration are most pronounced (dark blue shading). Also, since a well-balanced boat has a slight tendency to head into the wind—a phenomenon known as weather helm—the skipper must angle his rudder to hold the vessel on course. This causes a small local diversion of the flow, which in turn allows the rudder to create its own vital component of hydrodynamic force.

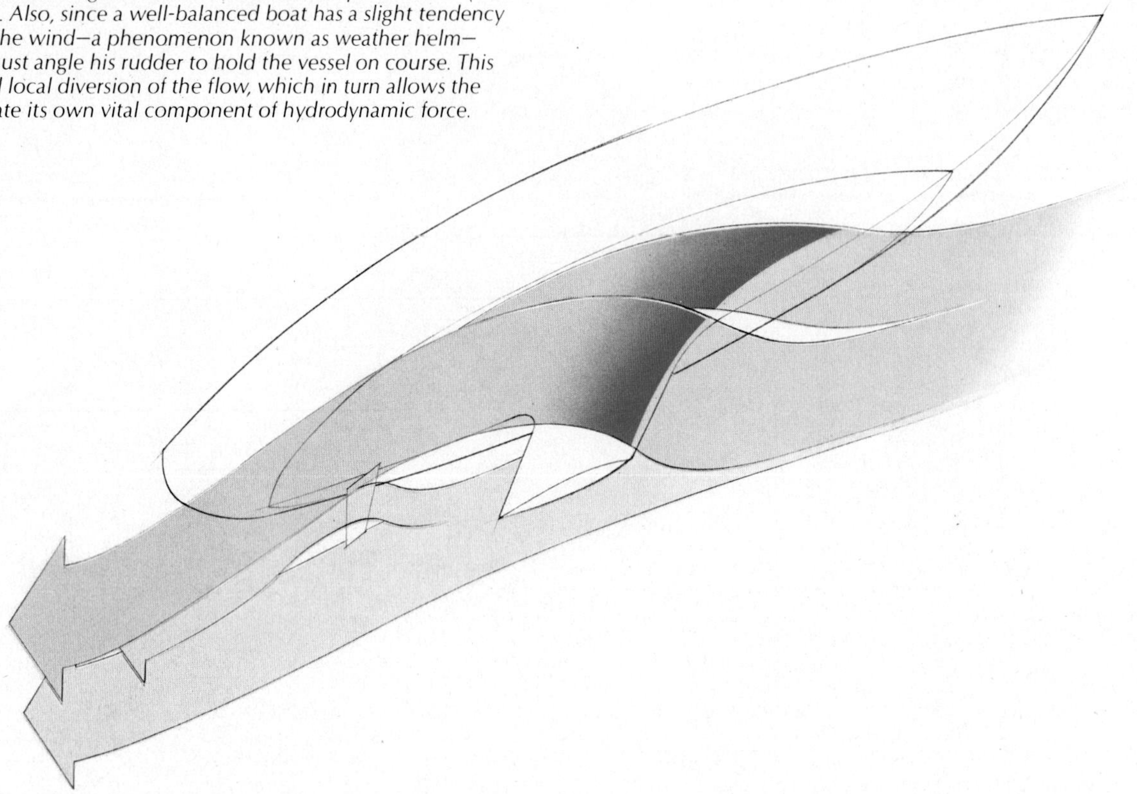

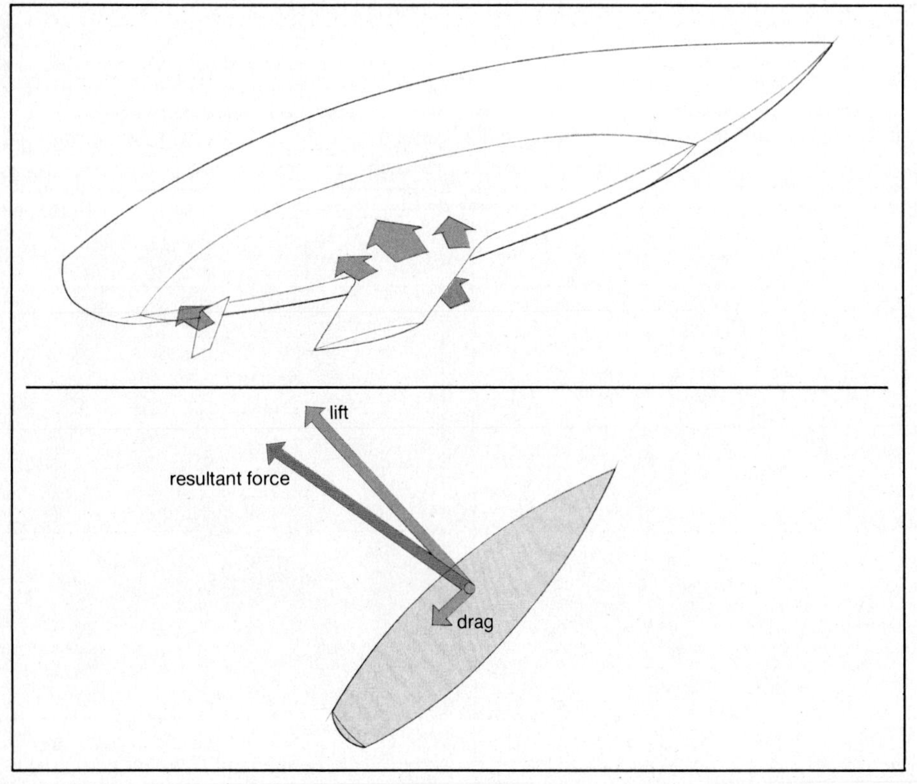

The drawings at left identify the specific hydrodynamic forces generated along the underwater surface of a boat's hull, keel and rudder (top). A powerful pulling force (blue arrows) sucks on the boat's windward side, and a much smaller force (gray arrow) pushes from leeward. These pressures can be summed up as a single resultant force (dark blue arrow, bottom), angled slightly aft. The resultant force can be split into two components called lift and drag, which counterbalance (overleaf) the side force and drive generated by the wind in the sails.

Forces of Water Flow

When a boat's sails fill with wind, the forces generated would, if unopposed, send the vessel skidding rapidly to leeward. The necessary opposition occurs below the waterline. It occurs in part simply because of water resistance against the broad surface of the keel or centerboard. But this resistance is only one element in a powerful set of hydrodynamic forces that develop along the hull and keel. Known as lift and drag, these forces are remarkably similar to the aerodynamic energies of side force and drive that act on the sails.

As a boat moves through the water, it travels both forward and also a bit to the side. This motion, in effect, cocks the vessel at a slight angle to its course, so that the bow points a few degrees to windward of the actual course. This angle, known as the angle of yaw, is what produces the key force of hydrodynamic lift—much the way a sail's incidence to the wind *(pages 28-29)* generates the power to drive the boat. Because of the yaw angle, water streams past either side of the hull and keel at different rates: pressure builds up on the lee side, slowing the leeward flow. At the same time, some of the leeward stream is drawn to the boat's weather side *(top left)*, and as it bends it accelerates. This increased speed in turn produces a low-pressure area on the weather side, holding the boat to windward. A similar lift develops on the rudder when the helmsman angles it to the flow of water.

For the lift on either the hull or rudder to operate effectively, the flow of water must be smooth and regular—a boat's underwater sections are streamlined for just this reason. Even so, under certain circumstances the flow will be disrupted, a stall will occur and the boat will lose its hydrodynamic efficiency. For example, if the helmsman angles the rudder too sharply to the moving water, the flow will break away into turbulent eddies and the rudder will no longer control the boat *(bottom right)*. A good skipper handles his rudder with restraint, therefore, turning it only as far as is necessary to keep on course.

The helmsman also has some control over a vessel's yaw angle, which depends on such factors as hull shape, sail arrangement and the maintenance of a proper course. Hull shape is bound into the boat's design, but the latter two elements can be influenced by proper sail trim and by a gentle, attentive hand on the helm. Failure in either area may turn the boat above its natural yaw angle, thus totally disrupting the underwater forces and stalling the keel *(top right)*.

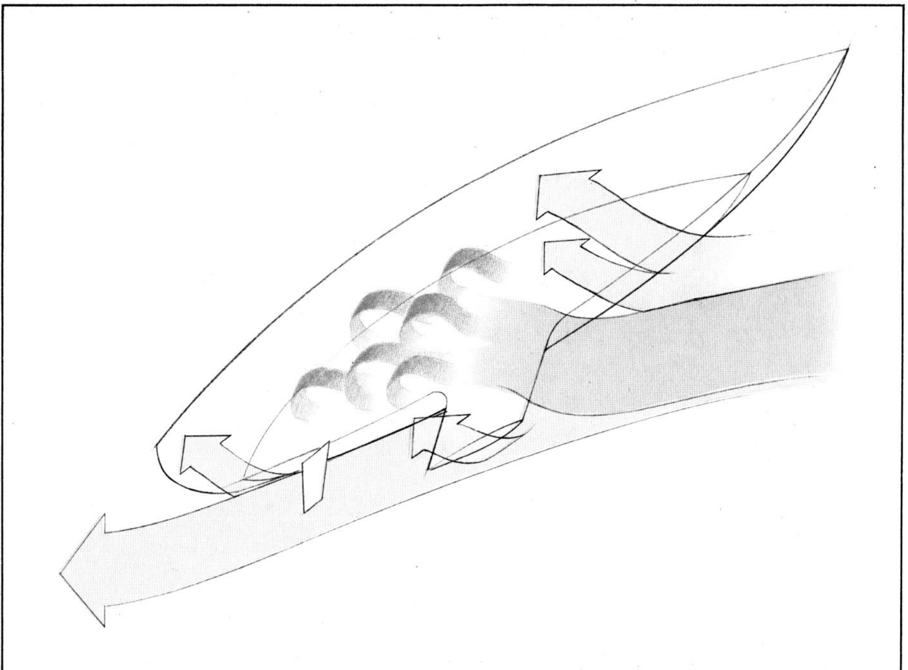

The most devastating type of stall occurs when a boat is angled too broadly to its path through the water, thus disrupting the stream moving past the keel. The stream breaks away prematurely from the keel's upwind surface, causing turbulent eddies (blue whorls) and drastically reducing the force of hydrodynamic lift—thus allowing the boat to skid to leeward. Keel stall may develop either when a skipper attempts to head too high, or when he overtrims the mainsail, or when he overpowers the boat by carrying too much sail in a stiff wind. Any of these tactics will slow down the boat and increase its leeway, in effect putting the vessel at too great an angle to its course.

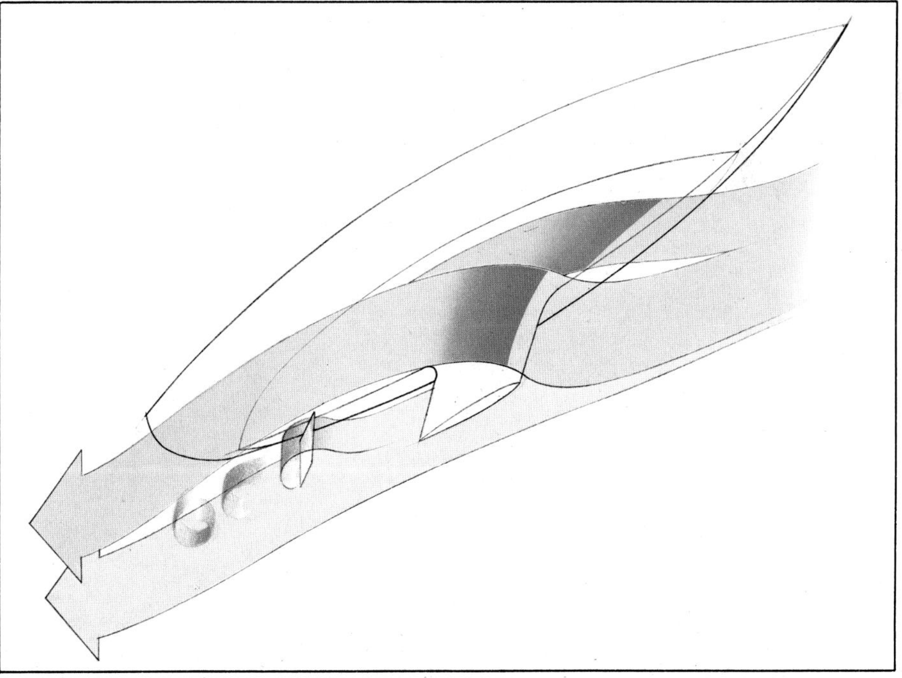

The more common underwater stall is the result of improper manipulation of the rudder—which, like a boat's hull, will not generate hydrodynamic lift unless it is angled correctly to the flow of water. Since a rudder angle of more than 10° will cause the flow to break away into turbulent eddies (blue whorls), the helmsman should avoid sudden, sharp movements such as jerking the tiller in a seaway or abruptly swinging it hard over to make a tight turn. If excessive weather helm develops, the skipper should correct it by shifting his weight or adjusting his sails—never by manhandling the tiller.

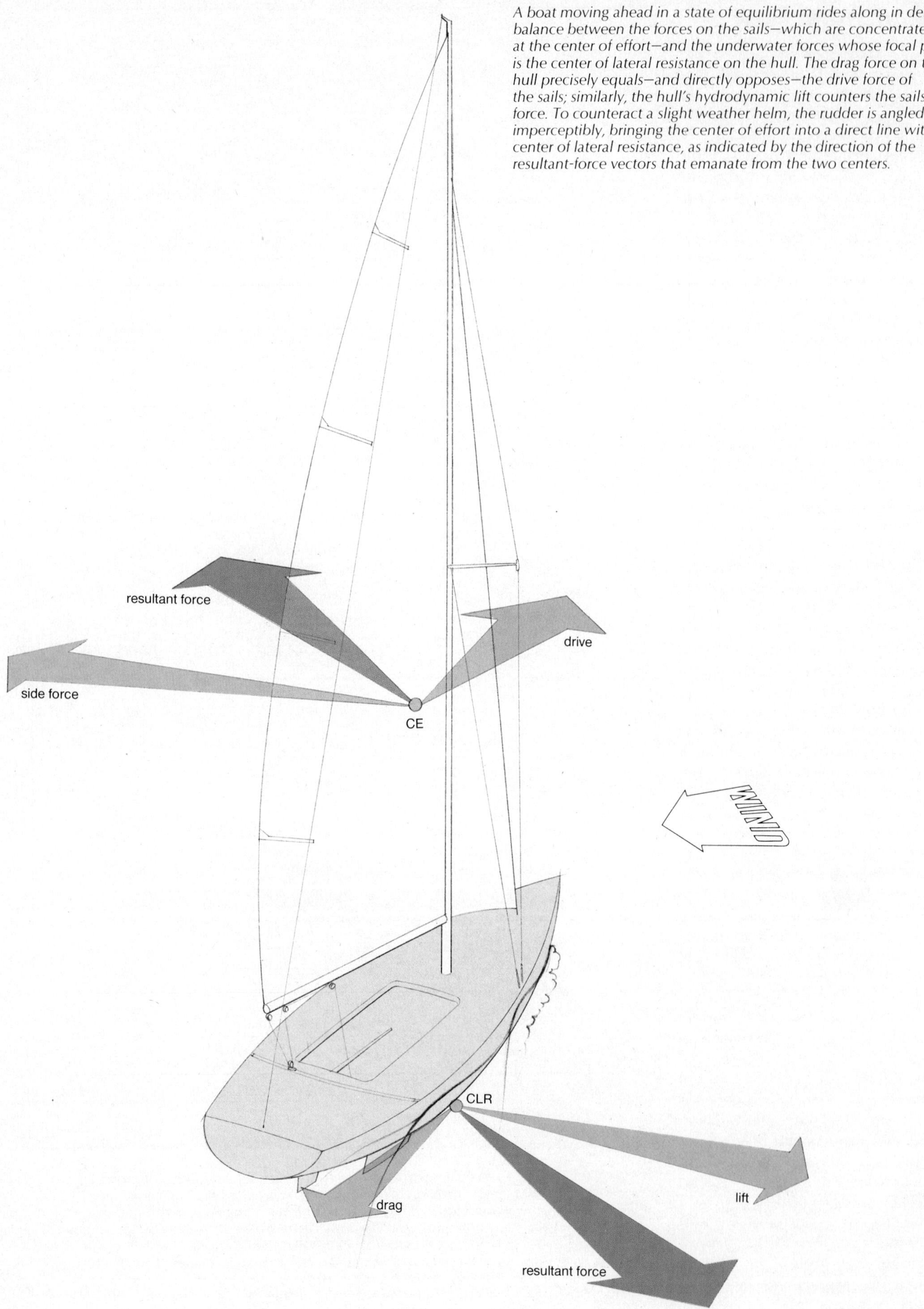

A boat moving ahead in a state of equilibrium rides along in delicate balance between the forces on the sails—which are concentrated at the center of effort—and the underwater forces whose focal point is the center of lateral resistance on the hull. The drag force on the hull precisely equals—and directly opposes—the drive force of the sails; similarly, the hull's hydrodynamic lift counters the sails' side force. To counteract a slight weather helm, the rudder is angled imperceptibly, bringing the center of effort into a direct line with the center of lateral resistance, as indicated by the direction of the resultant-force vectors that emanate from the two centers.

A Balance of Power

Whenever a sailboat moves forward at a steady speed, the forces acting on the hull and sails counterbalance each other to create a state of equilibrium *(left)*.

This balanced state is subject to constant change, however. If, for example, a skipper successfully adjusts his sails or alters his heading so as to pick up speed, the drive force in his sails increases, and the boat will accelerate. The acceleration continues until drag, in response to the faster flow of water past the hull, increases to match drive, and the boat settles into a new—and faster—state of equilibrium. Conversely, should a boat lose all headway the balance of forces will be totally disrupted, and the skipper must take measures *(right)* to get moving again.

In addition to placing the boat itself in an ever-varying state of equilibrium, the forces on the sails and hull contribute a second type of balance that acts on the helm. The sail forces are concentrated at a focal point called the center of effort (CE), the hull forces at a pivot point known as the center of lateral resistance (CLR). When these two centers are vertically aligned, with neither one ahead of the other, the helm is in balance and the boat will stay on course without any correction from the rudder. Normally, however, the CE is slightly aft of the CLR, and the boat tends to turn into the wind—a condition known as weather helm. Some weather helm gives the skipper a welcome feel of the rudder, but too much *(overleaf)* can render a boat unmanageable.

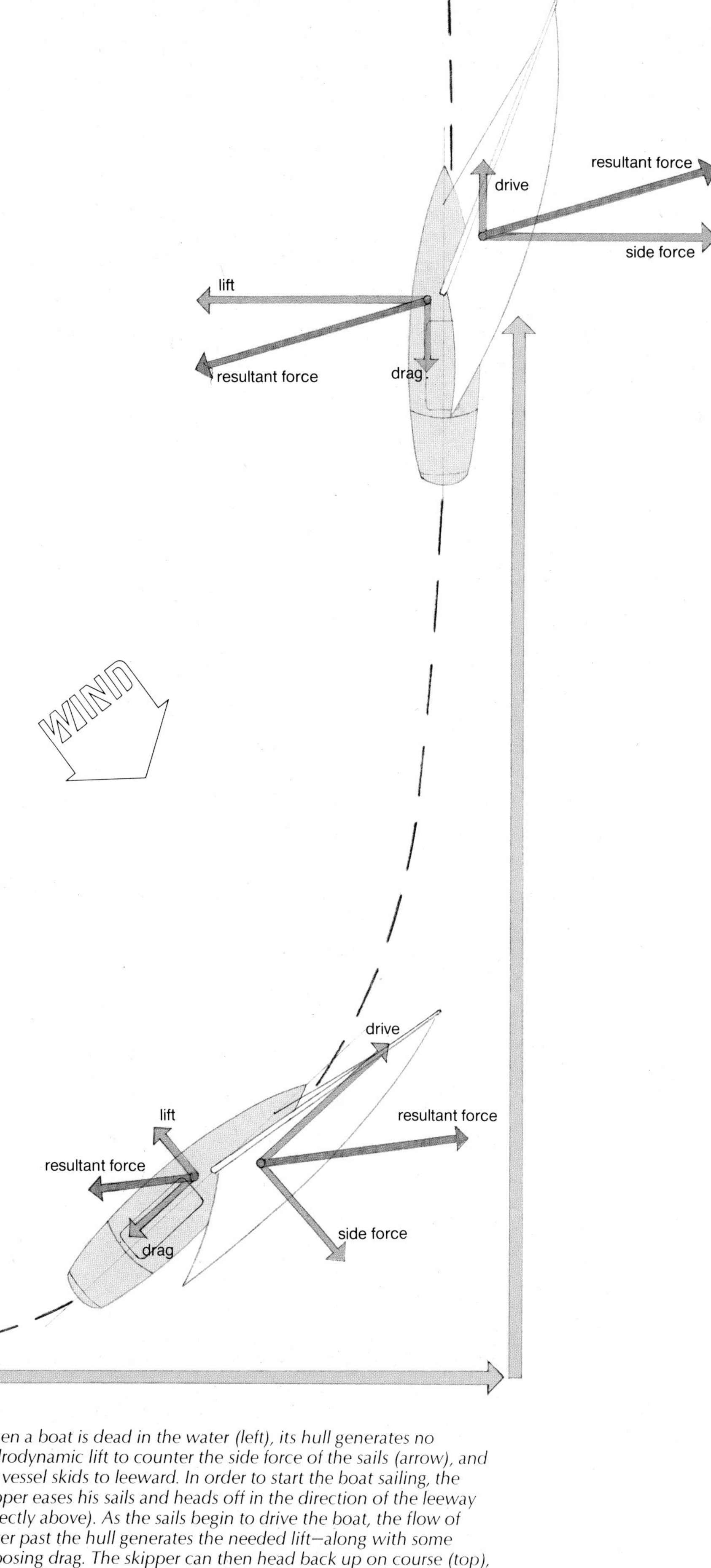

When a boat is dead in the water (left), its hull generates no hydrodynamic lift to counter the side force of the sails (arrow), and the vessel skids to leeward. In order to start the boat sailing, the skipper eases his sails and heads off in the direction of the leeway (directly above). As the sails begin to drive the boat, the flow of water past the hull generates the needed lift—along with some opposing drag. The skipper can then head back up on course (top), with the boat moving steadily forward and the forces in equilibrium.

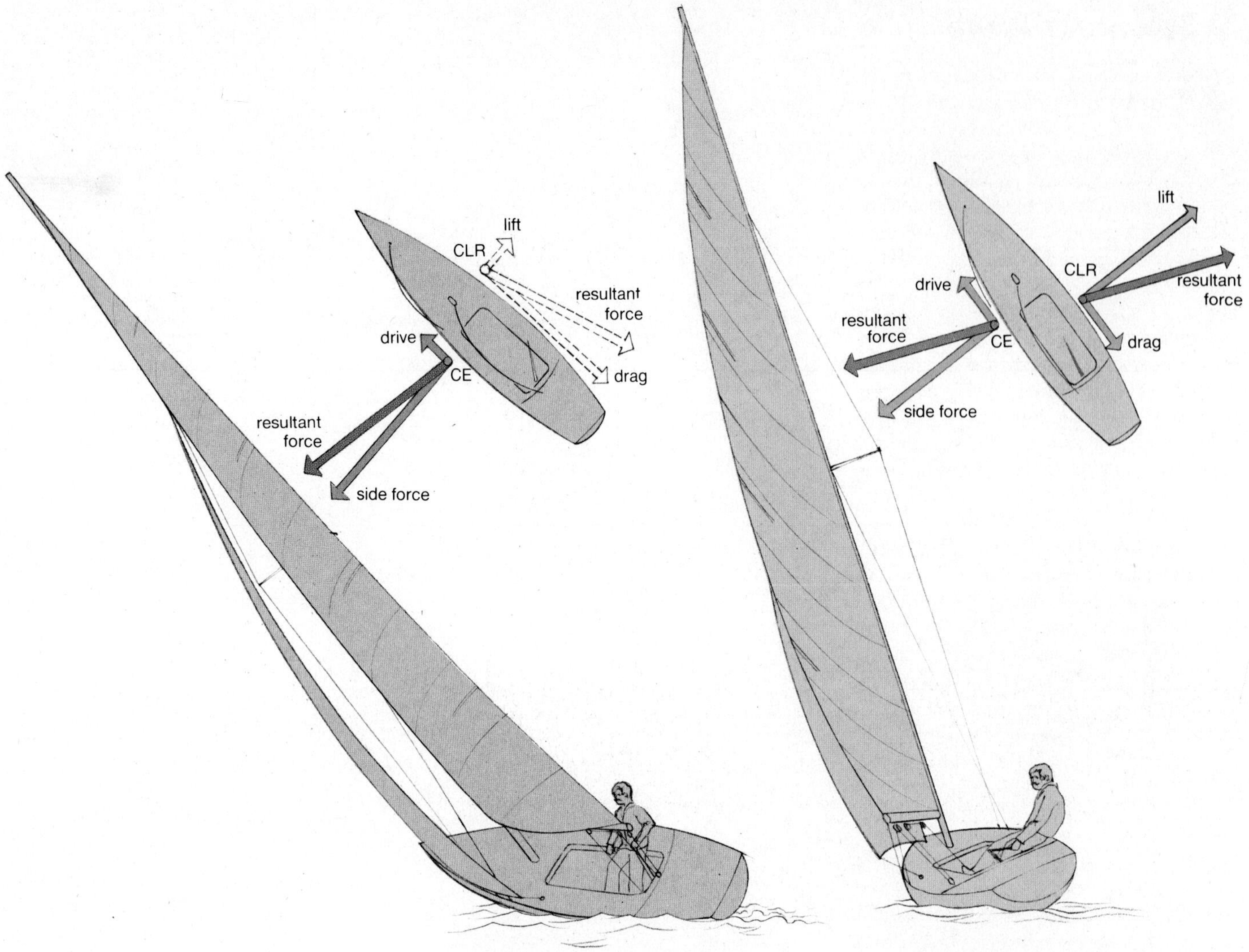

A boat heels excessively when the skipper allows it to become overpowered by the wind. Under these conditions, side force becomes severe, as shown in the diagram at top, and drive is reduced. As the boat slows down, the force of hydrodynamic lift diminishes, so that the boat falls off to leeward. At the same time the center of effort moves aft of the center of lateral resistance, and the boat develops a strong weather helm. In a mistaken effort to keep on course, the skipper shown here wrestles the tiller hard over, increasing drag and slowing the boat even more, thus compounding the problem.

To combat excessive heel, first feather up to weather, slack off the mainsheet and hike out to move weight to windward. If the heel persists, flatten both the mainsail and jib (pages 36-39), ease both sheets and move the traveler block to leeward. All three operations spill wind from the sails and thus reduce the side force. As the boat rights itself, the center of effort and the center of lateral resistance will fall into line, alleviating the weather helm. The skipper may now put his rudder back amidships, reducing drag and allowing the boat to move forward on a proper course at a faster speed.

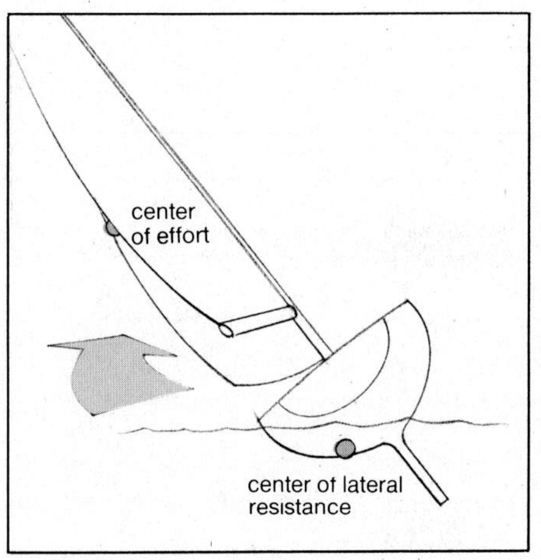

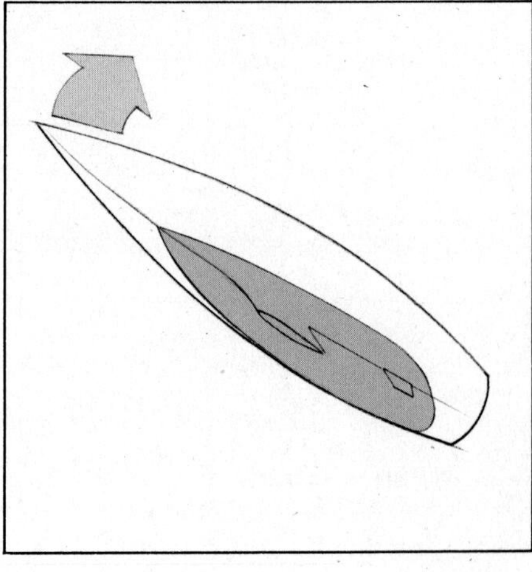

When a boat heels rail down, the forces on the sails and the hull put it in double jeopardy, generating weather helm on two accounts. The center of effort on the sails moves outboard (far left) and tends to lever the boat to windward (arrow) around its center of lateral resistance. In addition, since the boat is tipped beyond its designed limits (near left), the underwater shape of the hull becomes asymmetrical, and the flow of water against the curved lines of the leeward side turns the bow upwind.

The Right Attitude

No boat will perform up to its potential unless it rides in an even, stable attitude in the water. Excessive heel when going to windward *(opposite)*, or a side-to-side roll when heading off the wind *(right)*, will reduce the boat's speed dramatically.

Most keelboats are intended by the designer to be heeled no more than 30° to the perpendicular; for a centerboarder the critical angle is only 25°. Beyond either of these critical points, the vessel no longer sails on its designed lines, and enough drag will eventually develop on the hull to cut the speed. Indeed, the centerboarder may capsize. Too much heel also breeds the secondary problems of severe weather helm *(bottom left)*. And if the skipper, in an attempt to keep the boat on course, tries to outmuscle the helm, he may make the situation worse, perhaps causing the boat to heel more than ever *(top, far left)*.

When the wind heeling the boat is simply a sudden gust, the skipper can put the craft on its feet again by heading up momentarily, hiking out and, if necessary, by easing the main to spill wind. But if the gust turns into a strong, steady blow, the skipper must reshape and retrim both main and jib *(top, near left)*. This will not only right the boat, but will also bring welcome dividends of increased speed and maneuverability.

Another type of hull instability—an alarming phenomenon called downwind roll—is also created by poorly shaped and improperly trimmed sails, particularly the spinnaker. Here, too, the problem will be compounded by misguided helmsmanship: the skipper's normal instinct is to steer away from the roll, which only worsens it. The cure is to flatten the chute and trim it in, allowing it as little room as possible to swing back and forth. Then the helmsman steers with the roll—much as the driver of a skidding automobile steers with the skid—until the oscillation diminishes and the boat is under control.

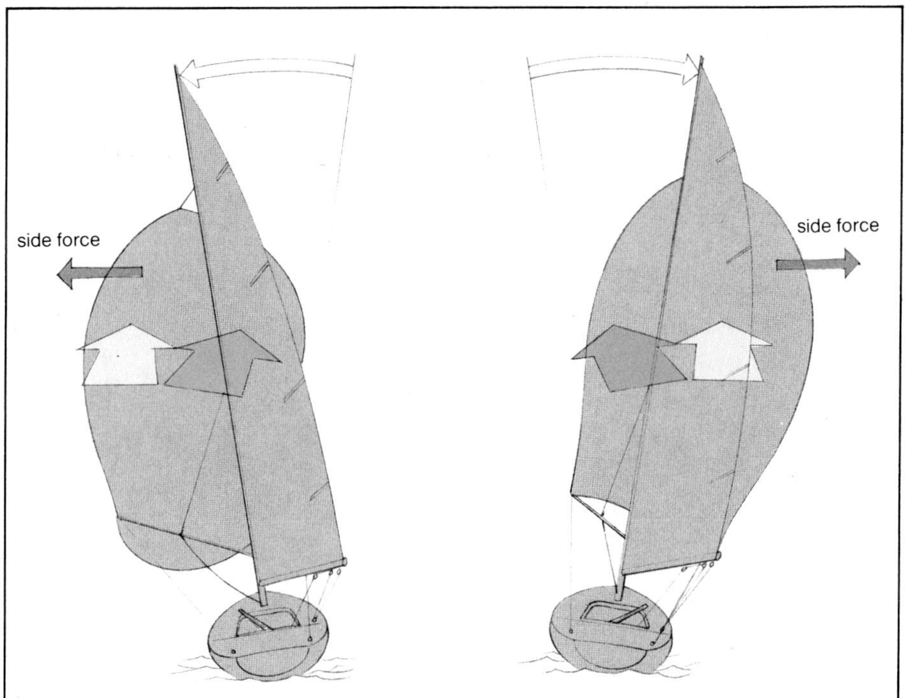

A violent downwind roll develops if a loosely trimmed spinnaker on a slack halyard is allowed to oscillate across the bow. As the sail swings back and forth, the speed of its movement brings about a local shift of the apparent wind (light blue arrows to dark blue arrows) on the sail. The new wind generates an unwanted force on the sail's forward side (dark gray arrows) that pulls the sail over and tips the boat all the more. Unless the mainsail is vanged down, it too will swing, accentuating the motion. An inexperienced skipper may try to counter the problem by steering against the roll; this only makes matters worse, as it steers the bow out from under the swinging spinnaker.

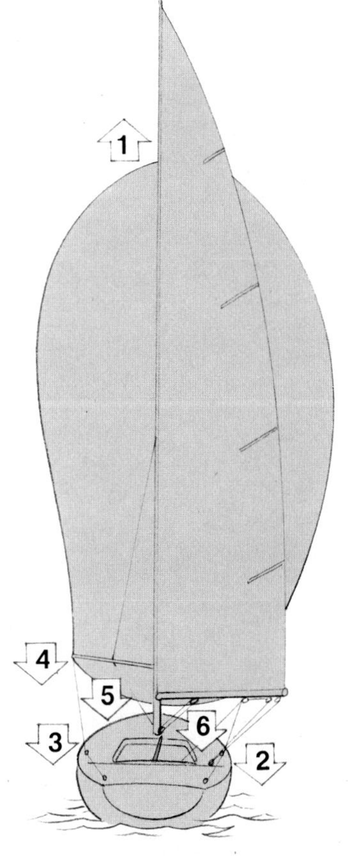

A proper solution to downwind roll is to flatten the spinnaker by first taking up on the halyard (1) and tightening the sheet (2) and the guy (3), then lowering the pole (4) and trimming in the foreguy (5). To prevent the mainsail from swinging and rising up, tighten the boom vang (6). Finally, steer in the direction of each roll; that is, when the boat is tipping to port, turn the bow to port as well. This keeps the hull directly under the top of the mast, and thus brings the oscillation under control.

THE LUSTY BIRTH OF SMALL-BOAT RACING

During much of the 19th Century, yacht racing was a rarefied sport for a handful of moneyed Easterners—many of whom relied on a professional skipper and crew to do the actual sailing of their splendidly large pleasure craft. Racing boats small enough to suit the purse of the common man were entirely lacking until shortly after the Civil War, when ordinary Americans looked around and discovered that serviceable vessels had been there all the time—in the form of catboats and other craft used by fishermen from Cape Cod to San Francisco Bay. Seaside residents soon began staging regular contests that drew enthusiastic crowds and often lasted well into the night.

At first the rules of these races were pretty much what the local organizer managed to think up, often on the spur of the moment. In some contests, boats anchored along a line for a standing start, their exact position in the row having been determined by drawing lots. Other races went off with no-holds-barred starts —epitomized by an 1883 race at Marblehead, Massachusetts, in which a stupendous fleet of 176 catboats battered its way across the line to the crunch of colliding vessels and the howls of outraged crews. After a contest, disputes were usually thrashed out—sometimes physically—at a local saloon.

By the close of the century, small-boat racing had left many of its rough-hewn ways behind. Rules had become systematized, and designers had begun creating standardized racing classes. Moreover, the sport had spread to inland waters, and international competition was underway. So thoroughly and quickly did the sport become both civilized and popularized that one emphatic spokesman for boat racing deplored the very existence of any other form of outdoor recreation "when Heaven has been good enough to send wind to sail with."

Yachting enthusiasts congregate on the steamboat pier at Oak Bluffs in Martha's Vineyard, Massachusetts, to watch a catboat race in 1875. During the heady youth of day racing, wealthy spectators sometimes placed bets as high as $50,000 on a single race; the wagering continued fast and furious throughout the contest, with the odds changing as the competing boats passed each successive mark.

The Work Boat Transformed

In the late 1860s, two particular types of commercial fishing boats gained popularity among the new breed of budget yachtsmen: the stubby-masted, round-bottomed catboats favored in rough New England waters; and the broad-beamed sloops designed for shallower, more sheltered environs. Quickly the desire for speed began to transform these boats' utilitarian rigs. Some catboats grew booms extending so far beyond their sterns that the mainsails could be reefed near the clew only by docking or having a dinghy come alongside. The owners of sloops followed suit with their booms—and devised huge bowsprits for their jibs. These over-canvased sloops were nicknamed "sandbaggers" because their crews heaved 50-pound sacks of sand from rail to rail when the vessel tacked. Even with adroit ballast-work, capsizings were common.

Despite their lack of seaworthiness, the catboats and sandbaggers remained racing favorites for three decades, and a man who regularly won in a boat he had bought for $250 could easily sell it to some other speed-hungry yachtsman for $600.

Ghosting along on a beam reach, a sloop with a crew of seven hunkered in the cockpit and a stack of sandbags on the weather rail cuts through Long Island Sound. On downwind runs to the finish, crews heaved their sacks of sand overboard if rules permitted; and if the rules forbade this ploy, bags were often lost "by accident."

Carrying large sails on outsized booms, 18-foot catboats compete off Marblehead, Massachusetts, in 1888. Overall length—with no consideration of sail area—was the usual criterion for sorting out competing boats. Nor was the sail plan necessarily a factor: catboats and sloops often raced one another.

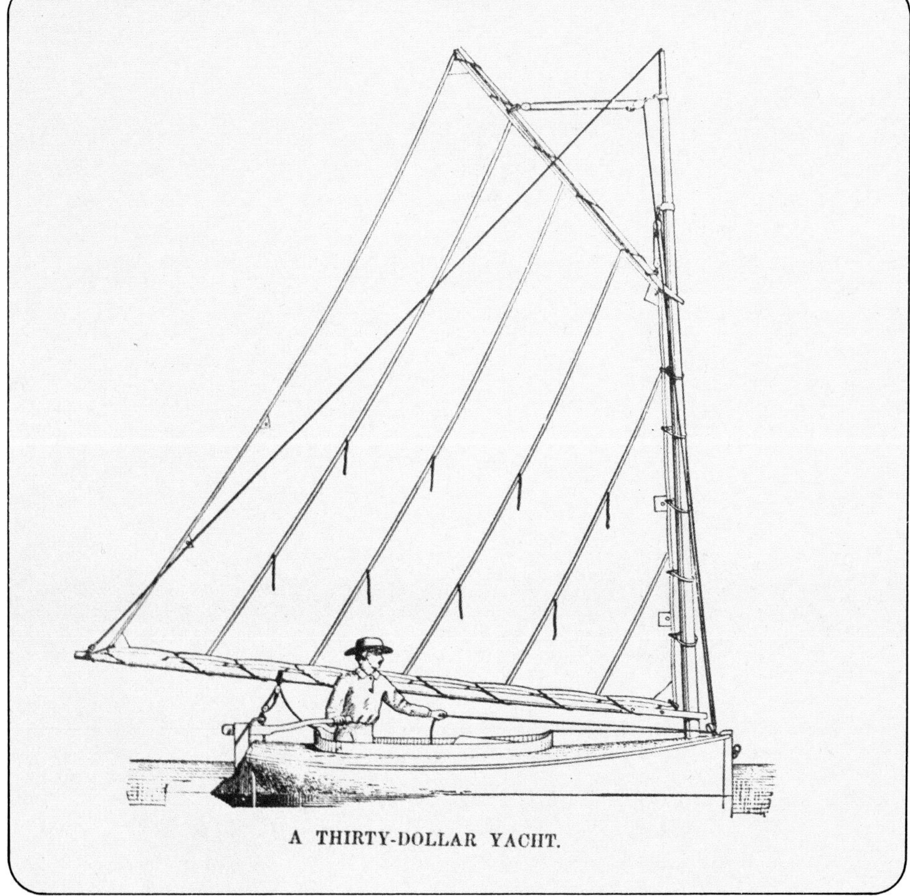

For would-be yachtsmen of modest means, an 1876 issue of Scientific American carried complete plans for building a $30 catboat. Lest even this price tag pinch, the magazine also provided do-it-yourself instructions for a $14 skiff and a $12 rowboat.

Newfangled Canoes

Another one of the oddities that raced in American waters during the late 19th Century was the transmogrified canoe, fitted with sails forward and aft. First developed in England in 1865 by a retired British Army officer named John MacGregor, the sailing canoe soon took on such rigging refinements as a bamboo mast and battens inspired by Chinese river junks; for stability, it acquired a ponderous metal centerboard and bags of shot as ballast.

In the early 1870s, a few of these vessels were imported to the United States, where they generated such excitement that dozens of canoe clubs sprang up to pursue the joys of racing and cruising in them. By 1880, the Americans had gone their own way in canoe design and were producing simpler versions of the original British craft. And when these new-world models were tested against the British in the contest shown here, the Yanks left no doubt as to who ruled the waves.

Skittish sailing canoes jockey for position at the start of the first British-American competition. The five-day, 19-race series was arranged by the infant American Canoe Association and staged off Grindstone Island in the St. Lawrence River during August 1886.

Warington Baden-Powell nestles down in Nautilus V, one of two British challengers in the 1886 race meet. Baden-Powell—whose brother founded the Boy Scouts—sailed "British style," stretching nearly flat in the canoe's tiny cockpit. Like the other British entry, his craft was stabilized by 100 pounds of ballast and a 56-pound centerboard. The Americans, however, dispensed with these speed-draining burdens and steadied their canoes by sitting up on the deck and shifting their weight as puffs of wind passed over.

Amid the tents and drying laundry of the canoeists' Grindstone Island encampment, big winner Robert Gibson poses with Vesper, bearing the American Canoe Association's silver trophy on her foredeck. Although Gibson did not bother to enter many of the 19 races, he walked off with the climactic Trophy Race. The best British canoe finished eighth—10 minutes behind Vesper—and the other British entry came in a minute later.

A Showcase Competition

In the final years of 19th Century small-boat racing, one competition stood above all the rest, both in prestige and in its stimulating effect on sailboat design—the Seawanhaka International Trophy for Small Yachts.

The Seawanhaka Cup began to take shape in January 1895 when the London Minima Yacht Club issued a sort of back-handed challenge to the Seawanhaka Corinthian Yacht Club of Oyster Bay, New York: Would the Yanks host a series of match races with the English "½-rater?" This class of boat, with a 15-foot waterline length and 225 square feet of sail, did not yet exist in the United States. But the Americans accepted the challenge and built six sloops to meet the restrictions of length and sail area. After strenuous trial races, the defense of the nation's honor was entrusted to *Ethelwynn,* the first American boat to carry a Marconi rig. And in the first race, in light winds against the gaff-rigged challenger, *Spruce IV,* she came in ahead by almost eight minutes.

When the Canadians challenged for the cup the following year, the Americans entered another advanced design—a mahogany scow whose bottom received a prerace smoothing by a piano finisher from the Steinway Company. But the Canadians had a still-swifter scow, which won handily. In subsequent years, Canada unveiled some even more exotic designs *(opposite),* and the Americans failed to retrieve the cup until 1904.

In a mere zephyr of a breeze, shortly after the start of one of the five races in the Seawanhaka Cup series in 1895, Ethelwynn—the creation of the renowned designer William P. Stephens—leaves Britain's Spruce IV astern. In heavier air Ethelwynn proved a bit slower, but won the series 3 to 2.

Although England issued the original challenge for the Seawanhaka Cup, the Americans set the rules in a "Declaration of Trust," and also provided the trophy. They stressed that the competition was to have a "Corinthian spirit"—meaning that only amateurs were allowed. The preamble to the declaration is reproduced at right.

DECLARATION OF TRUST

GOVERNING THE

SEAWANHAKA INTERNATIONAL CHALLENGE CUP,

FOR SMALL YACHTS.

☆

THIS INSTRUMENT, dated the first day of June, A. D. 1895, made by the SEAWANHAKA CORINTHIAN YACHT CLUB, a corporation duly organized and existing under and by virtue of the laws of the State of New York, hereinafter called the SEAWANHAKA CLUB.

WITNESSETH as follows:

The Seawanhaka Club, having offered an international Challenge Cup for the purpose of promoting small yacht racing and developing the Corinthian spirit among yachtsmen, hereby sets forth and declares the terms and conditions, which shall govern the tenure of the said Cup and the competitions therefor.

One of the fastest and most imaginative sailboats spawned by the Seawanhaka Cup was the 1898 Canadian challenger, Dominion, featuring a deep channel through the bottom that made her, in effect, a catamaran. Because she had much less hull in the water than her American competitor, she easily won—however, rule changes the following year barred such designs from further cup racing.

The First Look-alikes

While most early yachtsmen reveled in the triumphs of their own specially designed boats, in 1884 one, William Weld of North Haven, Maine, wearied of easy victories in a 14-foot dinghy he had created for local races. To develop worthy competition, he took a simple but radical step: he graciously allowed his opponents to build duplicates. The result was America's first one-design class *(bottom)*.

Although the cat-rigged dinghy never spread beyond its birthplace, dozens of other one-design classes began to appear, and racing flourished as never before. Weld may have regretted the development on one occasion. At a Grand Dinghy Race in 1887, all the male skippers of North Haven were trounced by a woman. The abashed losers gave her a sloop, perhaps to redirect her boating attentions.

By 1901, when these Herreshoff 15s were racing off Buzzards Bay, Massachusetts, one-design craft were commonplace in American waters. So too were races like this one, which featured female skippers. Although male crewmen were preponderant in the fleet, the winner—E-11—was an all-women entry.

High-sided North Haven dinghies reach toward the second mark during a 1919 race. Some of the earliest of these dinghies, built before the turn of the century, are still racing in the waters off the coast of Maine.

The 12-foot Butterfly class, shown here in a race on Long Island Sound in 1919, used the flattish hulls and sprit-rigged sails of 19th Century duck-hunting boats. Though the class failed to catch on around Long Island, virtually identical craft flourished in New Jersey's Barnegat Bay, where they still compete under the nickname of sneakboxes.

The Bug Becomes a Star

In the year 1906, an embryo yachting star was born quietly in a cluttered office in lower Manhattan. There, a yacht designer named William Gardner drew up plans for a 17-foot keel sloop with the rather undignified name of "Bug." He was acting at the behest of his friend George Corry, an avid racer who felt that the health of the sport would be well served by a yacht that was inexpensive, very fast but stable, and could be mass-produced as a one-design craft. The auguries for Gardner's creation were modest, however: while the Bug became a popular one-design class for a time, it was too small, wet and uncomfortable to gain lasting acceptance.

Five years later Gardner began designing a larger version of the Bug. The result this time was the first—and for decades the only—international one-design racer: the aptly named Star. Early Star boats were gaff-rigged, but the boat took on a Marconi-rigged sail in 1921. By 1970, that triangular sail and its distinctive red star could be seen on some 5,000 identical boats in fleets around the world.

Dressed in matching yachting uniforms, George Corry and his wife race the Star's predecessor—the 17-foot Bug. Although skipper Corry won almost all of the Bug races he entered, his greatest achievement was popularizing the Star—about six feet longer than the Bug—by forming the organization that grew into the present-day International Star Class Yacht Racing Association.

Gaff-rigged Stars race in a light breeze off Larchmont, New York, in 1920. A year later, after class rules were changed to allow jib-headed sails, the mast was lengthened and the boom shortened to complete the evolution of one of the most popular of all early one-designs.

J
6014

3

As the traffic jam of Blue Jays maneuvering around a mark in the photograph at left attests, yacht racing can be both tough and contentious. Like other highly competitive sports, it is governed by rules that bring sense and safety to the proceedings. These rules are elastic enough to allow for an almost infinite variety of competitive ploys. Nearly all races in the United States are held under a set of 72 regulations published in a 70-page blue booklet titled *The Yacht Racing Rules* and produced by the national authority for sailboat racing: the United States Yacht Racing Union. Encyclopedic in its thoroughness, this code covers virtually every aspect of the sport, from the

THE RACER'S RULE BOOK

administration of races by committees, through who has right of way under what circumstances, down to the proper size of identifying sail numbers. The rule book is divided into six parts, each dealing with a separate aspect of racing. The most important—and commonly misunderstood—of these bylaws are illustrated on the following pages.

The first part of the racer's bible, entitled "Definitions," spells out 17 fundamental terms—carefully noting, for example, that a yacht finishes "when any part of her hull, or of her crew or equipment in normal position, crosses the finishing line from the direction of the course from the last mark...." Part 2 of the book is addressed to race-committee officials, who are on hand for every contest, usually stationed on a boat that is anchored at one end of the starting and finish line. From a sailor's viewpoint, the most significant regulations set forth here are the signals used by the officials to inform competitors of the committee's on-the-spot decisions—such as postponing a race in bad weather or abandoning it completely. This section also empowers race committees to distribute leaflets of supplementary local information called sailing instructions *(overleaf)*.

The third part of the rule book lists all the steps a boatowner must take to qualify his vessel for a race—e.g., requisite lifesaving equipment, weight and ballast limitations, and so on. These instructions should be consulted long before race day, since it could take some time to fulfill all the requirements.

Parts 4 and 5 of the booklet contain the myriad boat-handling rules that must be observed by a skipper from the time he begins to sail in the vicinity of the starting line until the moment he finishes. Many of these strictures deal with right-of-way situations in a manner similar to worldwide maritime law. But yacht-racing rules are far more detailed, in order to account for frantic scenes such as the one shown at left or the even more harrowing moments when 60 or more ocean-racing yachts converge on a starting line that may be only 800 yards in length.

Part 6 of the rule book describes protest situations—the aftermath of one contestant's infringement upon the rights of another. Before a race, a contestant must be sure to check the sailing instructions to find out the penalty for breaking a rule; even though the traditional punishment is disqualification, some committees opt for milder alternatives, such as sailing through two complete 360° turns in open water. If a protested skipper wishes to contest a case and defend himself, he counterprotests, and the matter is settled at a race-committee meeting afterward.

No set of rules is completely just, and good tactical skippers can bend certain racing technicalities to their will. Watch out for the wily sea lawyer who wins races by outprotesting his rivals. And beware the cagey salt who, when approaching a boat on port tack, cries "starboard!" and bluffs an opponent into giving way; while his ethics might be questioned, the tactic is not unlawful, according to the book.

The sailors aboard these Blue Jays maneuver to avoid collision—as well as to gain competitive advantage—as they douse their spinnakers and crowd around a mark.

A Race-Day Fact Sheet

No sport is more diverse or more subject to circumstance than yacht racing. Races can last for minutes or months; they may circle a placid Kentucky reservoir or circumnavigate the globe's stormy seas; fleets may consist of majestic oceangoing craft or boards with sails. Though The Yacht Racing Rules *(previous page)* manage to oversee this entire spectrum of competition, they cannot cover every eventuality. Therefore they must be supplemented by additional bylaws concocted by individual race committees, spelling out the particulars of a given contest, such as the courses to be sailed, starting times for racers or time limits for finishing. These supplementary regulations, called the sailing instructions, are distributed to sailors before race day.

Instructions also give notice of any alteration of the rule book by the race committee; for example, if officials want to open a race to all comers, the sailing instructions must explicitly waive Rule 21, which states that all yachts in a race must have on board a member of a sailing club recognized by the United States Yacht Racing Union. Beyond these basic contents, officials can write up the instructions as elaborately as they please—offering information about tides or adding to the competitive zest with tantalizing descriptions of the winners' prizes.

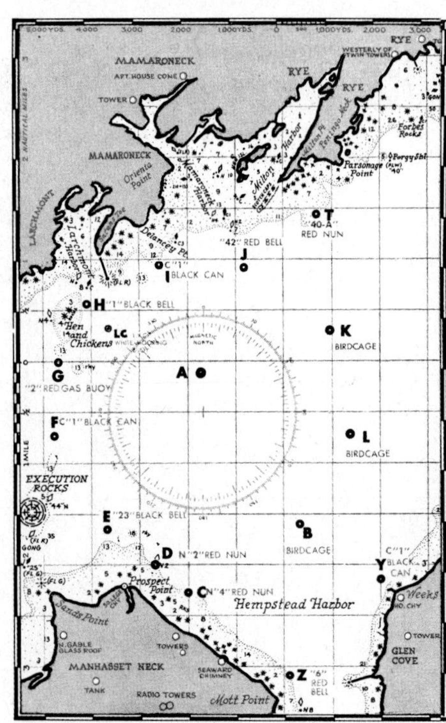

As a supplement to sailing instructions, racing organizations often distribute charts like the one above—issued by the Larchmont Yacht Club on Long Island Sound—locating marks and giving their identifying letters.

A typical set of sailing instructions, for a Labor Day regatta, is reproduced at right. As with all proper instructions, they contain nine entries, explained below.

Rules

The first element of every set of sailing instructions is a legalistic paragraph explaining that the race or races will be conducted under the International Yacht Racing Union Rules, and can be supplemented in three ways: by the United States Yacht Racing Union, by the race committee's instructions, and by the class associations (page 13). However, neither the race committee nor a class association can change provisions of Parts 1 (definitions) or 4 (right-of-way rules).

Courses

Three general types of race courses are commonly used. The type described at right, called selective, consists of several marks that may be chosen as rounding points by the race committee. The second type of course, called fixed, is used for point-to-point races—from one harbor to another, for example; it is described in full by the instructions. The third, or custom course, follows a geometric pattern —most often a triangle; it may be diagramed in the instructions.

Course Signals

These sailing instructions, dealing only with selective courses, offer a sample course-signal grid simulating the grid displayed atop the committee boat before the start of the classes. Reading down on the grid, skippers see that both the first and second classes, designated by numerals, must round marks A, B and C, while a third class must round D, E and F. Fixed and custom courses are signaled by a letter or number corresponding to a course description in the instructions.

Time

The starting time for each class is often included in the instructions in a table, which also indicates class names and starting signals.

Signal

When a series of classes is started sequentially, the starting signal for each can be either white, blue or red (page 68). At major racing events, huge classes may be broken into divisions; to avoid confusion, committees often add paired signals to indicate divisions.

Starting Line

A conventional starting line stretches between the committee boat and a mark—often brightly colored for visibility. Occasionally, however, a second mark may replace the committee boat.

Finish Line and Shortening Instructions

The finish line is designated in the same manner as the starting line —between a mark and the committee boat. Courses can be shortened, if the wind fails, by changing the position of the finish line.

Time Limit

To keep races from lasting into darkness in light air, a contest is considered valid only if completed within a stated time limit. Usually, only one boat needs to meet the time limit; however, an outside time limit may be added—for instance, "All yachts must finish by 7 p.m."

Scoring

A scoring system is necessary when classes are divided into divisions or when a race is part of a series. In the method shown here, the boat with the highest score wins. By awarding an extra one quarter point for finishing first, this system favors winners over skippers who amass high scores by often coming in second or third; it also penalizes rule breakers, giving them a lower score than a boat that fails to finish.

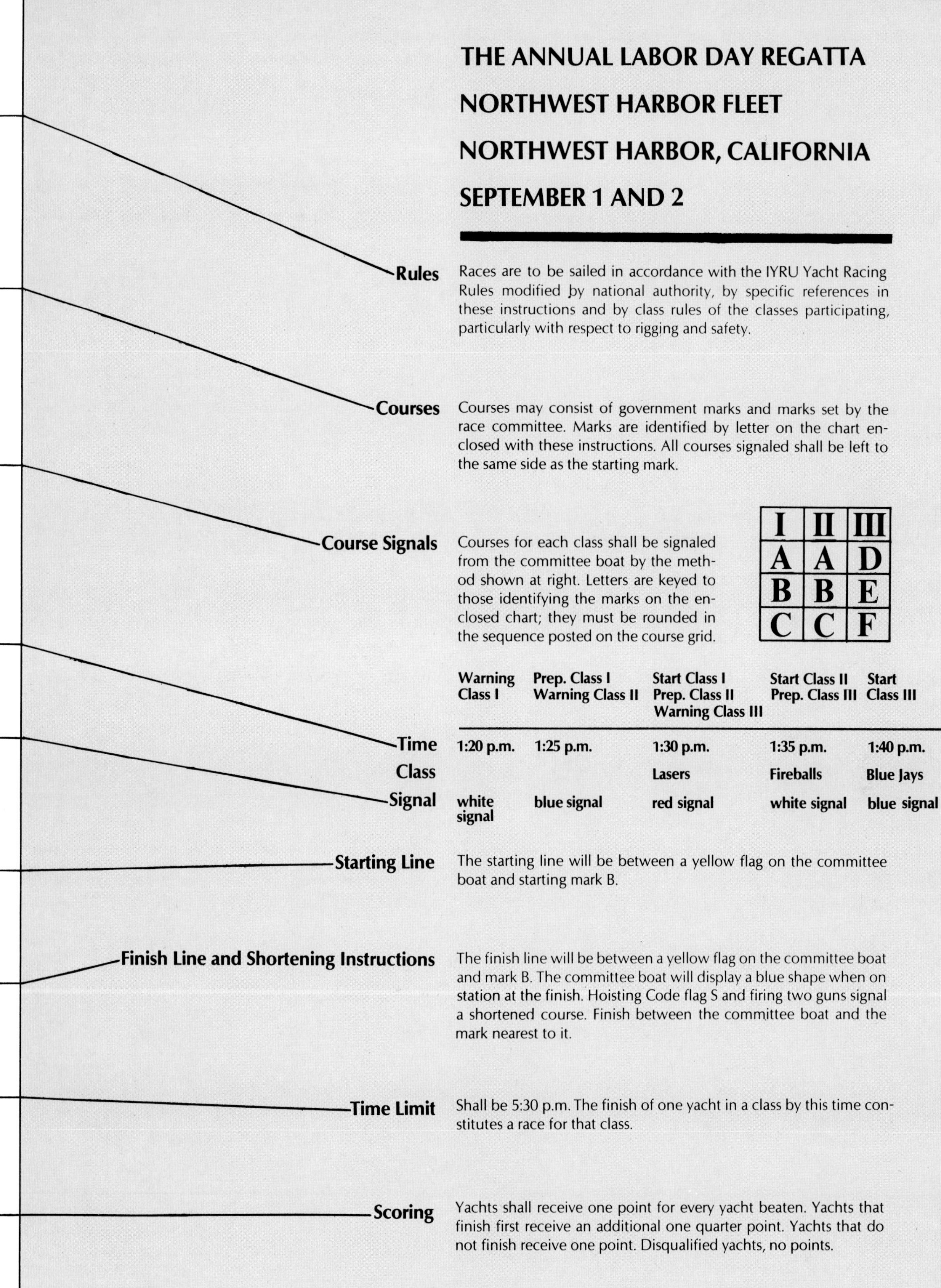

THE ANNUAL LABOR DAY REGATTA
NORTHWEST HARBOR FLEET
NORTHWEST HARBOR, CALIFORNIA
SEPTEMBER 1 AND 2

Rules Races are to be sailed in accordance with the IYRU Yacht Racing Rules modified by national authority, by specific references in these instructions and by class rules of the classes participating, particularly with respect to rigging and safety.

Courses Courses may consist of government marks and marks set by the race committee. Marks are identified by letter on the chart enclosed with these instructions. All courses signaled shall be left to the same side as the starting mark.

Course Signals Courses for each class shall be signaled from the committee boat by the method shown at right. Letters are keyed to those identifying the marks on the enclosed chart; they must be rounded in the sequence posted on the course grid.

I	II	III
A	A	D
B	B	E
C	C	F

	Warning Class I	Prep. Class I Warning Class II	Start Class I Prep. Class II Warning Class III	Start Class II Prep. Class III	Start Class III
Time	1:20 p.m.	1:25 p.m.	1:30 p.m.	1:35 p.m.	1:40 p.m.
Class			Lasers	Fireballs	Blue Jays
Signal	white signal	blue signal	red signal	white signal	blue signal

Starting Line The starting line will be between a yellow flag on the committee boat and starting mark B.

Finish Line and Shortening Instructions The finish line will be between a yellow flag on the committee boat and mark B. The committee boat will display a blue shape when on station at the finish. Hoisting Code flag S and firing two guns signal a shortened course. Finish between the committee boat and the mark nearest to it.

Time Limit Shall be 5:30 p.m. The finish of one yacht in a class by this time constitutes a race for that class.

Scoring Yachts shall receive one point for every yacht beaten. Yachts that finish first receive an additional one quarter point. Yachts that do not finish receive one point. Disqualified yachts, no points.

Committee-Boat Signals

Out on the water on race day, a race committee orchestrates the events in traditional nautical style: by raising and lowering Code flags, and/or other signals broadly known as shapes—brightly colored cylinders or spheres made of canvas or nylon. These signals are usually hoisted aboard a committee boat, though in some cases they may be displayed on a flagstaff ashore. Alert racing skippers memorize the complete vocabulary of messages and keep an eye out for any stirrings of the officials that might presage a new directive. Some may post a crew member as a committee-boat watch.

Signals are flown for two basic purposes —to mark normal racing procedures such as a start or finish *(pages 68-69),* and to convey information about postponement, cancellation and any other special procedures. In the former case, shapes are widely used instead of flags; they can be seen equally well from any direction and do not sag when the wind lets up. Special-procedure signals *(right)* consist of flags from the International Code (the normal meanings of the flags have little or no bearing upon their use as racing signals).

Visual messages are often accompanied by sound signals from a horn or a small cannon firing blank shotgun shells. Although a single horn blast or shot serves in most cases, changes in the expected visual directives are underscored by multiple sound signals. For example, one blast is sounded for a regular starting signal, two blasts for a postponement and three for the cancellation of a race.

The answering pennant of the International Code, normally used by ships when responding to a message, signals to yacht racers that all races not started have been postponed.

Code flag N hoisted over the first repeater—a triangular flag that betokens the repetition of the flag above it—means "all races have been canceled."

Code flag N flown alone indicates that the race or races already underway have been abandoned and declared void. The race committee then decides to resail or cancel them.

Code flag L means either "come within hail" or "follow me." It might be used to direct racers to a new starting area or to bring boats closer for essential verbal instructions.

Code flag S indicates the course has been shortened. If raised before the start, it refers to a course described in the instructions. Raised near a mark, it means "finish there."

Code flag R, when flown over a course signal, means "sail the designated course in the reverse direction." Reversals are usually prompted by a shift in wind direction.

The first repeater flying alone means that an entire starting class has been recalled to start over. The flag is used if many boats start early or if the start signal was in error.

Code flag M, when flown from a buoy, vessel or object like a stake, either designates a replacement mark for one that is missing or adds a mark to those listed in the instructions.

Aboard a well-draped committee boat, race officials signal a postponement due to threatening weather conditions by hoisting the candy-striped answering pennant over its bow and firing two blasts of a cannon. The yellow flag farthest forward marks the exact end of the starting line. Just forward of the bridge, Code flag D indicates that life jackets are mandatory for all racers. A blue-and-white-striped yacht-club burgee flies at the starboard yardarm. Atop the mainmast is a flag identifying this vessel as the committee boat. The grid on the cabin top aft spells out the courses: around marks F, A and I for the two classes that are racing. The third class has been canceled.

Starts and Finishes

Precisely 10 minutes before the start of the first class, at a time prescribed in the sailing instructions, competitors are given the so-called warning signal: a white flag or white shape (right, over the bow) is hoisted on the committee boat. A gun is fired at the same instant; but the visual directive is pre-eminent and remains in effect even if the gun is mistimed. In lieu of the traditional white signal, some committees opt for more eye-catching orange or yellow versions.

The hoisting of a blue preparatory signal and firing of a gun indicate that exactly five minutes are left until the start (the white warning signal has been dropped 30 seconds earlier to give racers some advance notice of the blue hoist). Race committees need not restrict themselves to the usual five-minute interval between signals, but any departure from it must be in the sailing instructions.

The hoisting of a red signal and simultaneous firing of a gun mark the start of the first racing class. This signal will also serve as the five-minute signal for the second class; a white shape will be its starting signal. If a third class is racing, white and blue shapes serve as the preparatory and starting signals.

A gun is fired on the committee boat as the first boat in a class crosses the finish line. Some committees sound a horn for each boat finishing thereafter; they may also announce sail numbers. Three blue cylinders on this committee boat inform racers that it is at the line; although the rules require one shape for the purpose, extras add visibility.

Instant Recall

When any part of the hull, crew or equipment of a boat crosses the starting line before the starting signal is given, the offender must come back over the line to start again —staying clear of all other boats while doing so. Here, the race committee signals a recall by hoisting a white shape with a red girth, sounding a horn to call attention to it and announcing the premature starter's sail number over the committee boat's public-address system.

This particular recall procedure is virtually foolproof, but committees often modify it slightly or omit some of the steps —especially if the fleet is a small one and the infraction is easily apparent. For example, announcing sail numbers is not mandatory, and the red-and-white Code flags V or F are sometimes used instead of the shape. Competitors should be sure, therefore, to check the sailing instructions of a specific race for recall details.

A vessel on starboard tack has the right of way over one on port tack—and port tack, shown here in blue, must give way. However, a boat on starboard tack may not alter its course so as to prevent the port-tack boat from keeping clear. The starboard-tack skipper also should hail the port-tack vessel if he intends to alter course unexpectedly.

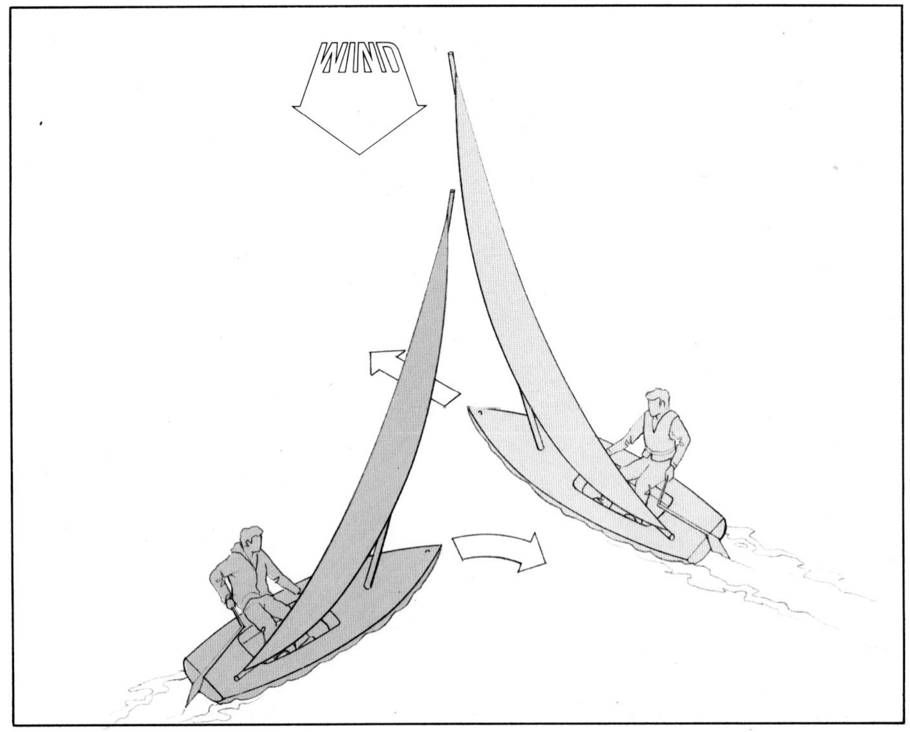

A boat to windward (blue)—that is, closer to the source of the wind—must give way to a leeward boat. But this rule is subject to certain refinements, particularly with respect to a maneuver called luffing (pages 72-73).

Basic Commandments

From the time a racing skipper begins to sail near the starting line until his boat crosses the finish line, he is subject to the right-of-way rules of Part 4 of *The Yacht Racing Rules*. The first three provisions of this section, called the fundamental rules and shown on these pages with one important corollary, serve a sober purpose: to prevent collisions during a race. As such, they are the keystones for safe, fair competition and for the more complex tactical rules *(bottom right and following pages)* aimed at preventing one boat from taking unfair advantage of another.

These three fundamental rules derive from a traditional nautical code known as the Rules of the Road, which dates back to the 19th Century and oversees right-of-way situations between all vessels. Happily, the racing fundamentals are so akin to their parent code that no major adjustment is required to switch from one to the other before and after a race.

Both sets of rules are founded on three so-called rights of passage: the right of a boat on starboard tack—with the wind on its starboard side—over a boat on port tack; the right of a vessel to leeward over a boat nearer the source of the wind—or to windward; and the right of a boat being overtaken over its overtaker.

The Rules of the Road do not elaborate upon these basic rights. In the noncompetitive environment of the open sea or an inland cruising ground, good will and common sense prevail between seamen. In racing, however, where the primary objective is to win, the elementary regulations are not always enough to restrain highly competitive rivals. For example, a skipper on starboard tack might be tempted to intentionally brush a boat on port tack in order to protest it out of the race. *The Yacht Racing Rules*, therefore, contains a succession of clauses carefully worded to discourage such bloodthirsty tactics; e.g., "a right-of-way yacht which fails to make a reasonable attempt to avoid a collision resulting in serious damage may be disqualified."

Such clauses help greatly to ward off the acrimonious chaos that might develop; but such interpretable terms as "reasonable," "serious" and "may" leave room for plenty of aggressive gamesmanship.

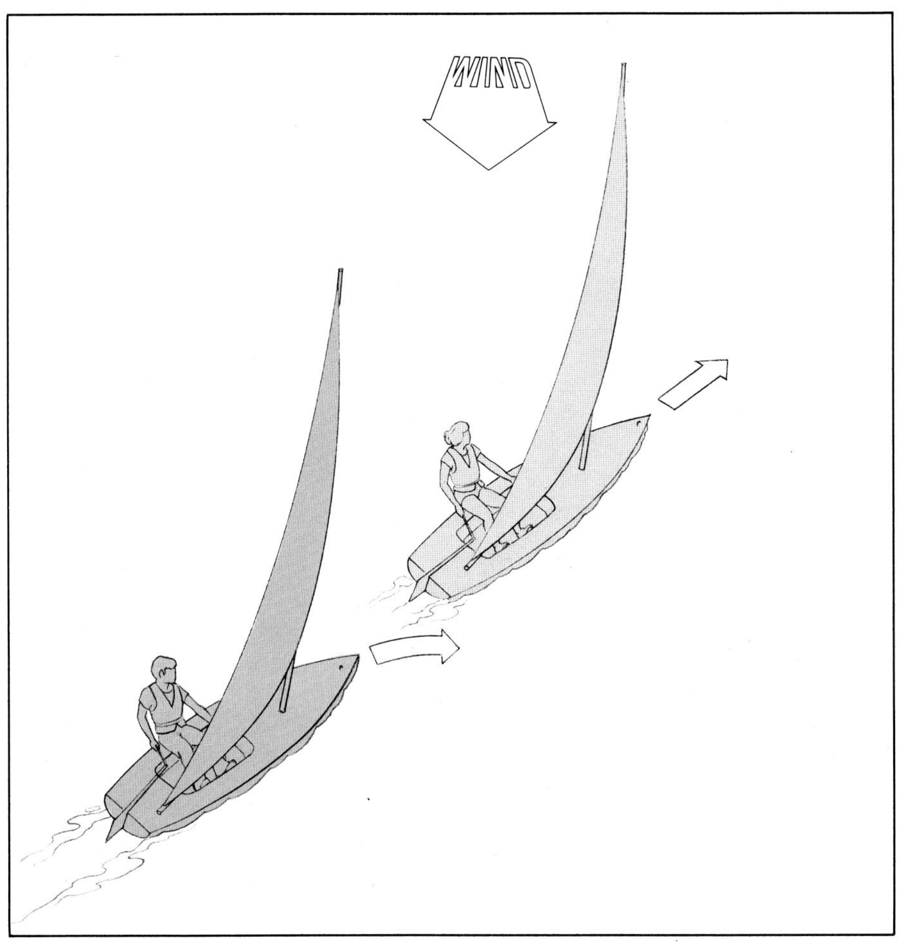

A boat that is overtaking another from astern must avoid the vessel it is overtaking. Once it has established an overlap—that is, when some part of the blue boat overlaps some part of the gray boat—other rules, like the one described below, take effect.

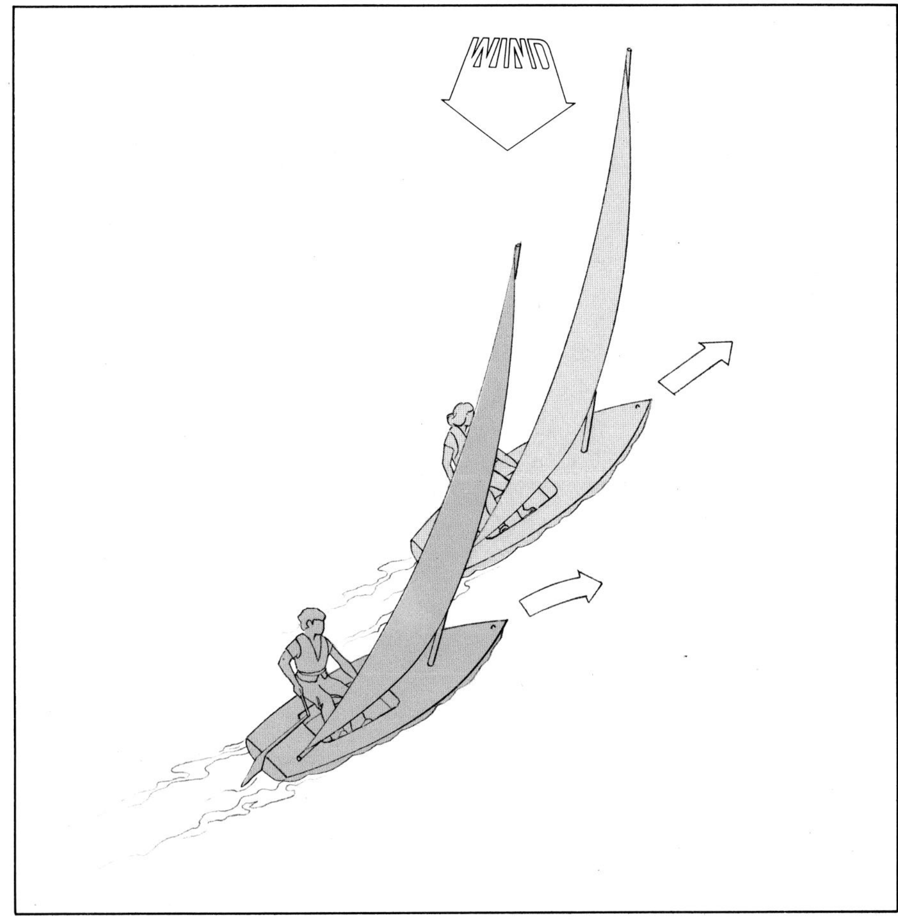

After an overtaking vessel has established an overlap to leeward, she may not assert her rights under the leeward-rights rule by sailing upwind of the course to the next mark. Without this rule, a yacht overtaking to leeward might intentionally attempt to ram her adversary from a leeward position in order to cause a protest situation.

Luffing Rules

Perhaps the most frequently applied of the tactical rules are those that relate to luffing—or, as the rule book defines it, "altering course toward the wind until head to wind" (until the boat is pointing directly into the wind). This maneuver is often done intentionally by a leeward boat to head off a boat overtaking her to windward. According to the fundamental rule allowing leeward boats right of way, the windward boat must keep clear. And luffing by the leeward boat quickly erases the windward boat's advantage.

If, however, the leeward boat were able to luff continually, it would maintain an unfair advantage, in that the windward boat might never be able to pass. Furthermore, in turning toward the wind, after a certain point the windward boat would no longer be able to steer clear of the luff, and the leeward boat could force a foul by touching the windward boat's quarter, thus disqualifying it from the race.

For these reasons, a provision of tactical equality is added to the luffing rule. If the windward boat advances so far ahead of the leeward boat that the skipper of the windward boat, sitting in a normal position at the helm, is able to sight directly abeam at the leeward boat's mast *(bottom diagram),* the leeward boat's skipper may no longer luff.

The overall consequence of this rule and its variations is that a boat being overtaken to windward is favored—up to the point that it gains an unfair tactical advantage; whereupon, its privilege to luff is revoked. However, these luffing rules, like the other tactical regulations, tend to be complex and subject to interpretation. As a result they often become objects of protest, counterprotest and hard feelings between skippers who might have overlooked, misused or misunderstood a portion of them. Therefore, smart racing skippers read and reread the rules with meticulous care.

After starting, a craft that is ahead and to leeward (blue boat) of another may luff —head up abruptly toward the source of the wind—to prevent the competitor's passing to windward. The windward boat must stay clear to avoid violating the leeward-rights rule. And by quickly heading back on course, the leeward boat can also gain ground.

Once a windward boat (blue) has pulled ahead to a position in which its skipper, when sighting abeam from his normal position at the helm and sailing parallel to the leeward boat, is abreast or forward of the leeward vessel's mainmast, the skipper shouts, "Mast abeam." At that point, the leeward boat may no longer luff.

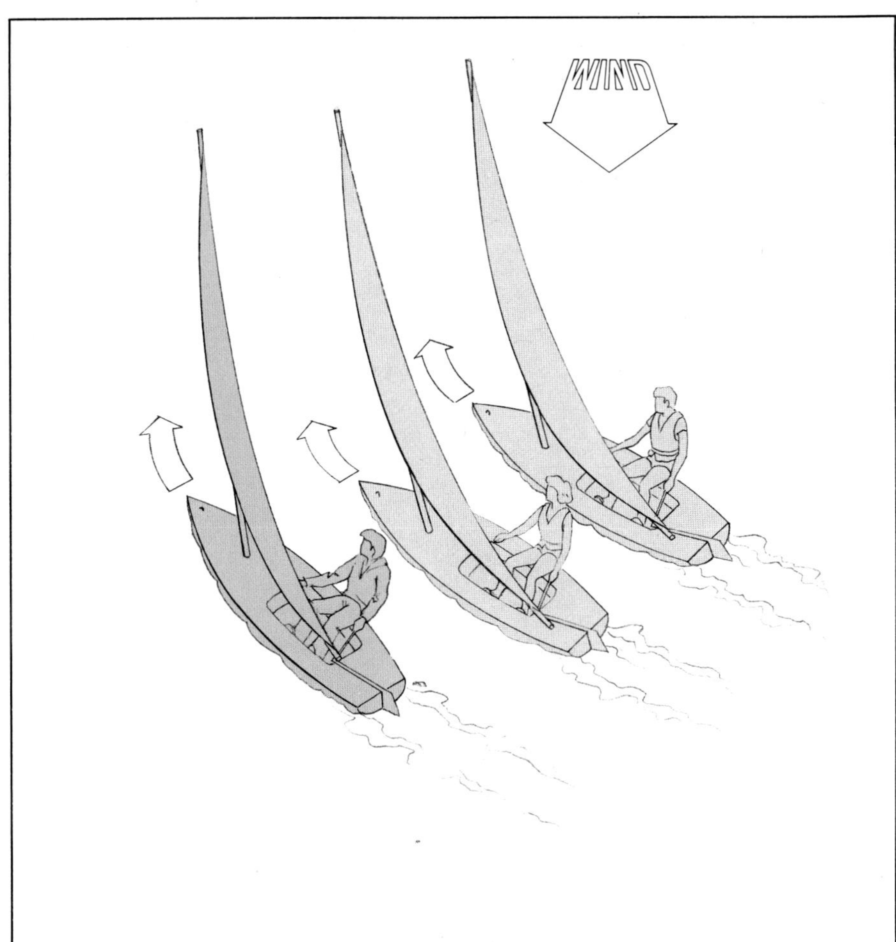

When more than two boats are sailing side by side—common immediately following a start—a leeward boat (blue) may not luff the vessel immediately to windward unless the leeward boat has luffing rights over all craft to windward that would be affected by the luff. But if the leeward boat has rights over all those to windward (as here), then they must all respond to the luff, even if they otherwise would have no right to luff the boats to windward of them.

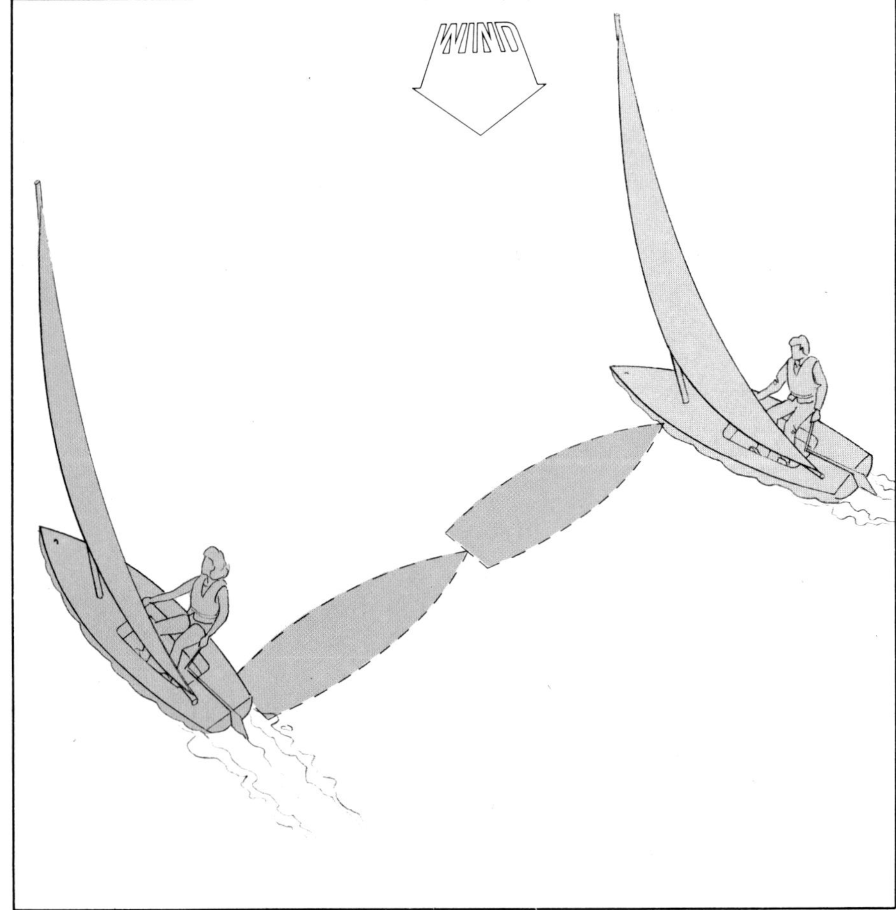

A fine point in the luffing rules specifies that an overlap for the purposes of achieving mast abeam is said not to exist if the two boats in question are farther than two boat lengths apart. As one consequence of this variation, luffing rights may be established by a leeward boat (blue) converging upon a windward one, even if the windward boat has been forward of the mast-abeam position before moving inside the two-boat-length barrier.

Rounding Marks

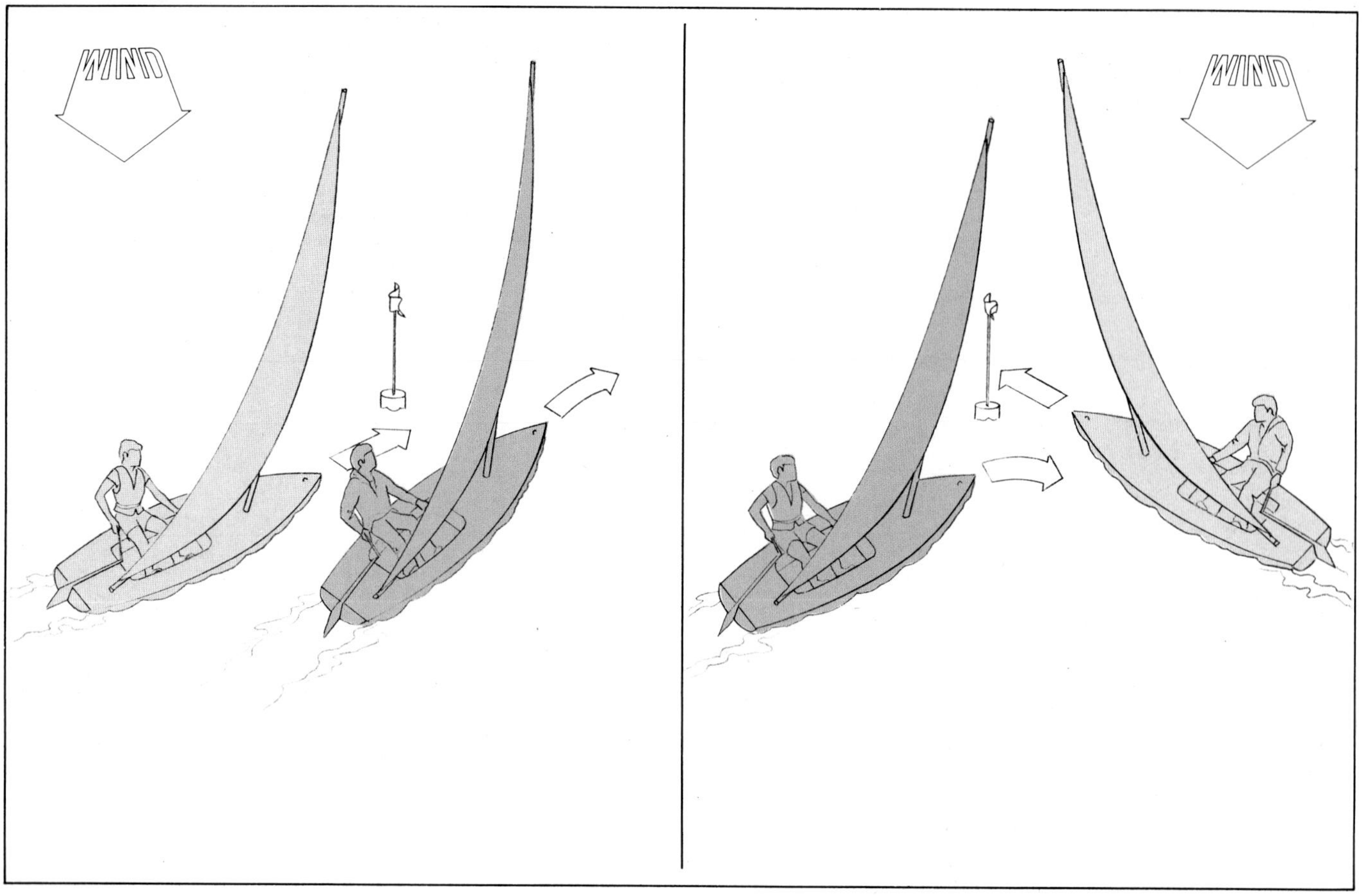

Regardless of the fundamental rules that give rights to leeward boats and boats on starboard tack, whenever two boats on the same or opposite tacks near a mark of the course, the boat farthest to the outside (blue, directly above) of the mark must give the inner boat room to pass or to round it, provided the nearer yacht has an overlap. However, if the two boats are approaching a mark on opposite tacks when close-hauled (above, right), the fundamental right of starboard tack prevails, and port tack (blue) must give way, even though it is inside.

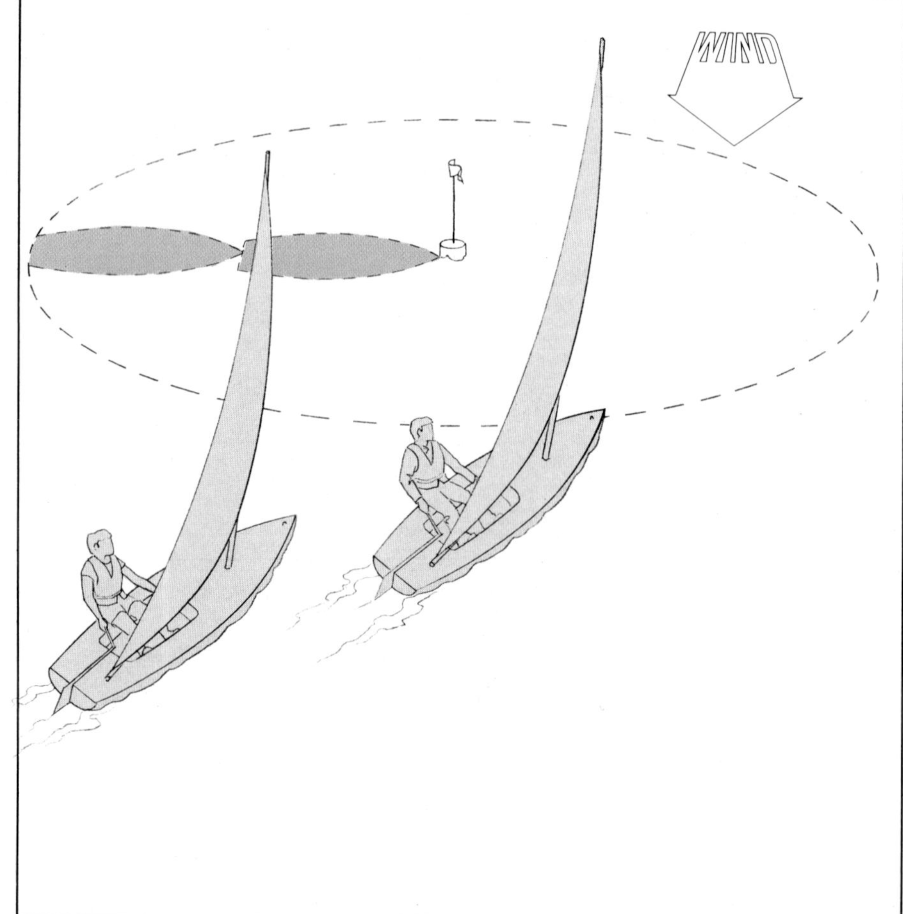

If, in a rounding or passing situation, the inside boat has been unable to establish an overlap before the leading boat is within two boat lengths of the mark, the inside boat has no rights to room, even if it subsequently is able to slide into an overlap position. On the other hand, if an inside boat enters the two-boat-length margin with an overlap, the inside boat does not lose its rights even if the overlap is later broken by the outside vessel.

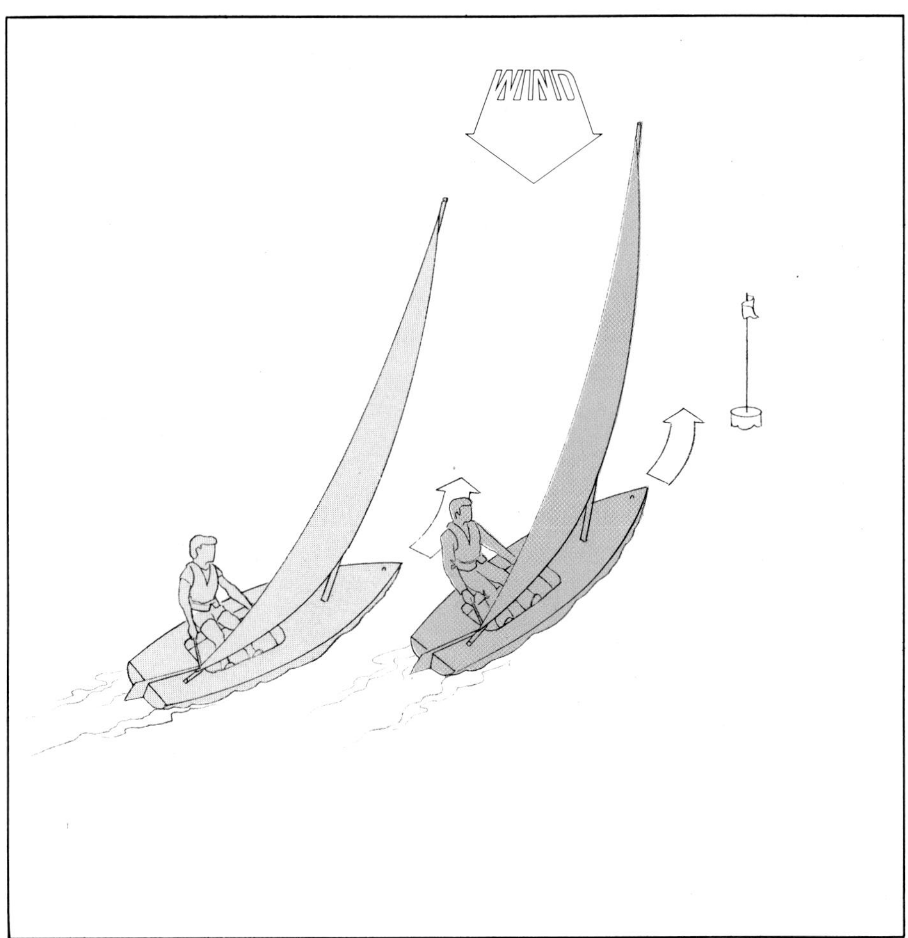

A leeward boat (blue) that is outside of one to windward in a rounding situation may claim luffing rights, and can luff its rival to the wrong side of the mark so long as the maneuver commenced outside the two-boat-length margin. The luffing skipper must also hail the windward skipper that he intends to luff; and finally, the luffing boat must pass to windward of the mark, as well. After this time-consuming tactic—used primarily in match races—both boats have to veer back and round the mark properly.

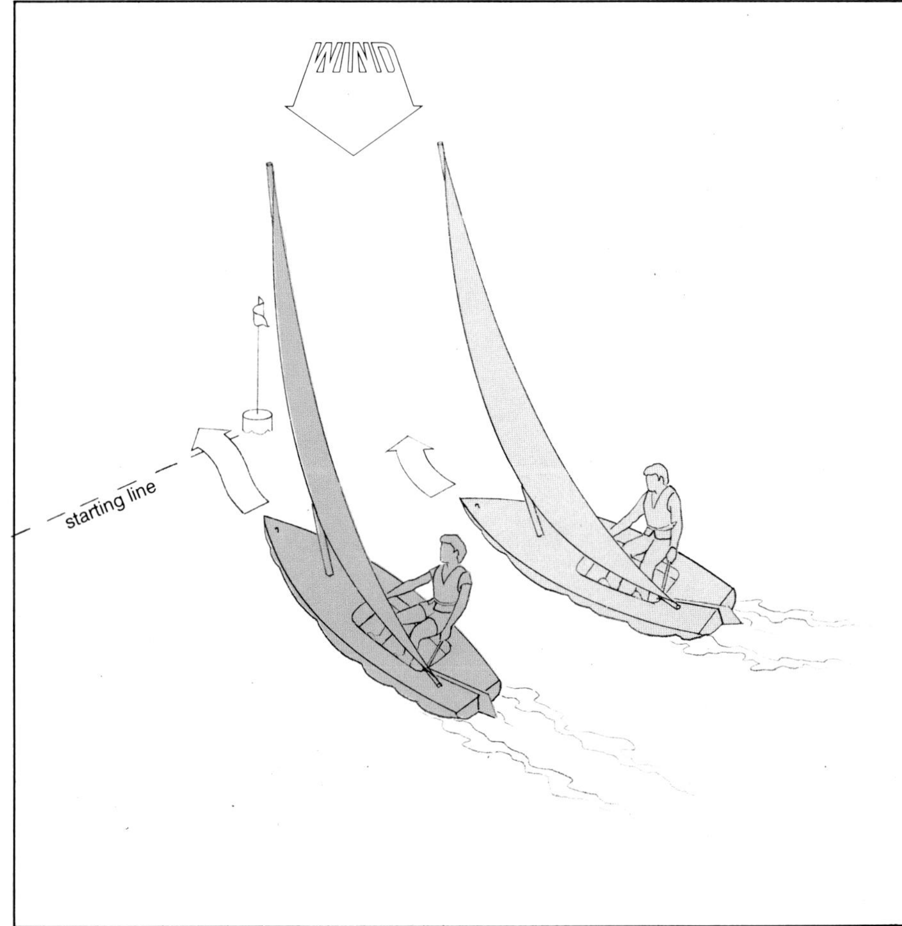

An exception to the room-at-the-mark rule (opposite, top) may occur immediately before the start. A leeward boat is not required to give a windward boat room at a starting mark; it may even attempt to close out the rival, as here. But the maneuver must be very carefully timed, for after the starting signal is raised, attempts by the leeward boat to deprive the windward yacht of room at the mark in this manner must cease; leeward may no longer sail above a direct course to the first mark—or above close-hauled.

Room at Obstructions

When two boats are close-hauled on the same tack and the leeward boat (blue) must come about to avoid an obstruction like the rocks shown here—but cannot do so without blocking or colliding with the windward yacht—the leeward skipper may call for room, shouting the words, "Water to tack." (In other circumstances, boats in the process of tacking have no right of way.) After hearing the hail, the windward boat's skipper either must tack as soon as possible, or he may respond, "You tack," after which he may hold his course; but he assumes the responsibility of staying clear.

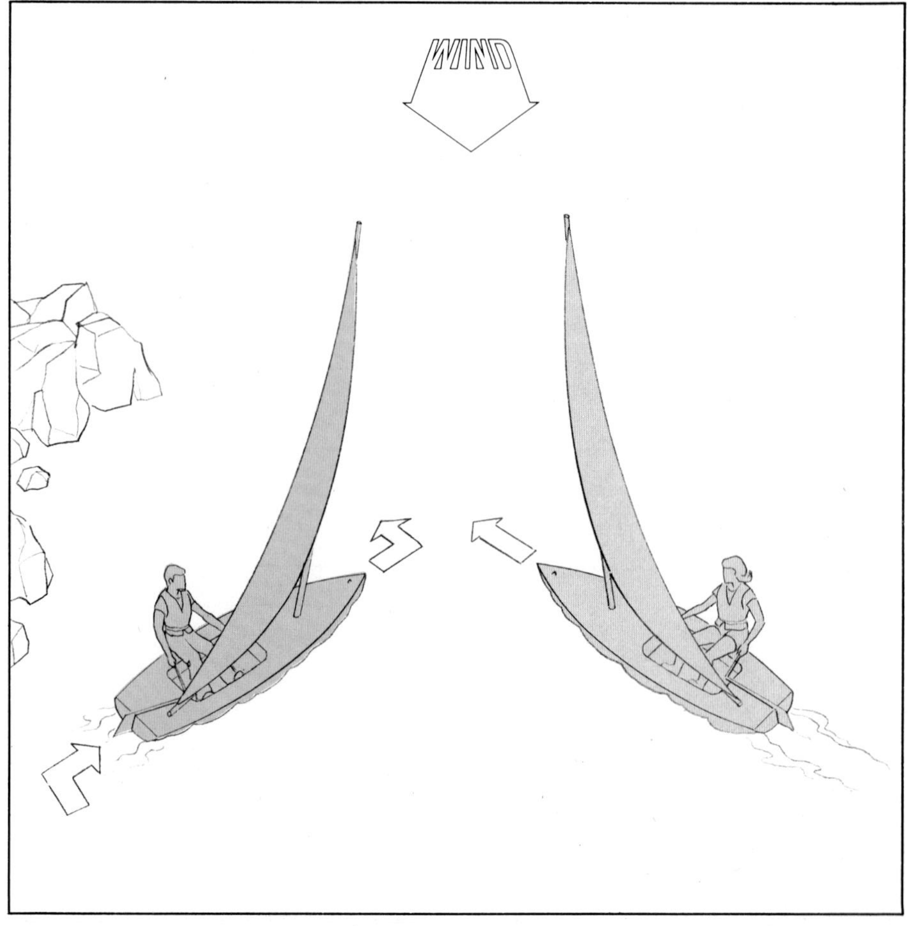

If a leeward boat (blue), tacking to avoid an obstruction, is far enough away from a windward boat on starboard tack so that it can tack and then tack again in the intervening space, the windward boat's skipper may refuse a call for room to pass after the leeward boat's first tack. However, if the leeward boat, having tacked twice, is still unable to clear the obstruction, leeward's skipper may call again for water to tack, and the windward boat must oblige. This rule prevents a skipper from taking advantage of an obstruction to override the fundamental right of starboard tack.

If two boats are passing to leeward of an obstruction, rounding and passing rules (pages 74-75) apply. The outside boat (blue, at above, left) is obliged to give room to an insider with an overlap. The same rule applies when two boats on port tack approach a boat on starboard tack (which is legally considered an obstruction). If the leeward, port-tack boat (blue, at right) does not hail for room to tack, the windward port tacker may expect room to pass to leeward of the starboard-tack boat.

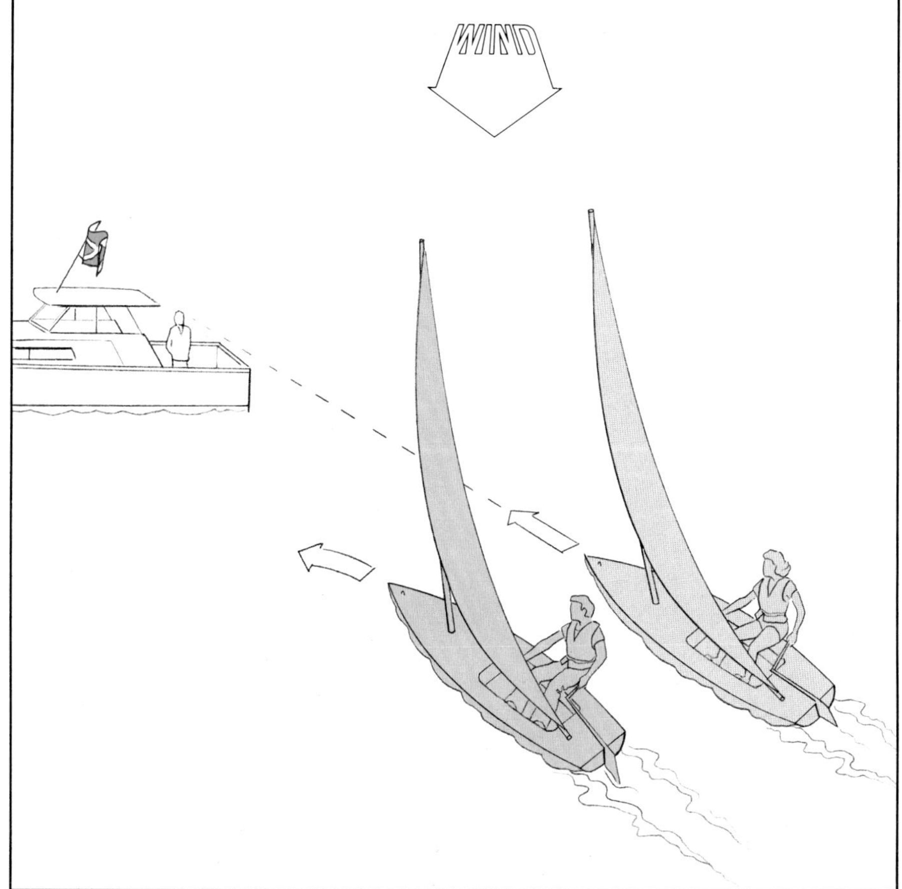

If the obstruction to be avoided is also a mark (as in the case of the powerboat here, displaying Code flag M to indicate its status as a replacement mark), certain obstruction rules do not apply. Should a leeward boat (blue) be unable to clear the mark without tacking, its skipper may hail for room to tack; but if the skipper of the windward yacht believes that he can fetch the mark without having to tack himself, he can refuse the hail, forcing his rival to circle and approach again. For windward to hold course, however, is risky: if it does not fetch the mark, it must take the applicable infringement penalty.

Supplemental Strictures

The list below is a shortened version of the 18 "Other Sailing Rules," with the actual titles in bold type, followed by a summary of each rule.

Fair sailing, *as defined in the other rules, requires boats in a race to attempt to win only by superior speed, skill and—except in team races—individual effort.*

Ranking as a starter *in a race is established simply by a properly certified boat's presence in the vicinity of the starting line after the preparatory signal is given. This rule ensures that boats entered in a racing series will be penalized for any infraction committed before the start of any given event.*

Sailing the course *consists of starting and finishing (defined in Part 1 of the rule book) and rounding marks on the required side and in the correct sequence.*

Touching a mark *results in disqualification unless the mark is rerounded.*

Fog signals and lights, *as described in the International Regulations for Preventing Collisions at Sea, must be properly observed by every racer.*

Setting and sheeting sails *is restricted to booms and spars regularly used for this purpose. A spinnaker may not be set without a pole. And only one mainsail and one spinnaker may be set at once (except when changing sails).*

An owner steering another yacht *must have the permission of the race committee to do so if a boat he owns also competes in the race.*

Boarding a yacht *is forbidden except between two vessels that are fouled, or unless an ill or injured crew member needs attention.*

Leaving a man overboard *is forbidden: a boat must finish a race with the same people that were aboard at the start—unless an ill or injured crew member must be removed for his safety.*

Rendering assistance *to another boat or person in peril is mandatory.*

Outside assistance *is prohibited except as specified in other racing rules.*

The means of propulsion *that a boat may use while racing is restricted to the natural action of the wind on the sails, spars and hull, and water on the hull.*

Soundings *may be taken, provided that the rule on the means of propulsion is not infringed upon.*

Manual power *alone may be used to work a boat in all normal racing situations; however, power winches may be used to weigh an anchor or pull clear after fouling an object or another boat. Auxiliaries may use power bilge pumps.*

Anchoring *is permitted at any time during a race—in a foul current, for example. If possible, the anchor must be recovered. A vessel shall not be made fast by any other means—such as a crew member holding a lobster buoy.*

When aground or afoul an obstruction, *a boat may use any of its resources to get clear. But it may not seek assistance except from a vessel fouled with it.*

Skin friction *of the hull on the water may not be reduced by releasing any substance—such as a polymer—into the water.*

Increasing stability *by using a trapeze is forbidden unless specifically provided for in class rules. Crew members may not station themselves outside life lines other than momentarily.*

Questions of Ethics

Part 5 of *The Yacht Racing Rules* is a compendium of 18 disparate statutes entitled "Other Sailing Rules." In large measure, this grab-bag section is designed to plug up loopholes left by the other rules; it prohibits, for example, such productive though questionable tactics as sculling through a calm by pushing the tiller to and fro. It also counters ploys that might be dangerous, such as hiking out on boats that have life lines but no trapezes (in careful phraseology, the pertinent rule forbids a crew member from projecting "any part of his torso" outside the perimeter of the life lines "other than temporarily"). The section also includes an umbrella provision that is all too familiar to artful dodgers: the fair-sailing clause, which may be invoked to disqualify a competitor who strays beyond ethical bounds in beating the rule book.

The table at left offers an abbreviated version of these other rules for quick, easy reference. Serious racing skippers should become closely acquainted with these strictures, both to prevent an inadvertent violation on their own part and to curb dubious behavior by others. Two particularly important provisions are further explained at right.

If the skipper of a singlehanded boat falls overboard during a race and is clearly imperiled, a nearby boat must give him all possible assistance, as specified by Rule 10 in the all-important Part 5 of The Yacht Racing Rules. Racers who rescue others are often rewarded with more than thanks: race committees may grant them a special dispensation for all the time lost or correct their finishing position in the fleet.

A vessel that hits a course marker is disqualified—unless the skipper exonerates himself by rerounding the mark, without touching, before proceeding on course. In big-boat races, however, this rule may be waived by race committees in order to prevent dangerous maneuvering.

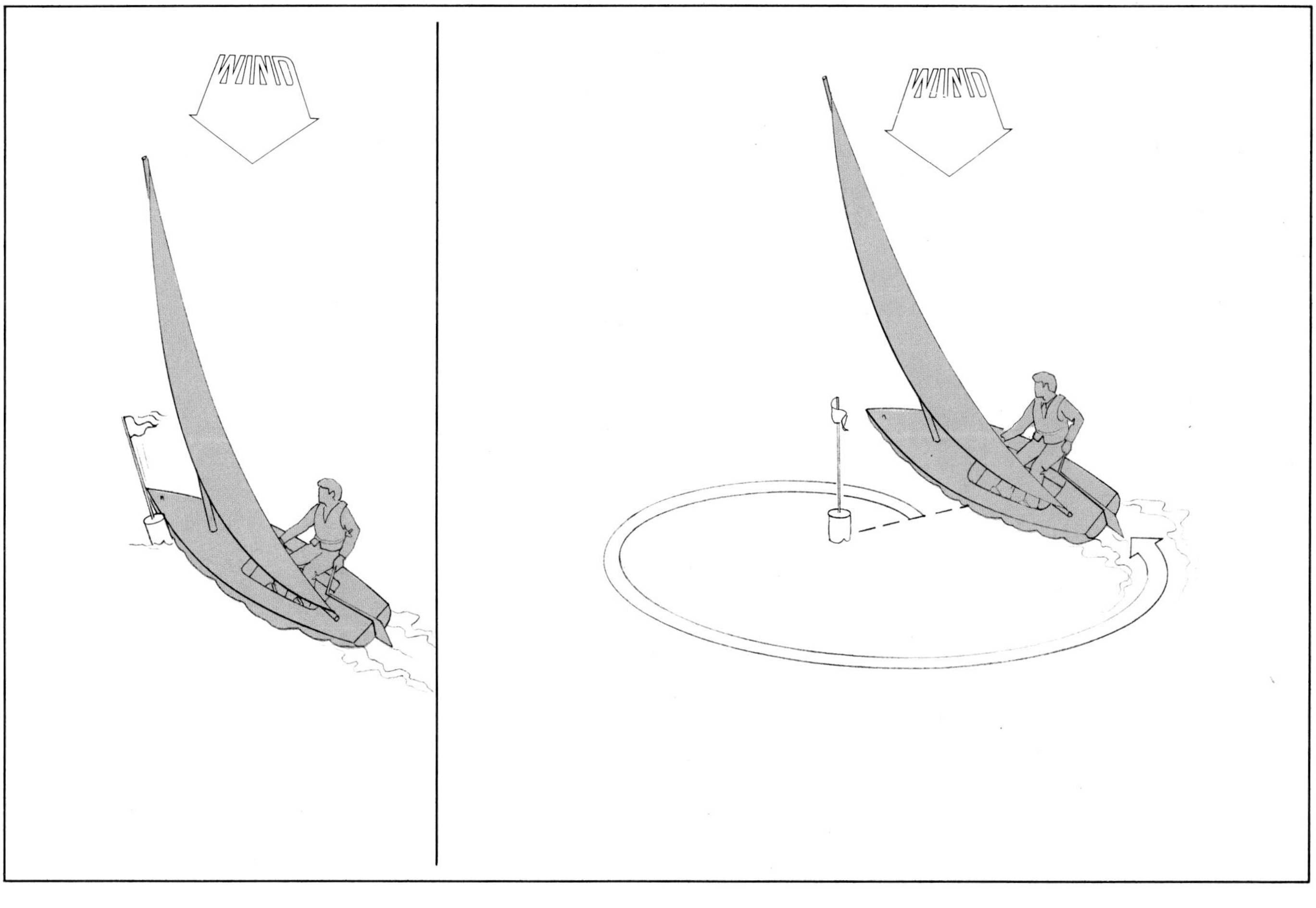

WIND

WIND

Trial by Committee

Although law and order sometimes appear to break down in the heat of a racing competition, the rule makers have evolved a reasonably fair and efficient system aimed at making sure that justice prevails. Race committees are empowered to disqualify boats if committee members witness an infraction—usually at the start or finish, when the committee has a close-up view of the action. Competitors can voluntarily levy penalties against themselves if they know they are guilty of some infraction; the offender may either withdraw from the race on the spot or—if the sailing instructions permit—take a lesser punishment, such as sailing two 360° turns in open water.

The rule book also allows one boat to bring charges against another. This process, called protesting, begins out on the course. If a skipper thinks he has been fouled by a rival or believes he has seen an infraction, he may lodge a protest by flying a flag prominently in his rigging—a signal to the race committee that an accusation will be forthcoming. After the race, he submits his charges to the officials in writing, and the case is then heard by either the race committee or a specially appointed protest committee.

The hearing is a formal affair, based upon the model of trial by jury. All skippers involved present their side of the issue, calling witnesses when necessary and questioning one another's testimony. Then the committee meets privately to decide on the case—either by disqualifying the boat that has been protested, or by throwing out the charges entirely and leaving the official finishing order of the fleet unchanged.

When minor brushes like this light bow-stern collision occur, where maneuverability is impaired by lack of wind or an adverse current, the race committee often declines to find fault. However, the skippers involved should protest nonetheless, for the rule book decrees that a collision must result in either a withdrawal, a protest or a penalty—and offending skippers can be protested by a third party if this provision is not met.

Believing that she has been fouled by another boat, a skipper flies a protest flag from her starboard shroud, a traditional site for the signal. She must continue to display the flag until it is acknowledged by the race committee at the finish; and she must also attempt to notify the protested boat of her intention. If these duties are not carried out, the committee may refuse to hear the case.

A Classic Controversy

Even the world's premier racing sailors occasionally break a rule—and sometimes even exchange a little hull paint, as in the notorious incident depicted at left. Fifteen seconds after the starting gun of the second race of the 1970 America's Cup challenge match off Newport, Rhode Island, Australian contender *Gretel II* banged her nose into defender *Intrepid's* port beam, bounced free and went on to finish 1 minute 7 seconds ahead of her irate rival. Both yachts protested, touching off one of the most explosive controversies in more than a century of competition.

The following day, Race Committee Chairman B. Devereux Barker III signed a decision disqualifying *Gretel II* for violating Rule 42 *(page 75).* This provision forbids a leeward boat from depriving a windward rival of room at a starting mark, either by sailing above a close-hauled course or above the course to the first mark after the starting signal. The judgment brought forth a deluge of telegrams and letters in support of *Gretel II.* Although the decision proved to be irrevocable, hard feelings still lingered—exacerbated by the fact that the Australians, having been swept in four straight races by *Intrepid* in the last series, had finished ahead of the Americans for the first time since *Gretel* had beaten *Weatherly* in the second race of the series that was held in 1962.

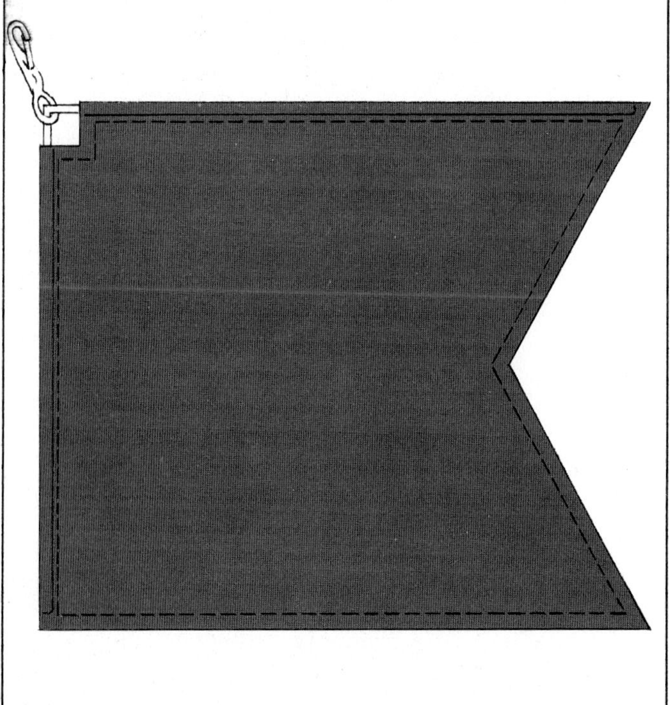

STANDARD PROTEST FORM

PROTESTOR: Sail No. Yacht's Name Class

Helmsman *print* Signature

PROTESTEE: Sail No. Yacht's Name Class

Helmsman *print* Whom I have have not tried to inform

Sponsoring Club Race date & number

Time and whereabouts of incident

Rule(s) applicable

Direction & Strength: Wind Current

Time protest flag was shown

Witnesses

Received by Time Date

Address: Protestor

Tel.

Protestee

Tel.

Although the rule book is not specific about what constitutes a suitable protest flag, it does note the acceptability of one candidate, International Code flag B—a blood-red swallowtail, shown here with stays sewed into its lining to hold it open and a clip to facilitate its attachment to the rigging.

No more than two hours after a race, a protester must deliver a written report on an alleged violation to the committee. Some racing groups provide standardized forms like the one above, but any report must include: the date, time and place of the incident; the rule thought to have been broken; a description; and, if applicable, a diagram.

FJ
US35
FJ
US 32
FJ
US36

4

Winning sailboat races is an acquired skill, and almost every successful racing sailor will cheerfully confess that during his first year or two of competition he finished far back of the leaders in practically all the contests he entered. No amount of time spent tuning a boat or studying the rule book will prepare a neophyte for the full array of complex, split-second decisions he must make out on the race course; and even familiar boat-handling maneuvers like tacks, jibes and spinnaker sets will require extra precision and coordination to be effective in the heat of competition. Inevitably, a large portion of a racing skipper's reactions are forged by trial and error: having encoun-

RACING STRATEGY AND TACTICS

tered a particular situation before, and having made the wrong move, he quickly learns how to make the right one.

For many beginning skippers, the main hurdle to be surmounted is the fear of colliding with other boats—especially at the start. The first time or two out, he should not hesitate to stay on the outskirts of the fray that develops just before the gun, remembering that it is usually best to approach the line on starboard tack in order to maintain right of way. Another major difficulty for novices is gaining a sense of direction on the water. With only an occasional landmark and a damp racing circular to go on, a skipper has to locate marks that are often miles apart and may look exactly like other flags or government marks that have nothing to do with his course. In these circumstances, a beginner who stays reasonably close to the rest of the fleet at the start, finds the right marks and rounds them in the right order will have scored his own personal victory.

As the skipper gains experience, he begins to appreciate the competitive subtleties of the various phases of the contest. Typically, a race opens with a windward leg, followed by one or more leeward legs and closes with another leg to windward *(pages 84-85)*. Each of these legs suggests an overall plan, or strategy, by which the skipper can capitalize on shifts of wind and current to get to the next mark most quickly. In his first few races, for example, a newly fledged racer may notice that the boats in the fleet that sailed close to shore came out ahead. Gradually he figures out why, under certain conditions of wind and current *(pages 98-103)*, the inshore tack is the best one—and, similarly, he learns the circumstances under which the fastest course would be to stand off toward open water.

Such considerations of strategy provide the skipper only with a set of guidelines, to be modified as he meets and contends with rival vessels. In competing with other boats on a one-to-one basis, he turns to tactics—aggressive or evasive maneuvers—to protect or improve his position in the fleet. Proceeding almost like a chess player, a skilled racing skipper can call upon a large repertoire of moves and countermoves. They may help him gain an advantage at the start, capture a favored inside slot at each mark or use his sails to block a rival's wind.

At times, a specific tactic may conflict with the dictates of strategy. Should a skipper near the front of the pack sail for an expected wind shift that might effectively offer a shortcut to the next goal, or should he concentrate on maintaining his position vis-à-vis his rivals? Since the answer often depends on how far along the race has progressed (tactics take precedence over strategy on the last leg, for example), the following pages are grouped into the various legs that make up the natural divisions of a race. The principles they offer will help to guide any skipper, whether he is fighting to win a national championship or simply making an effort to stay out of last place at the Sunday races of the local yacht club.

Driving to windward on the first leg of a championship race for Flying Juniors, three skippers and their crews tensely play every nuance of the breeze as they vie for the lead.

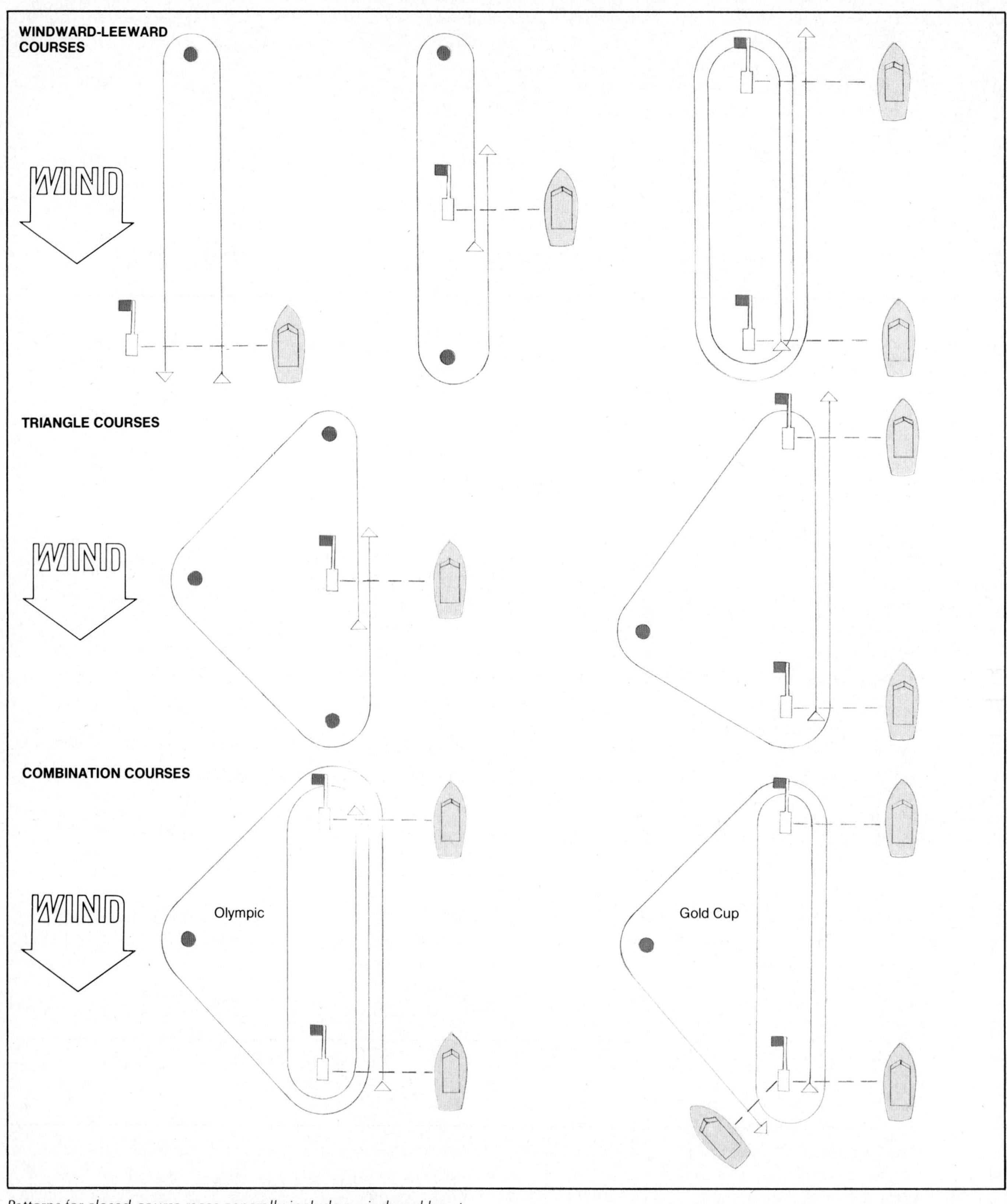

Patterns for closed-course races generally include a windward leg at the start, followed by one or more downwind legs, and frequently an upwind finish. Simplest are straight windward-leeward courses (top), ranging from a single beat and run to multiple up-and-downwind legs. Triangle courses (middle) substitute two reaching legs for a dead run. Combination courses (bottom), with standard patterns and names such as Olympic and Gold Cup, combine windward-leeward and triangle courses in order to incorporate all points of sail. The precise shape, and start and finish-line positions of any course, however, may vary at the discretion of the particular race committee.

Courses and Marks

Most races among one-design boats are run over carefully prescribed courses, specifically calculated to test the competitors' abilities on the various points of sail. Laid out by the race committee on the day of the contest, these so-called closed courses *(left)* may be simple windward-leeward types, triangular configurations or intricate combination patterns. Normally the committee sets up a course so as to make the first leg—and in most cases the last leg—a beat to windward, with at least one downwind leg in between.

On any particular course, each turning point is indicated by a buoy, flag or other such marker. Sometimes the race committee makes use of permanently placed government aids like nuns, cans or beacons. Frequently, however, the course is arranged around a club's private marks *(right)*—highly visible shapes that ride on an anchored buoy or other floating object. The course is generally designed so that all the marks are rounded on the same side; most often they are left to port *(below)*. Such specifics as mark rounding, course patterns and any modifications thereof are usually announced in the race's sailing instructions *(pages 64-65)*.

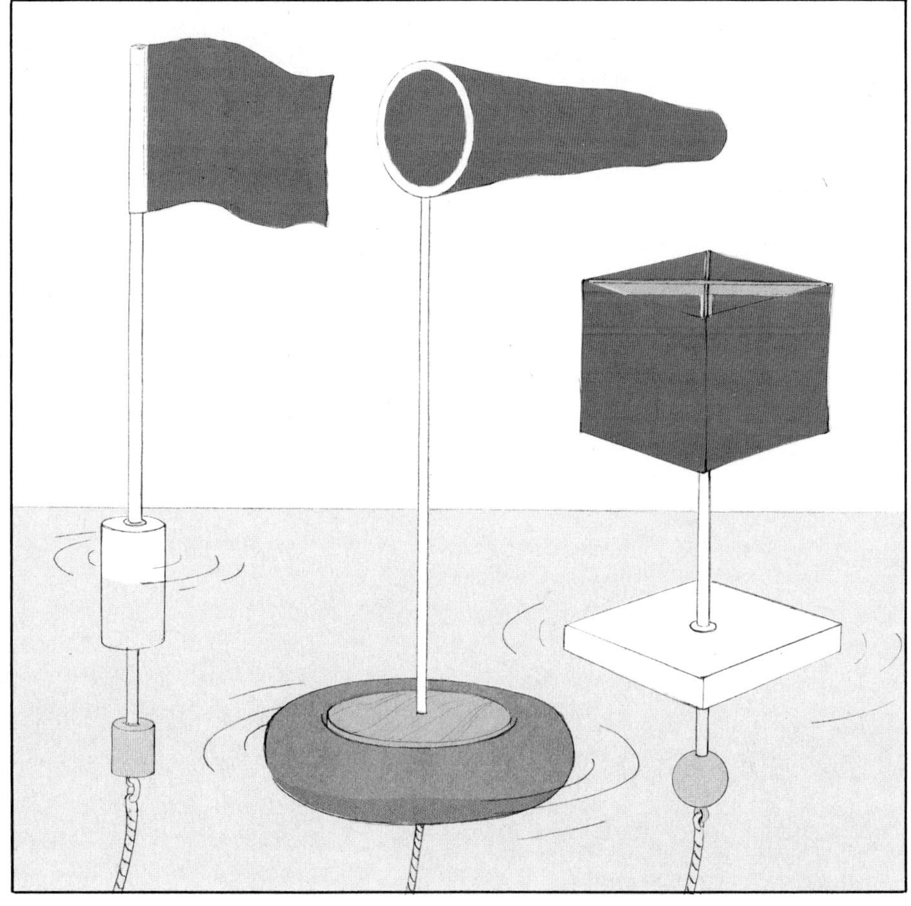

Private marks set out by the race committee to mark a course may consist of almost any distinctive, brightly colored shape supported by some variety of flotation device—such as the inner tube or Styrofoam buoys shown above. The simplest and commonest mark is an orange or red flag (left); a wind sock (middle) provides slightly greater visibility. Since both flags and wind socks require a breeze to give them shape, some race committees use a more elaborate boxlike marker (right), consisting of cloth stretched around a wooden frame for maximum visibility from all sides and in light air.

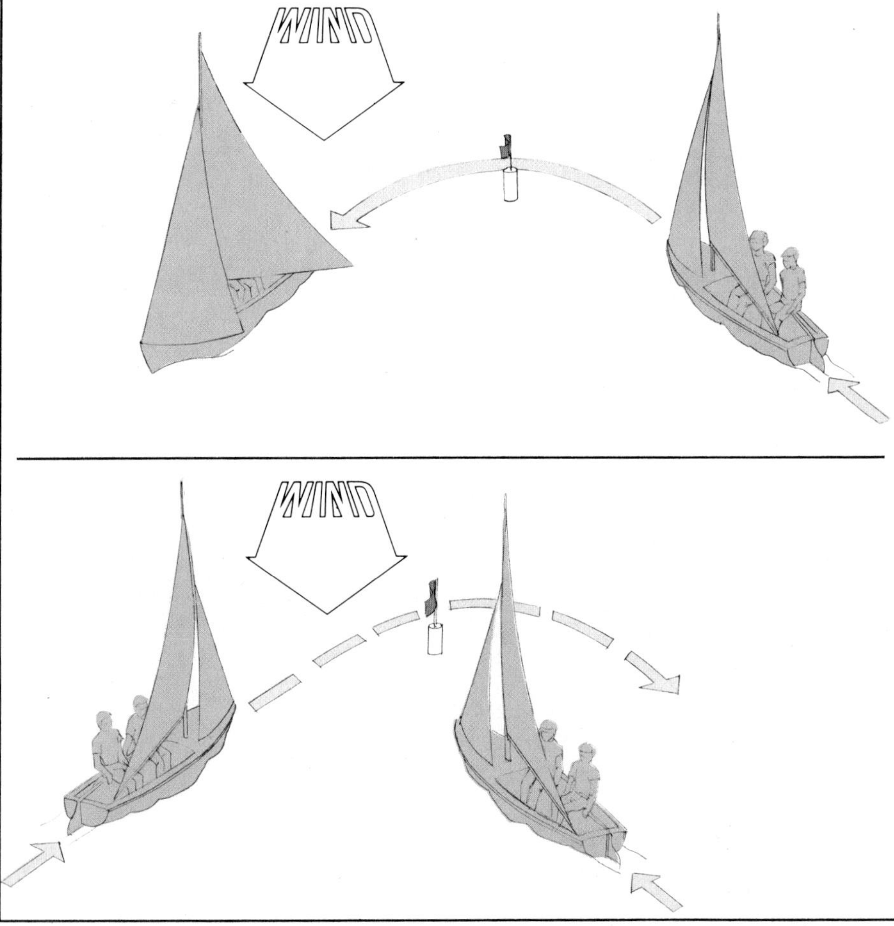

Closed-course marks are almost always passed to port (above, left) for reasons indicated in these diagrams. A skipper approaching a weather mark on starboard tack can maintain his right of way and then bear off around the mark on the same tack. A starboard rounding (left) is more complicated. A skipper making a port-tack approach—the tack on which he must round—has to give way to boats on starboard tack; and starboard tackers must themselves come about to round the mark. The resulting melee can lead to collision and protest.

The Crowded Start

Battling for a split-second edge at the most crucial moment of the race, Flying Juniors shoot across the starting line on Lake Charlevoix, Michigan. Skippers who manage to start in front get the critical advantage of sailing in unimpeded wind, and thus stand a fair chance of staying on top to the finish. But boldness at the start carries grave risks: in this picture, boat 3103 (foreground) arrived at the line early and will have to jibe around and come in behind the fleet.

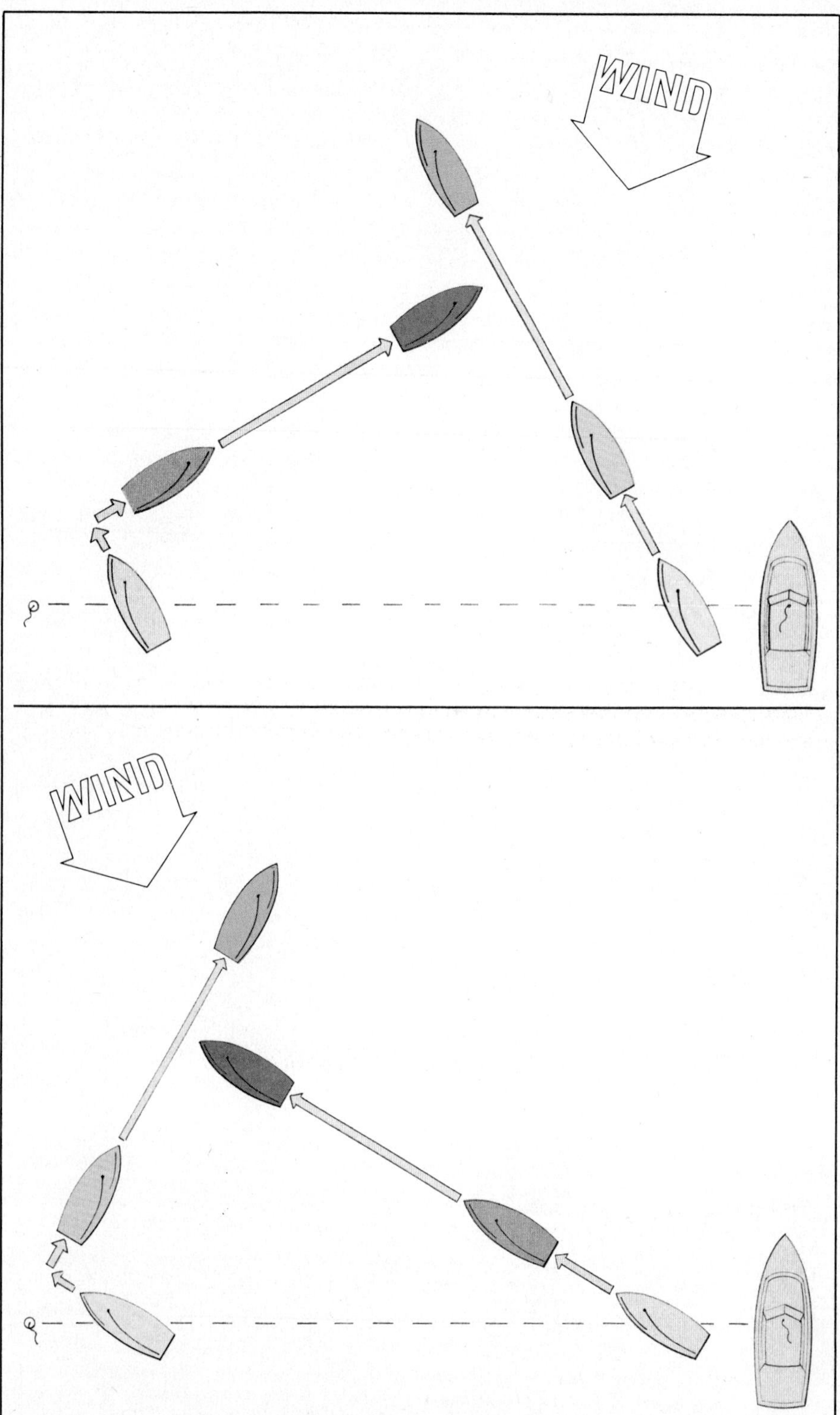

Whenever the starting line is angled to the wind, a starting position as close to the source of the wind as possible yields an instant advantage. If the wind has shifted clockwise (top), a boat starting from the starboard end of the line will cross in front of a boat coming from the other end on the opposite tack. A counterclockwise shift (bottom) favors the port end: when the port-end starter tacks he will be ahead of a skipper who started at the starboard end.

Finding the Favored End

In formulating a strategy for a successful start, a racing skipper should always know the relationship between the wind and the starting line. Race committees try to set the line perpendicular to the wind, but some shift in the wind direction almost always occurs. When this happens, the upwind end of the line is said to be favored, because a boat that starts there naturally needs to sail a relatively shorter distance toward the wind source in order to reach the windward mark.

Although the shift that creates this advantage may be slight, racing skippers can usually detect it by any one of the methods described on the opposite page. To allow time to work out a starting plan, a wind test should be made as soon as the race committee sets the line; a final check as near in time to the starting gun as possible will indicate any last-minute shift.

The decision about the best starting position on the line is not always a cut-and-dried matter, however. For example, strong currents will sometimes favor one side of the course so markedly as to outweigh any advantage offered by the favored-end start. And potential traffic problems are another consideration: a skipper in a large, aggressive fleet might be better off starting near the middle of the line, where he can gain an unimpeded start in clear wind by avoiding the jumble of boats all aiming for the same coveted upwind point.

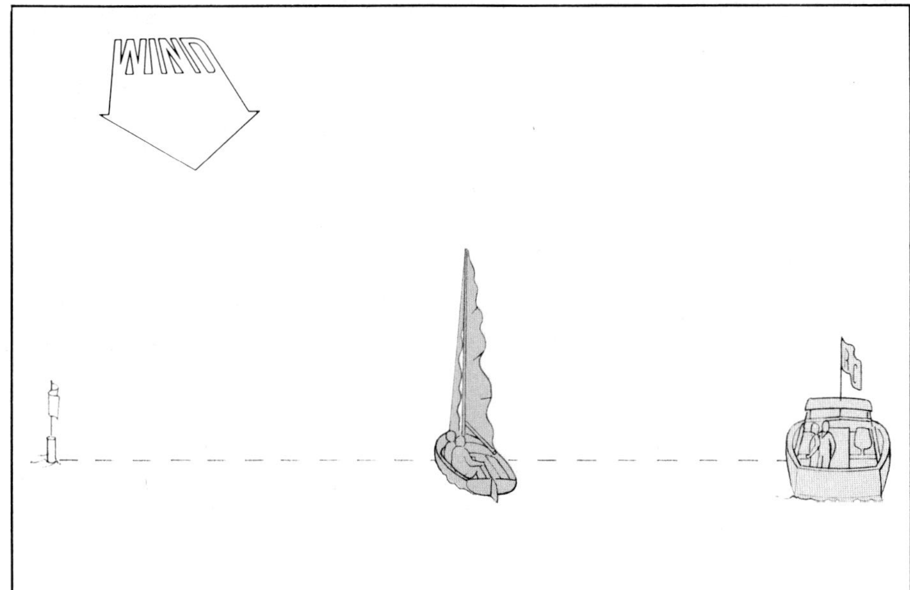

An easy, freehand way of determining the favored end of the starting line is to sail to the line and then head directly into the wind. The bow of the boat will incline toward the upwind end. Slight shifts are most easily detected when this wind-direction test is made near the middle of the line.

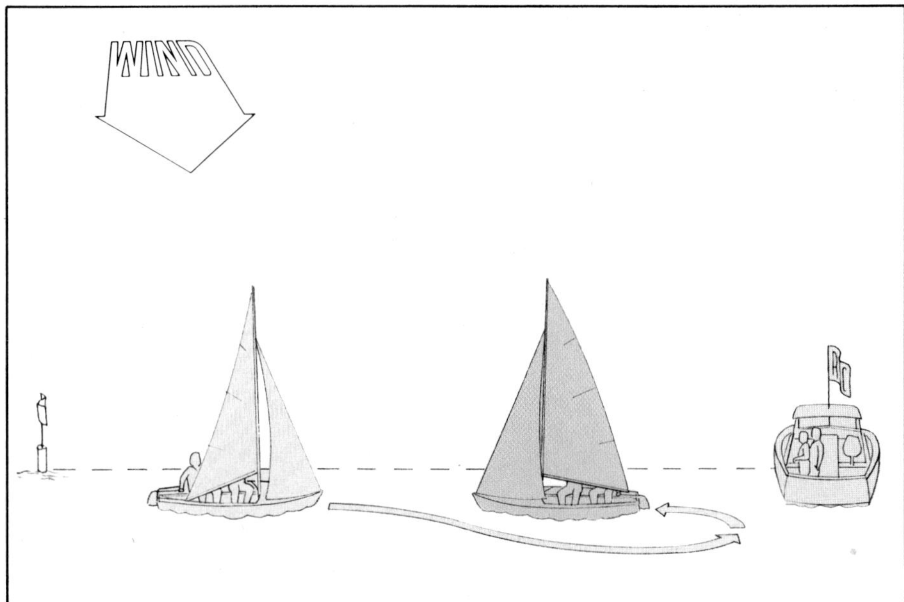

Another equally quick and rough method of finding the favored end is to sail back and forth parallel to the starting line, trimming the sails just off a luff. The favored end is the one toward which the boat is sailing when its sails are most closely trimmed (dark blue).

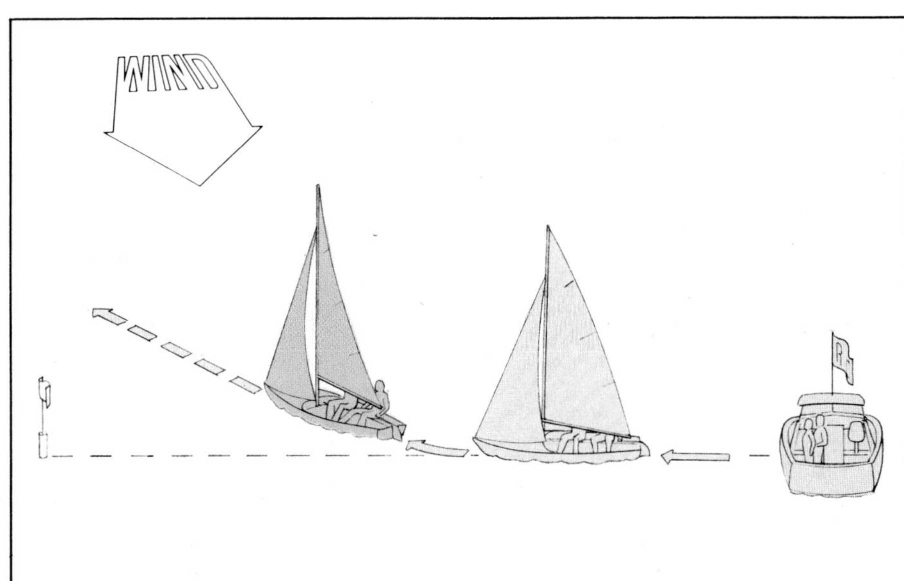

A compass injects an element of precision into finding the angle of the wind to the line. In using it, first note the compass heading when traveling directly down the line—here, toward the port end. Then harden up and note the compass bearing of the close-hauled course (dark blue). If the difference in the two readings is less than the boat's best close-hauled sailing angle—usually about 45°—the port end is favored; if the difference is greater than that angle, the starboard end is favored. The advantage of this method is that once the line's compass bearing is known, the wind angle can be checked anywhere on the course.

On a port-end start, the fleet usually gathers near the starboard end about one minute before the gun and begins to reach down the line on starboard tack (1). The skippers luff to control speed and avoid being over early, while the crews call out the time every 15 seconds and count down the last 10 seconds. When the gun fires, the fleet trims in and heads across the line close-hauled (2); the boat crossing at the favored end with clear air (far left) has made the best start.

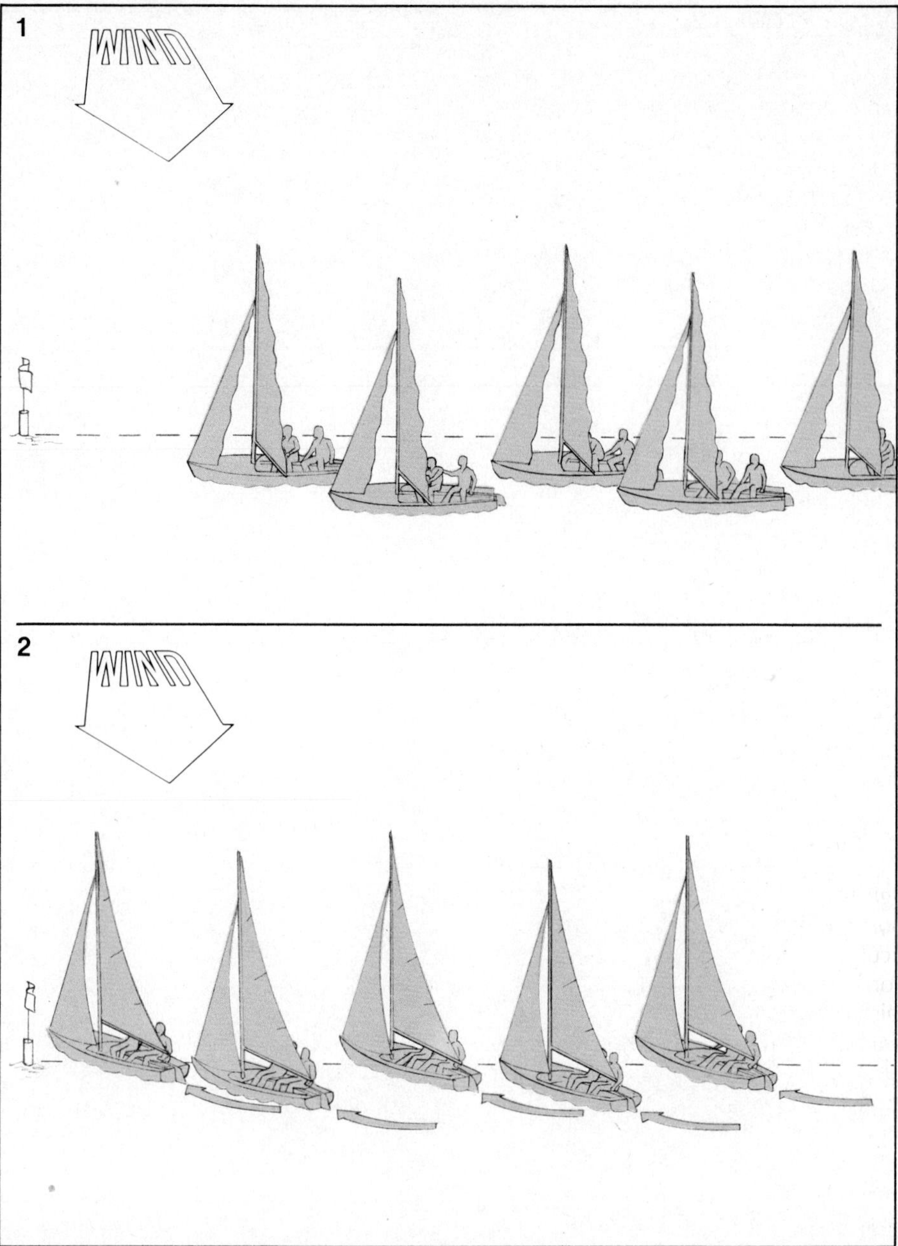

The Vanderbilt Start

Although the timing of most starts is more art than science, one method can claim a little more science than the others: the Vanderbilt, or timed-run, start, developed by tycoon sportsman Harold S. Vanderbilt in the early 1900s. His formula was designed to answer the need of large yachts to sail some distance in order to hit the line with good speed. Several minutes before the start, the skipper crosses the line going in the wrong direction. At that instant, he notes the amount of time remaining until the gun, and subtracts the time it takes to jibe or tack —determined in advance. He then sails away from the line for half the time left, turns, and sails back for the remaining half, theoretically hitting the line with full way on just as the gun goes.

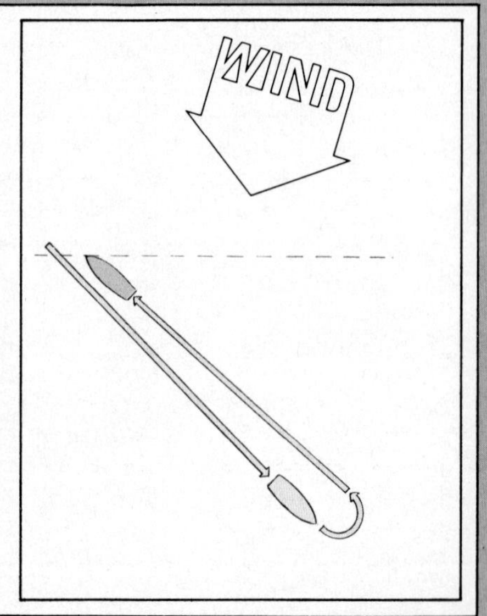

Hitting the Line

Finding the favored end of the line is only part of the battle of a racing start. Another key element is knowing how to get there in a crowd—and how to get there just as the gun fires.

Any number of techniques have been evolved for achieving well-timed starts—including a special formula *(box, bottom left)* devised primarily for big boats by the famous America's Cup skipper Harold S. Vanderbilt. However, when the port end of the line is favored, most skippers choose a simple yet flexible method called running the line *(1 and 2, left)*.

Beginning somewhere near the far end of the line, the skipper sails along on a starboard-tack reach, parallel to the line and about a boat length below it to prevent leeward rivals from luffing him up and forcing him across too soon. Near the port-end mark, he hardens up and crosses the line as the gun goes off. To time this sort of start properly, he naturally needs to know how long it will take to reach the favored end; the approach interval is determined in advance by a trial run—or several, just to be on the safe side.

A start at the starboard end *(1 and 2, right)* is a more chaotic situation than a port-end start and a good deal more difficult to time. In order to cross at the favored end on starboard tack—thus maintaining right of way—most of the fleet starts its approach beyond the end of the line. When the gun goes off, some boats in the fleet, such as D at right, may find themselves with no line to cross—a situation that is less likely to occur on a port-end start.

Though The Yacht Racing Rules allow leeward boats to deny room to windward boats trying to barge in between them and the mark, windward skippers nevertheless regularly try to thrust their way in. As a result, starboard-end starts are often filled with stentorian claims to right of way and the unhappy sounds of collision. To avoid this situation, many race committees try to anticipate any wind shift that will favor the starboard end; as added insurance, they may even set the line to favor the port end.

An essential ingredient in any starting situation is knowing how to slow down in order to avoid being over the line early. A skipper can reduce his speed either by luffing or by sailing a sharply oscillating course. And, if need be, a panic brake can be applied by releasing the mainsheet and shoving the boom out to back the main—first making sure that no boat is close enough to be fouled by this maneuver.

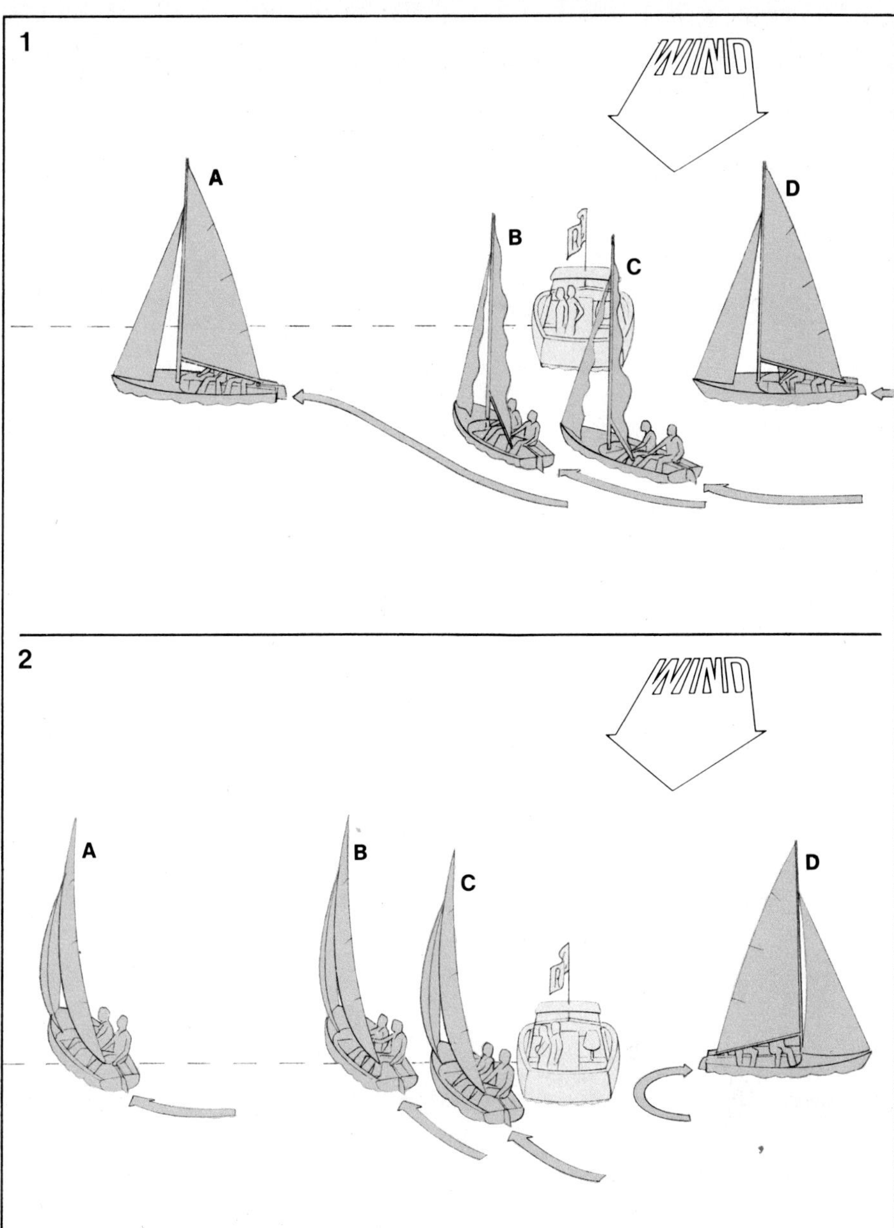

When the starboard end of the line is favored, a contentious crunch often develops near the mark as boats approach on the starboard tack. In diagram 1, the skipper of boat A has elected to stay out of the fray at the favored end; boat B is heading close to the wind, hoping to deny room at the mark to windward boats C and D. When the gun goes off (2), boat A has achieved a creditable start in clear air; B has done better, having crossed the line near the starboard mark—and also with clear air; C has managed to sneak inside, but will be slowed by the disturbed air spilling off B's sails; while D, denied room, must jibe around and reapproach the line.

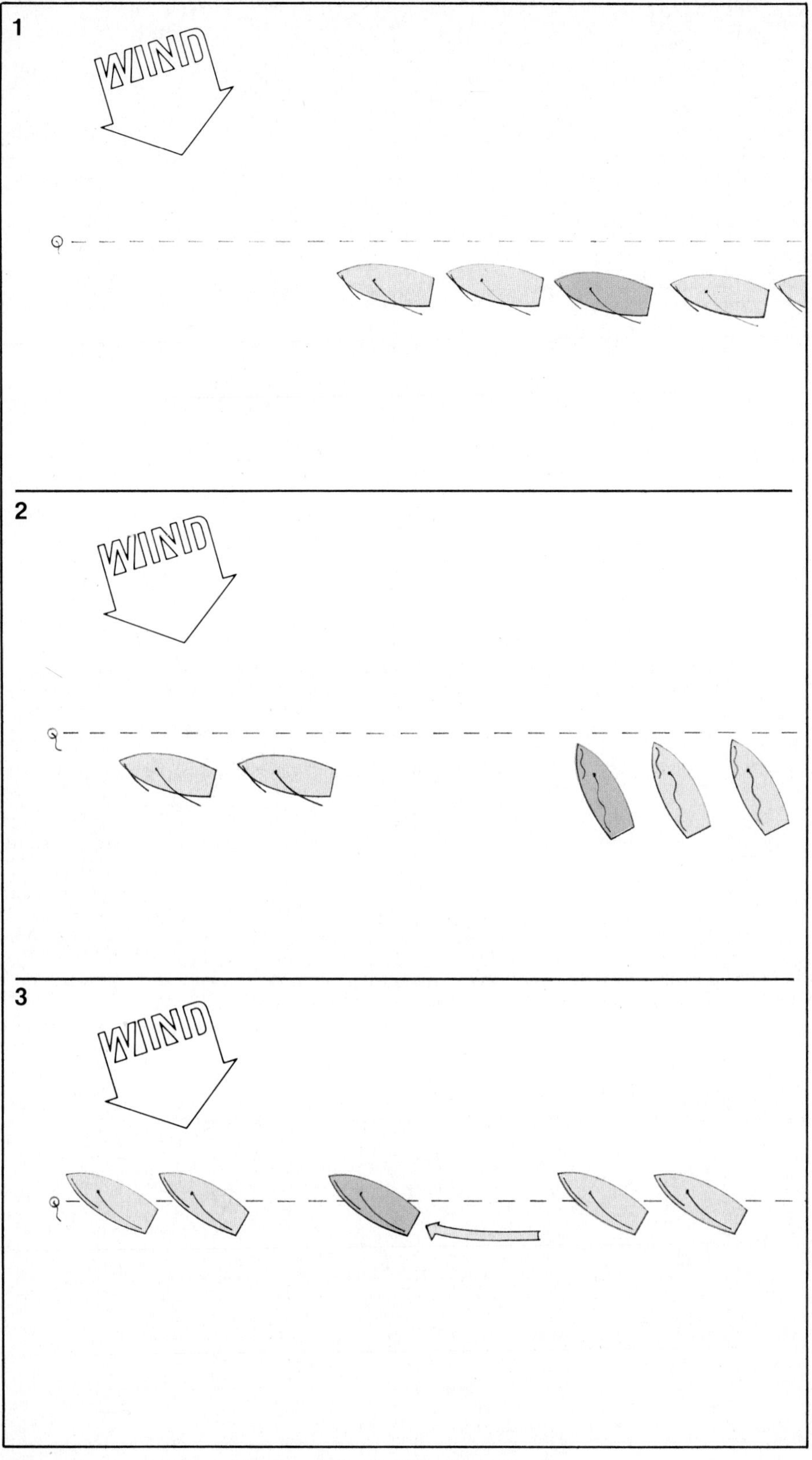

When a skipper finds himself in the middle of a line of boats heading for the favored end (1), he can increase his chances for a good, fast start by making a hole for himself. To do this he heads into the wind, slowly luffing up the boats to windward. As he holds them in check, the rest of the fleet sails on, leaving a hole to leeward (2). With about 10 seconds to go, the skipper bears off into the hole, reaches along the line for five seconds or so in order to pick up speed, then quickly hardens up to cross the line close-hauled at the starting gun (3).

Aggressive Starts

The racing skipper who plans to make the ideal start by simply crossing the line at the right place and the right time soon discovers that he must contend with the equally eager plans of his rivals. But aggressive maneuvers may, nonetheless, raise him above the multitude. If, for example, he is caught somewhere back in the fleet while running the line, he can exercise leeward-boat luffing privileges to create room in which to pick up speed before the starting gun *(1, 2 and 3, left)*.

A more creative, and frequently overlooked, way of getting an edge on competitors is to stay out of the starboard-tack fleet and approach the starting line on port tack *(top right)*. From this vantage, a skipper can see whether or not other boats are timing their own approach correctly and can judge when to tack onto starboard and slide into a hole in the pack.

A skipper with a fast boat, steely nerves and exquisite timing can sometimes outwit the fleet by forswearing right-of-way safety altogether and holding his port tack all the way across the line *(right, center)*. This risky ploy is best used when a last-minute wind shift makes it difficult for boats to cross the line on starboard tack. While the rest of the fleet doggedly tries to pinch over the line, the port-tack starter will have full way on at the gun and can sweep past all his rivals.

The brave at heart may also be tempted to try a maneuver called the dip start *(bottom right)*. Because the skippers near the middle of a long starting line cannot easily tell precisely where the line is, they often hang back to avoid going over early. This nearly always leaves a gap between the fleet and the line, and the gap will be accentuated if a strong current is running into the fleet. Under such circumstances, a skipper starting from above the line can sail with the current and then dip down into the space left by the wary, getting a fast start in clear air. If the gap has disappeared by the time he gets to the line, he can usually manage to find a saving hole between boats that will allow him to bear off, sail under a rival's stern and harden up for a later start.

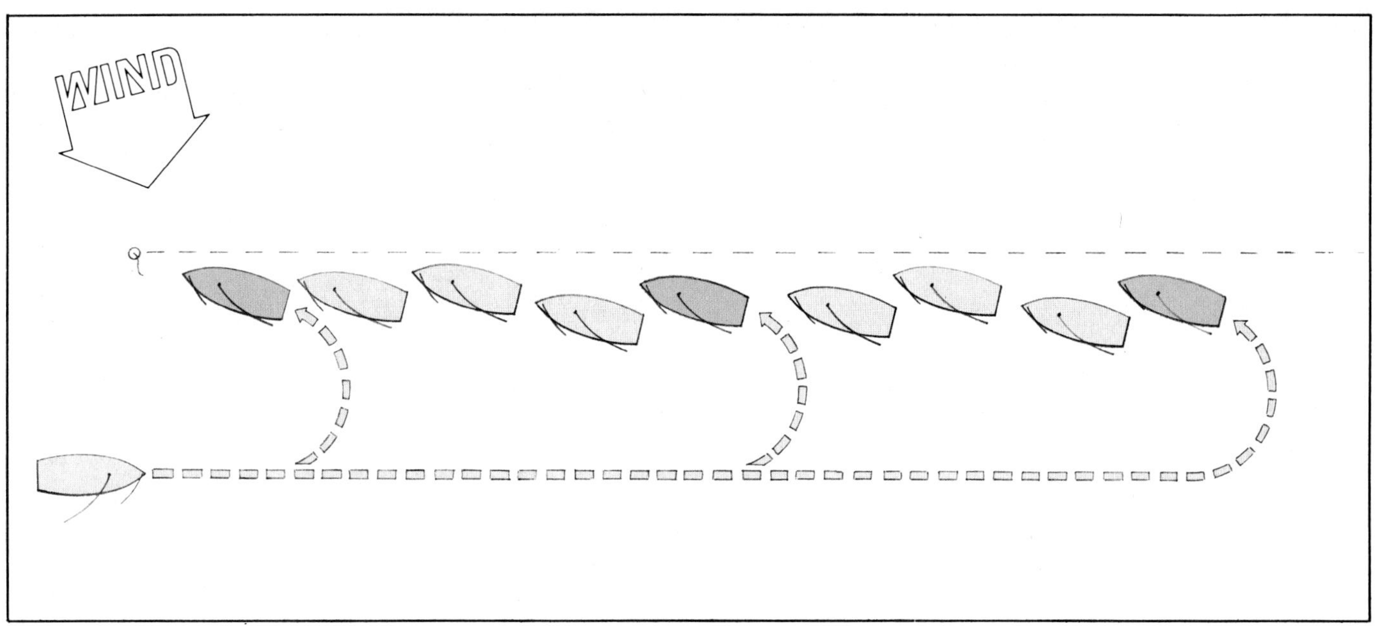

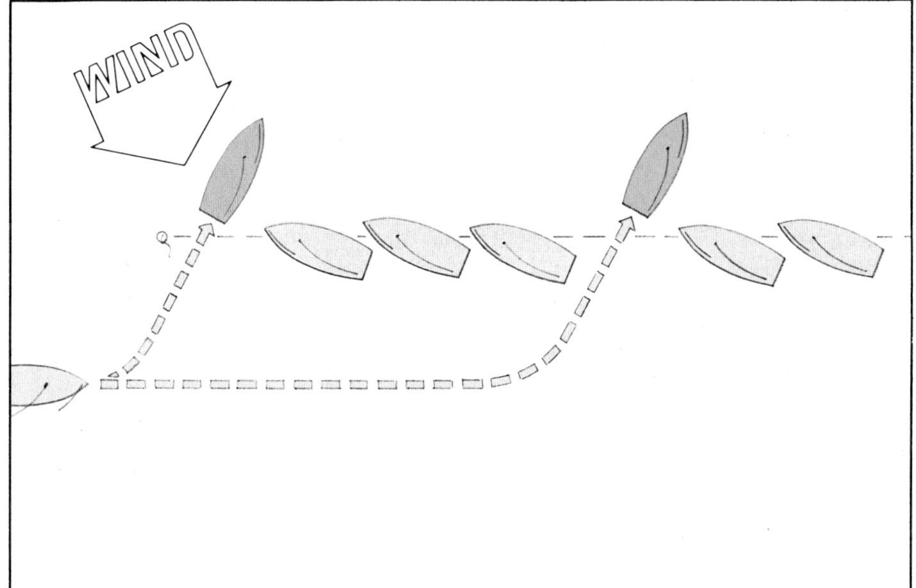

A port-tack approach offers the skipper several opportunities for a good start. He may tack in front of a fleet (above, left) made late by light winds or an adverse current. If the fleet has timed the start well, he may find a hole not too far behind the leaders (above, center). And if the fleet is early, he can tack in behind them (above, right) and make up ground as the skippers ahead maneuver to keep from crossing the line before the gun.

A port-tack start is potentially the most fruitful of the various aggressive starting maneuvers, but the risk of a right-of-way violation is high. Before the gun, the skipper reaches toward the line from beyond the port end. If the fleet is late, he aims directly for the mark and sails across the line in first place (far left). If there is no room at the mark, he can reach along under the starboard-tack boats, hoping to find a hole to shoot through.

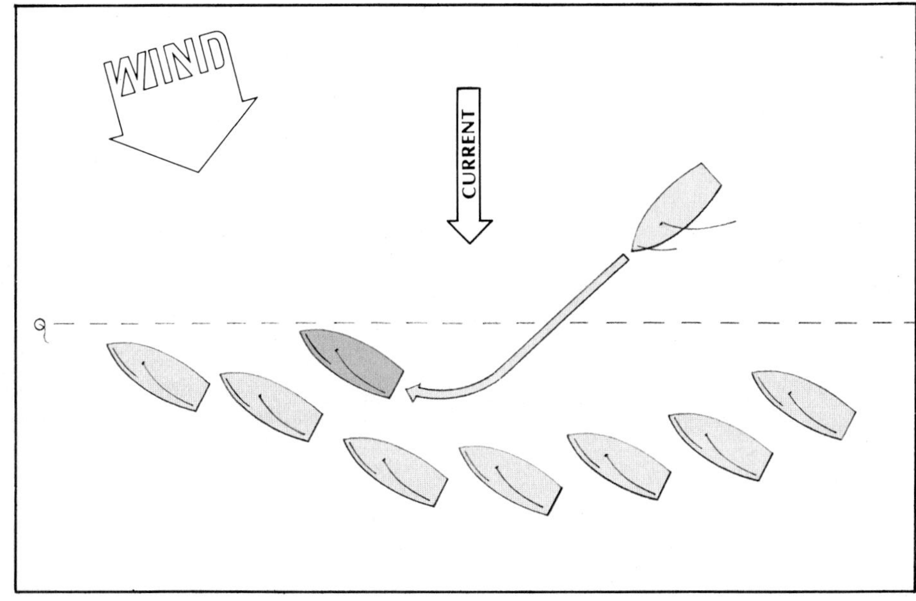

The so-called dip start, involving an approach from above the line, is most easily pulled off when a strong current is running into the starting line. The skipper, on starboard tack, sails toward the port end looking for a current-induced gap between the fleet and the line. As soon as he spots one, he starts toward the line on a broad reach, crosses into the hole, rounds up gently to maintain momentum and recrosses close-hauled.

The Windward Legs

Nearing the end of a windward leg, Flying Juniors converge at the mark, the red flag directly ahead of the third boat from the right. Amid the traffic, the skipper of boat 3210 has worked his way into an ideal position. With right of way on starboard tack, he can force most of his opponents either to tack or to drop off below him, assuring himself one of the top positions as he rounds the mark.

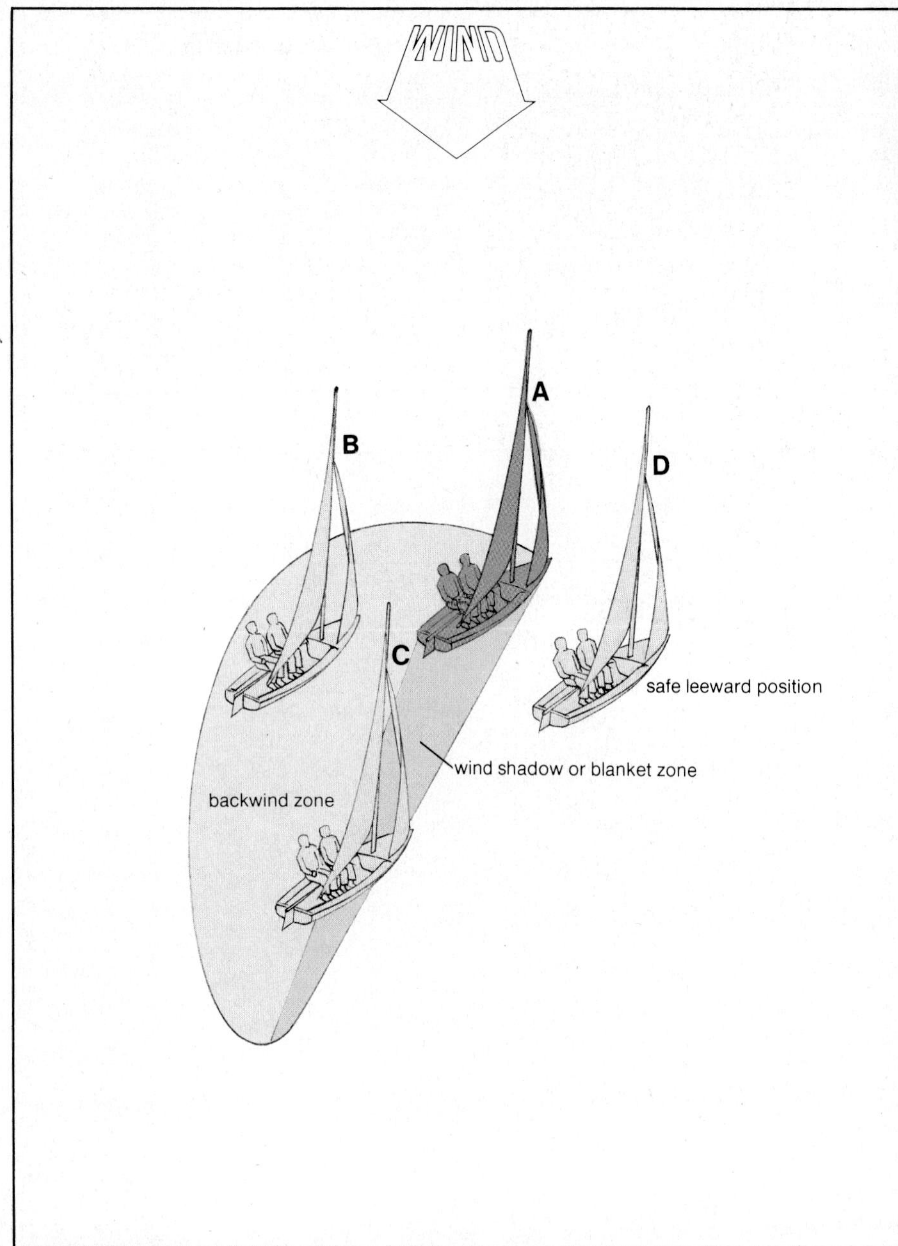

Each boat on an upwind leg can exert a major influence on the performance of nearby boats by interfering with their wind. For clarity, only boat A's area of disturbed air is diagramed here. The boat generates two areas of disturbed air: a backwind zone (light blue) where the wind eddies off its sails, and a blanket zone or wind shadow (dark blue), where it has blocked off virtually all the wind's flow. Boat B, caught in A's backwind, will begin to drop astern and to leeward. Boat C, in the smaller wind shadow, will drop off even more quickly, but will be free of disturbed air sooner. Boat D is in the so-called safe leeward position, where it is unaffected by boat A.

Finding Clear Air

Racing sailors agree that the windward leg is the most demanding of the race, because a skipper must deal with so many variables. Unable to steer directly for the mark, he has to choose a course based on his best estimate of present wind direction and possible shifts; and sometimes he must take into account current conditions as well. Then he must sail his boat as close to the wind and as fast as possible, often with no competitor nearby against whom to monitor his performance.

On those occasions when other boats are in a competitor's immediate vicinity, they create another sort of problem: their sails, by interrupting the wind's flow, change its force and direction over a sizable area *(left)*. A skipper sailing in this area of disturbed air glancing off the sails of another boat cannot get the best speed out of his own craft, and will not only fail to pass his rival but will also lose ground to boats sailing in undisrupted wind.

Top racing skippers can often ensure clear air for the windward leg by making an outstanding start. But most sailors find themselves in the middle of the fleet after the gun and must resort to other measures. The easiest method is known as sailing through the lee *(top right)*: a skipper simply sacrifices some distance to windward in hopes of making up this ground —and more—when he is free of wind interference from his rivals.

An alternate escape technique is to tack away from the disturbed air; but unless the skipper has a good continuing reason for staying on the new tack—such as certain knowledge of a coming wind shift or favorable current *(pages 100-103)*—he should tack back again quickly. This is because it is generally wisest to stay with the fleet early in the race, even though the temptation on the windward leg is to do the opposite of what the leaders are doing in hopes of catching up through some fluke of wind or current. An all-or-nothing gamble should be saved for later, when a skipper has exhausted his chances to gain a lead by outsailing his rivals or outmaneuvering them at the marks.

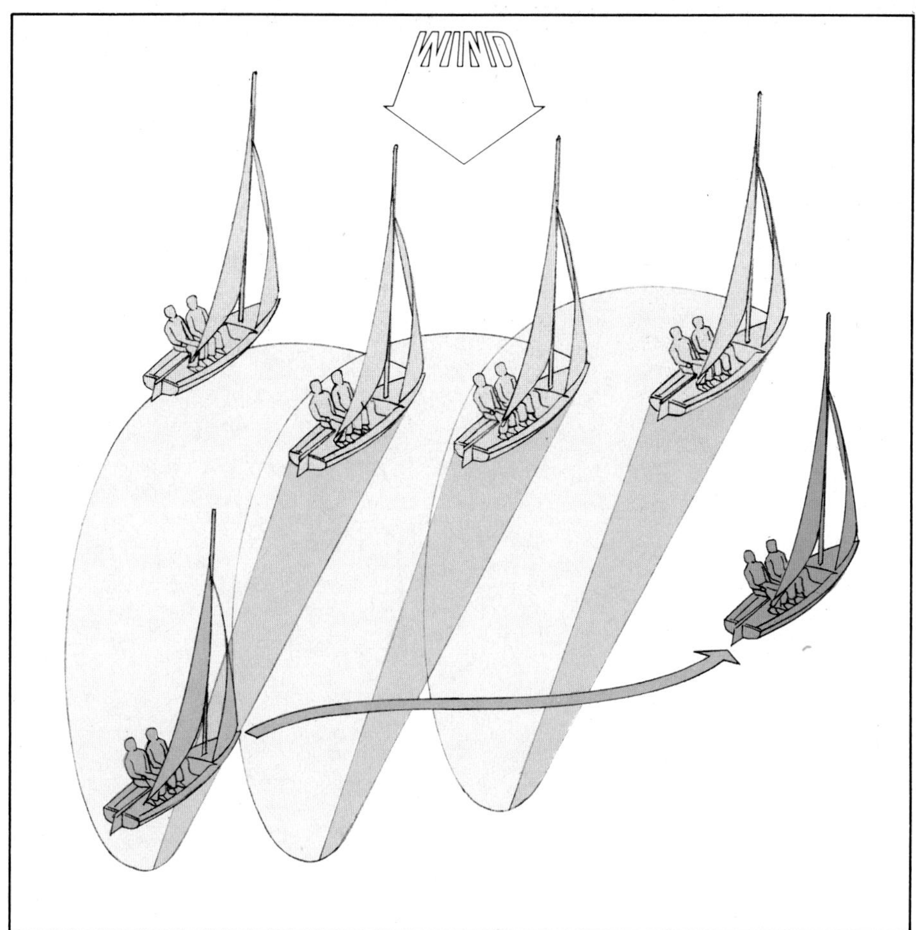

One course to sail in escaping from the disturbed air caused by the fleet lies to leeward, below and outside the bad air. Here, the lagging boat (blue) bears off on a close reach to gather speed, sailing for the outside of the wind shadows where the effects of blanketing are less serious. When the skipper is safely past, he retrims the sails, heads up and tries to work his way back to windward.

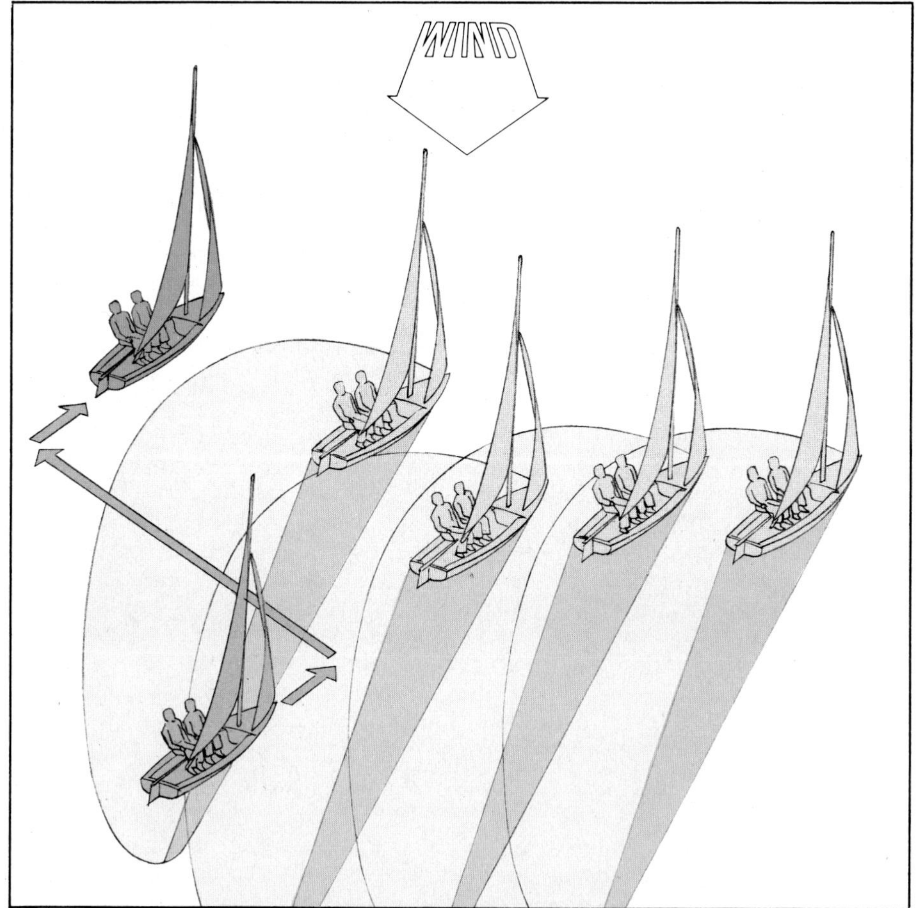

Another way for a skipper to free himself from a fleet's bad air is to tack, first making sure that the maneuver will not merely place him in another boat's disturbed air. After attaining clear air by putting a distance of about two boat lengths between himself and his nearest rival, he should tack back to remain with the fleet—unless he has a compelling reason to strike off on his own.

A wind shift that moves aft on a boat sailing close-hauled (below, left) is called a lift, since it enables the boat to point higher. When two boats are lifted, the windward one always benefits: thus the blue boat at right, originally to windward and even with its rival, is still to windward—and clearly ahead—after the lift.

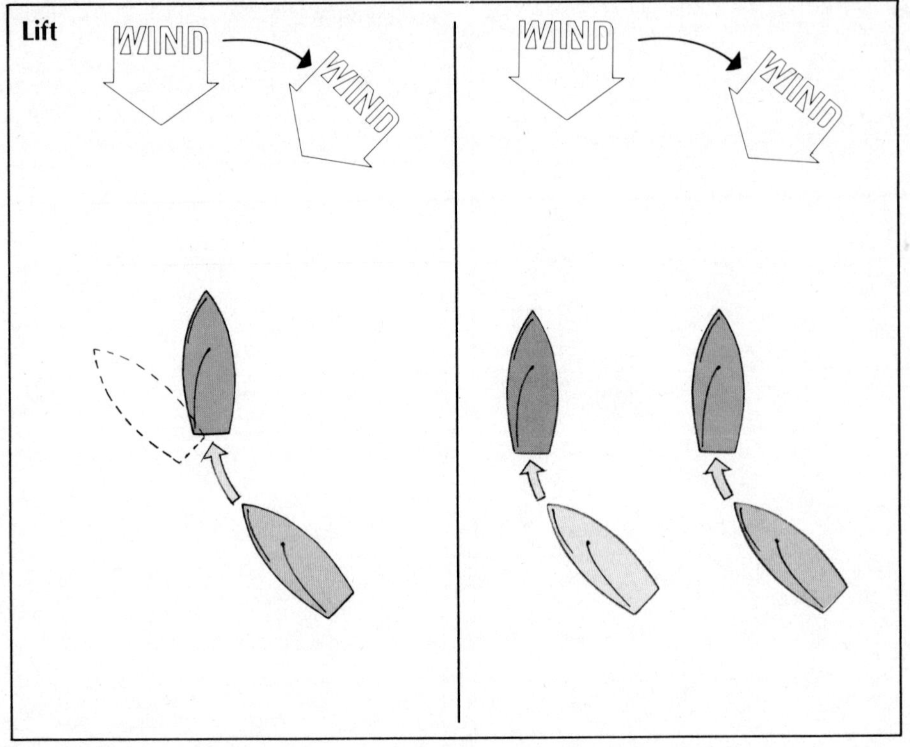

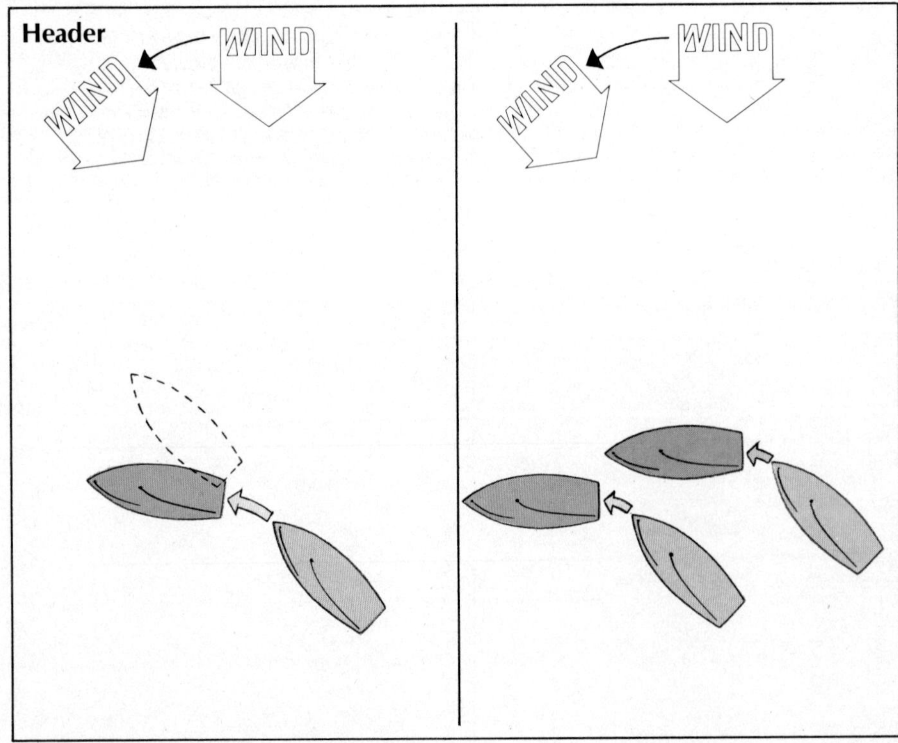

A wind shift forward on a boat is called a header; it forces the boat to head lower to keep its sails full (above, left). A leeward boat gains over a windward rival in a header. The blue boat at right, originally to leeward, is clear ahead after the shift: the farther apart the boats are, the greater the gain.

Lifts and Headers

Although skippers in a race have a choice of routes to the windward mark, most of them tend to follow the same general pattern. After crossing the starting line—presumably near the favored end—they will either tack or bear off to get clear air. They will then make a relatively long tack toward one side of the course to take advantage of the wind or current direction. A series of tacks thereafter serves to hold them on that side of the course; and a final tack places their boats on the lay line —the path that will bring them right to the mark *(pages 112-113)*.

When a skipper executes this sequence, perhaps his most important decision is to pick the direction for the tack that will carry him to one side of the course. A key factor in selecting the right tack is the prospect of wind shifts. While sailing a windward leg, a skipper can count on experiencing a number of minor wind shifts, and even major shifts of 30° or more are common. Sailors call a change in the wind's direction either a lift or a header, depending on its directional relationship with their boat's path. Either kind of shift may not only result in an instant reshuffling of the positions of boats in a fleet *(left)* but may also dramatically shorten the distance a boat must travel in order to reach the mark.

Even if a skipper has no way of anticipating the direction of a shift, he can position himself to receive a bonus, nevertheless, by following a simple rule: his long tack to one side of the course should be on whatever heading takes him most directly toward the mark. As demonstrated in the simplified diagrams at right, this will enable him to benefit from both clockwise and counterclockwise shifts.

Other considerations may override this general rule for defending against unforeseeable wind shifts. For instance, in very light air the main factor in choosing a tack toward one side of the course is the relative abundance of wind: if a skipper knows where he is likely to find more wind, he should go there. In heavy air, the most advantageous side of the course may be the one in the lee of a land mass, where milder waves allow him to keep his boat pointing high and moving fast.

But no matter what the conditions, he should usually commit himself to one side or the other. Sailors who select a compromise route down the center of the course are likely to miss some sort of opportunity out on the margins; furthermore, they lose ground by having to make many short tacks to stay in the middle.

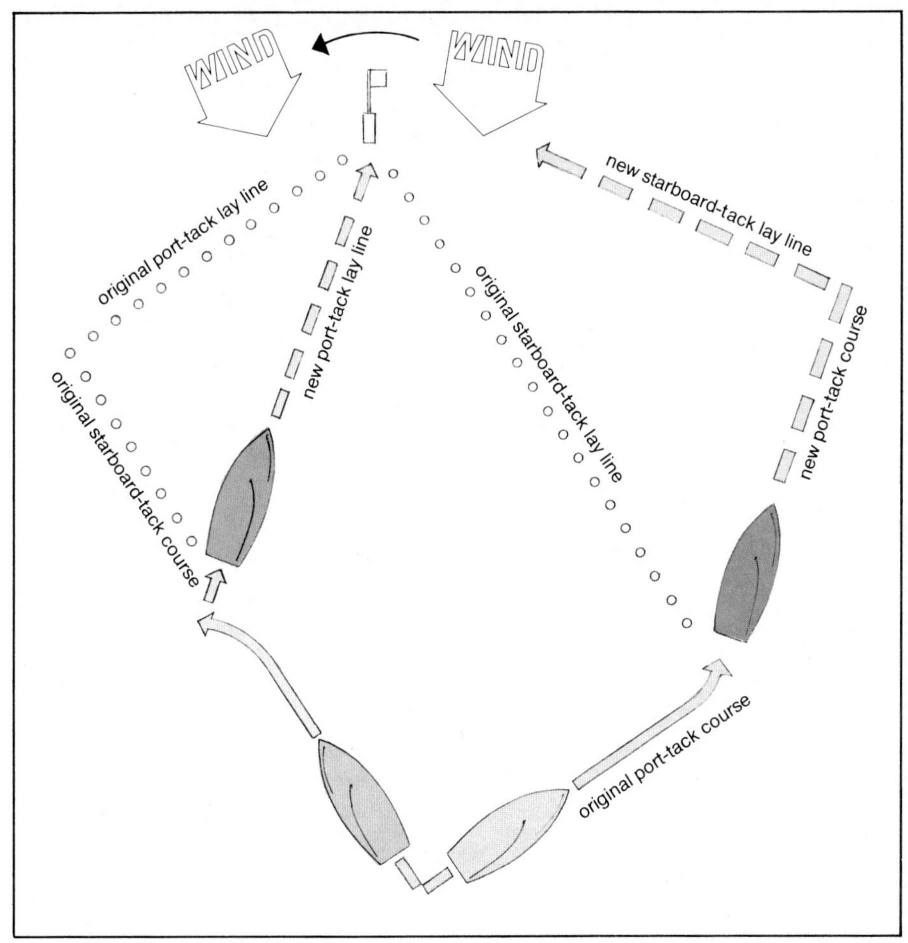

When sailing for a mark that is not straight upwind, a boat (blue) whose first tack is aimed more nearly toward the mark stands to gain from a counterclockwise wind shift, as shown in the simplified diagram at left. The boat, on starboard tack, will be headed by the shift; but the skipper simply comes about onto port tack, putting him on or near the lay line. A boat (gray) whose first tack carried it farther away from the mark is lifted by the shift, but not enough to fetch the mark on port tack. This boat now will have to make at least one more tack and will end up sailing a greater distance to fetch the mark.

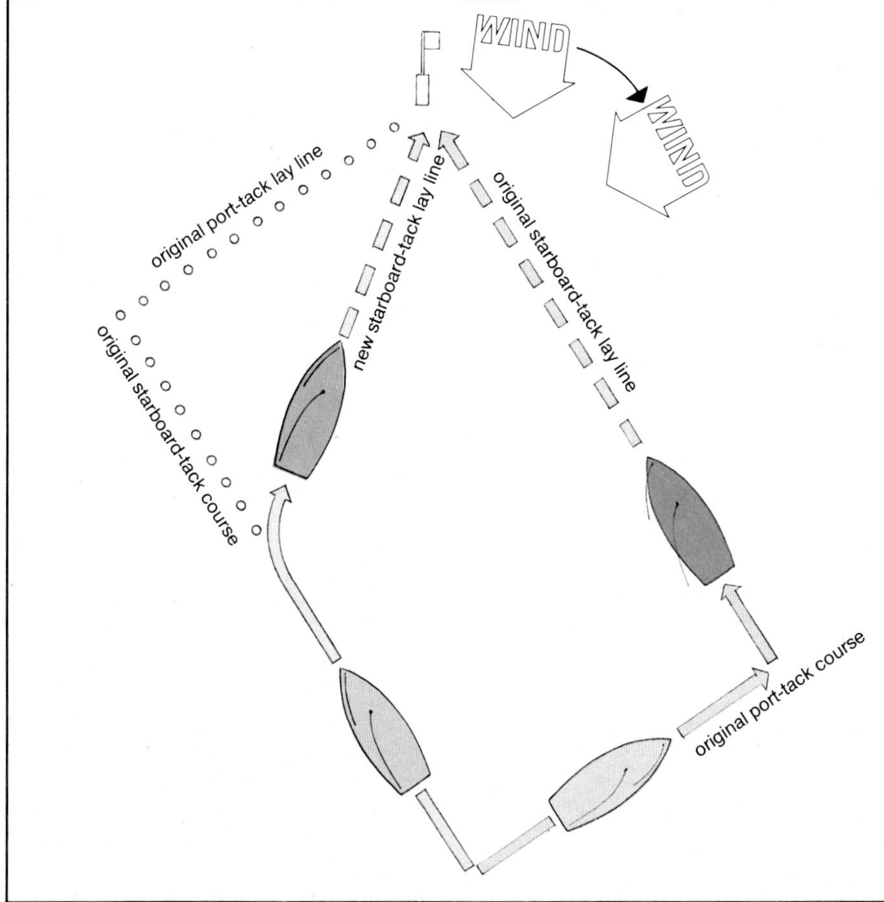

A boat that chooses the most direct tack toward a mark also stands to gain from a clockwise wind shift. In the situation at left, the starboard-tack boat (blue) has been lifted enough to fetch the mark. A port-tack boat (gray) can come about to receive the lift, but if, as here, it was already close to the lay line when the shift occurred, the skipper has, in effect, overstood—sailed farther than necessary to fetch the mark close-hauled. He can now reach to the mark, but has farther to sail and will arrive behind his rival.

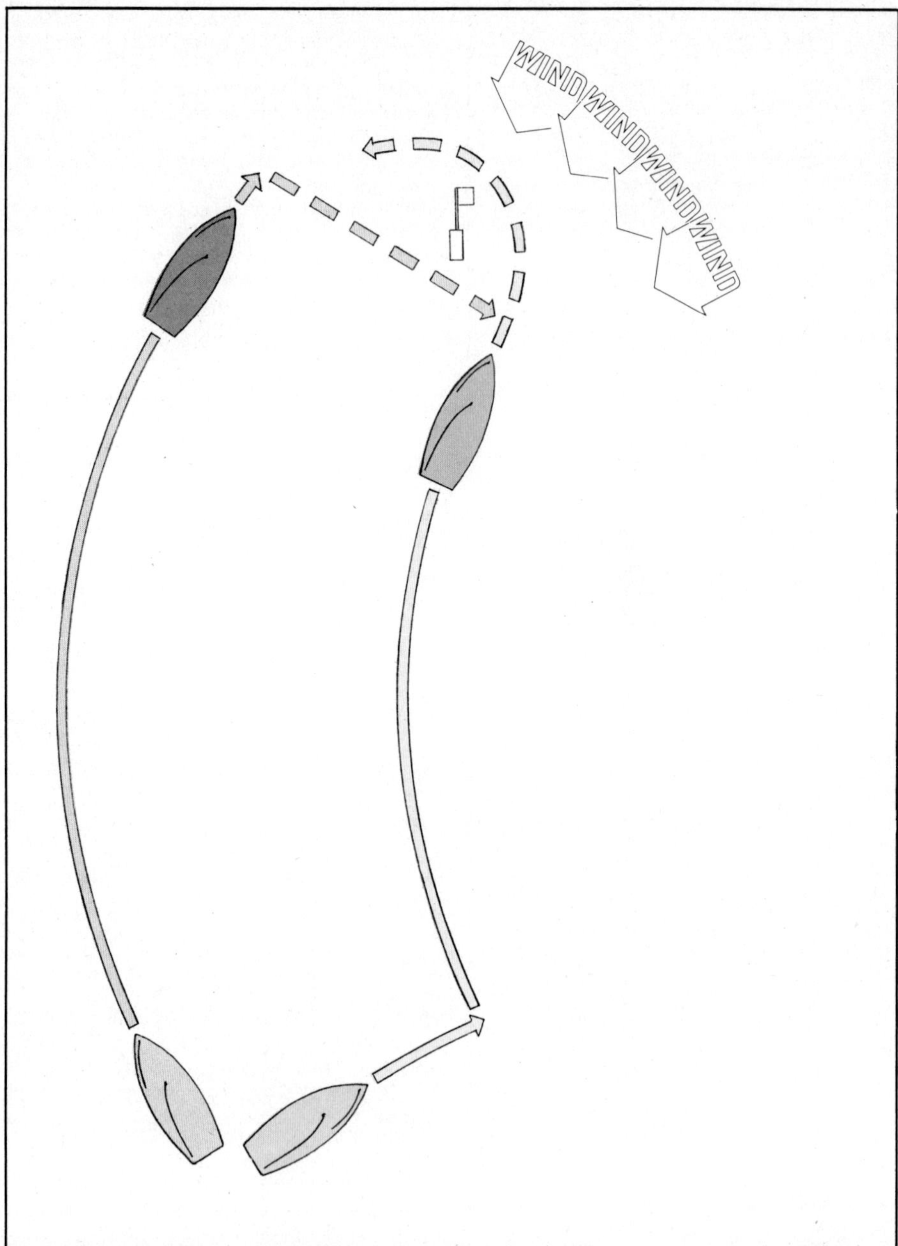

If the wind steadily shifts in any one direction during a windward leg, every skipper will find himself at one time or another sailing into a header while trying to fetch the mark. Under these conditions, the best strategy is to accept the header sooner rather than later. The skipper of the blue boat above has made a short tack toward the shift just after the start, allowing himself to be headed away from the mark; but after he comes about, the continuing shift will lift him in a curving track to his goal. The gray boat's skipper is lifted from the outset; but at the end of the leg, he must accept a more severe header than his rival, because of the change in the wind's angle.

Using the Wind Shifts

Although wind shifts often seem capricious, a racing sailor can sometimes forecast what the wind will do and thereby steal a march on the opposition. A continuing shift, for example, may be detected by getting out on the course before the race and sailing a long tack to windward. If the skipper notices that the wind is consistently moving clockwise or counterclockwise a few degrees at a time, he should adopt the strategy shown at left. By making a brief tack in the direction of the shift after the start, he will arrive at the mark ahead of a rival who chooses an opposite initial tack.

Another sort of predictable shift occurs when the wind blows obliquely offshore. The breeze is first slowed by the friction of the land, then speeds up again when it reaches the water. This creates an area of reduced pressure along the shore, and the wind fills the partial vacuum by altering direction slightly—offering a potential lift to the weather mark *(below)*.

Sometimes the wind oscillates back and forth from one side of the course to the other. If, when sailing a long test tack before the start, a skipper is first lifted, then headed, his best strategy is to find the lifted tack at the start and then tack whenever a major header is encountered *(top right)*. However, even a good sailor will occasionally tack on a very minor shift, putting himself out of phase with the major oscillations. His best recourse is to keep sailing on that tack, waiting for the next major header to get him back in phase. By then he will have given up ground to leeward, but the reshuffling of the fleet's order by the shift *(pages 98-99)* may result in an impressive gain.

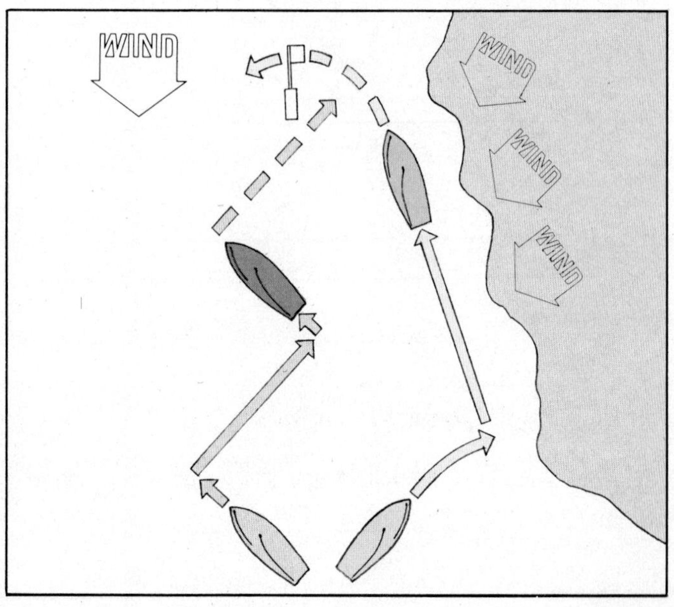

Wind blowing diagonally off a shore will tend to shift in a direction more perpendicular to the land, to fill a low-pressure area created by differences in land and water friction. To utilize such a local shift, a boat (blue) simply sails inshore, tacks when headed and is lifted to the mark. A boat (gray) that stays away from shore must travel a greater distance to reach the mark, since it receives no lift.

When the direction of the wind shifts back and forth—a circumstance most common in a breeze blowing directly offshore—the favored tack changes regularly as well. The skipper of the blue boat at left, aware of the wind's behavior, has promptly tacked each time he is headed, transforming the wind shifts into lifts and sailing a short route to the mark. The gray boat's helmsman has failed to perceive the oscillating pattern and spends much of his time being headed away from the mark; thus he makes far less progress to windward than his rival.

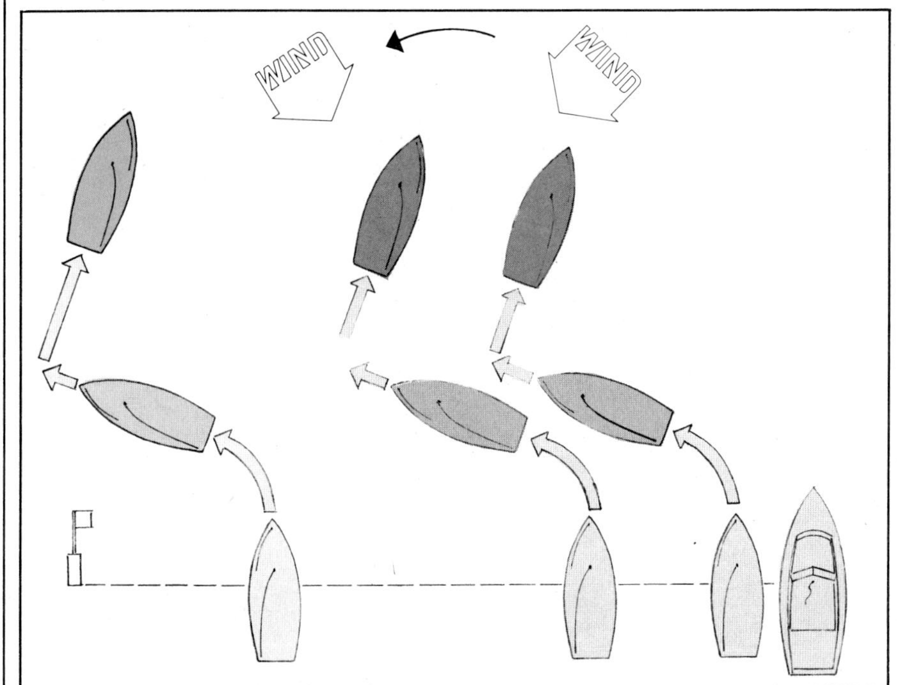

A Delayed Payoff at the Start

An oscillating wind may dictate special starting tactics. If the starting line is set square to the median wind direction, the end of the line that is favored at the gun will not be favored a few minutes later. Anticipating the shift, the skipper of the blue boat above starts at the unfavored end, avoiding the jam-up at the other end. Then when the wind swings around, heading the boats and forcing them to tack, he ends up in a good position, to windward of his rivals.

When the current is running evenly on the course, a boat (light blue) that first takes the current on its lee bow arrives at the mark no sooner than a boat (light gray) that takes the current to weather. Both boats—angled to their actual course to show the course they steer—are equally set to windward on starboard tack and to leeward on port. However, the blue boat's path does offer an advantage. Although when the wind blows directly from the mark, neither tack heads closer to it, here the current sets the starboard-tack course toward the mark. The blue boat will gain from any wind shift.

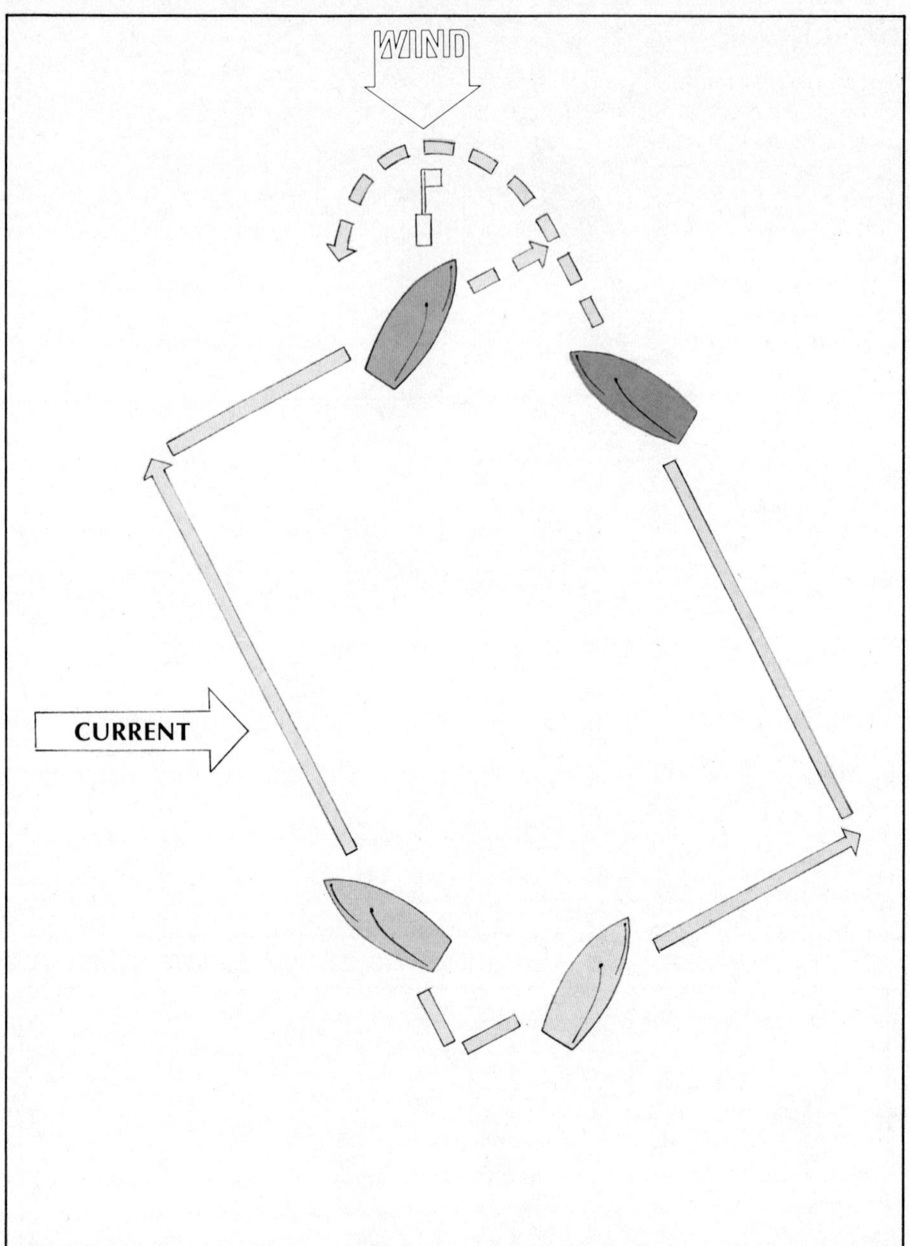

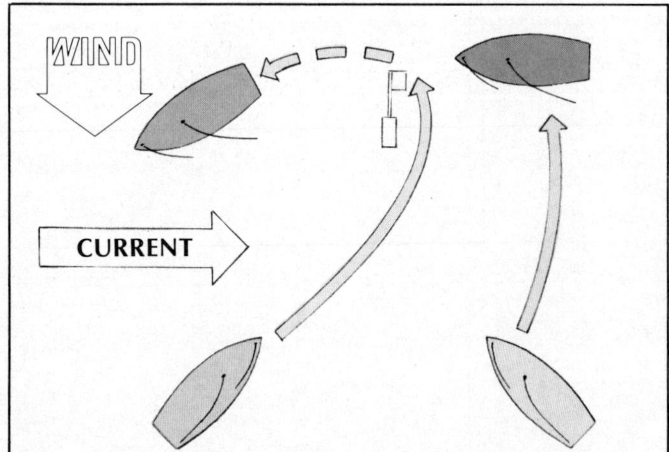

Nearing the end of a windward leg in a strong crosscurrent, a boat (blue) that approaches the mark from upcurrent avoids the danger of overstanding. His opponent, approaching on the other tack, is pushed past the mark and must reach toward it against the current.

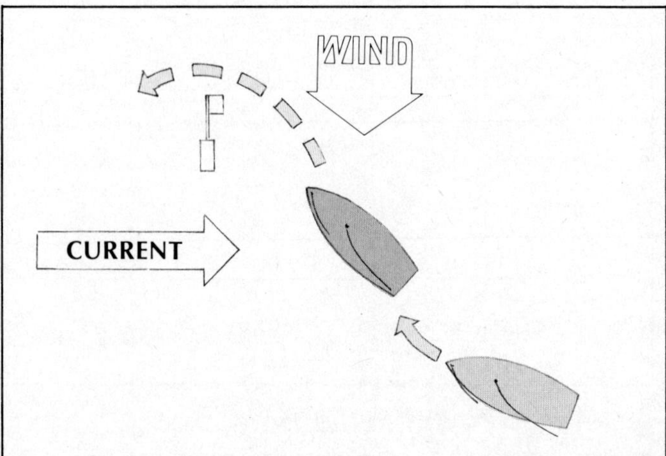

A boat that is very close to the mark but unable to fetch it can often use a current on its lee bow to squeeze out the extra distance to windward. The skipper pinches slightly and allows the current to carry him up to the mark, avoiding the need to make two more tacks.

Playing the Current

Preoccupied by sail trim, wind shifts and by their competitors' maneuvers, sailors competing in salt water sometimes ignore the effect of tidal currents on their racing strategy. But they do so at some peril, for current can be a critical factor, especially in light air.

To cope with this subtle but powerful force, a skipper needs some foreknowledge of its behavior at the time and locale of the race. Most racers rely initially on tidal bulletins—giving times of high and low water—published in table form by local newspapers and broadcast on local weather stations.

They supplement this information with their own on-the-spot observations. For example, a skipper can tell the direction of current by watching it flow past a buoy. Another technique is to line up a buoy with some point on land, then observe the movement of the landmark while steering toward the buoy: if the shoreside reference moves to the right, the current is setting the boat to the left—and vice versa.

A common misconception among racers is that, when beating upwind, a boat should keep the current on its lee bow as much as possible. Theoretically, the current then helps push the boat toward the mark ahead of its rivals. But in fact, this notion is badly flawed. All boats in the fleet must spend the same amount of time on a given tack to attain the windward mark, and as long as the current is even all over the course, it gives them equal benefits *(top left)*. However, the decision on whether or not to take the current on the lee bow may become an important tactical consideration in the immediate vicinity of the mark *(bottom left)*.

Usually, current is stronger on one side of the course than the other. When flowing around a curve of land, for example, the water at the outside of the curve moves faster than at the inside. Current is also much stronger in deep water than shallow, where it is slowed by friction against the bottom. And behind a large point of land, the current may actually eddy in a direction opposite to the main flow. All of these factors provide opportunities for outsailing an opponent. In a favorable current, the winning strategy is simply to stay in the strongest current as long as possible; in an adverse current, a skipper should try to get out of the current *(right)*. And if the air is so light that an adverse current begins to set the fleet backward, a skipper should instantly drop anchor and hold position until the wind or current changes.

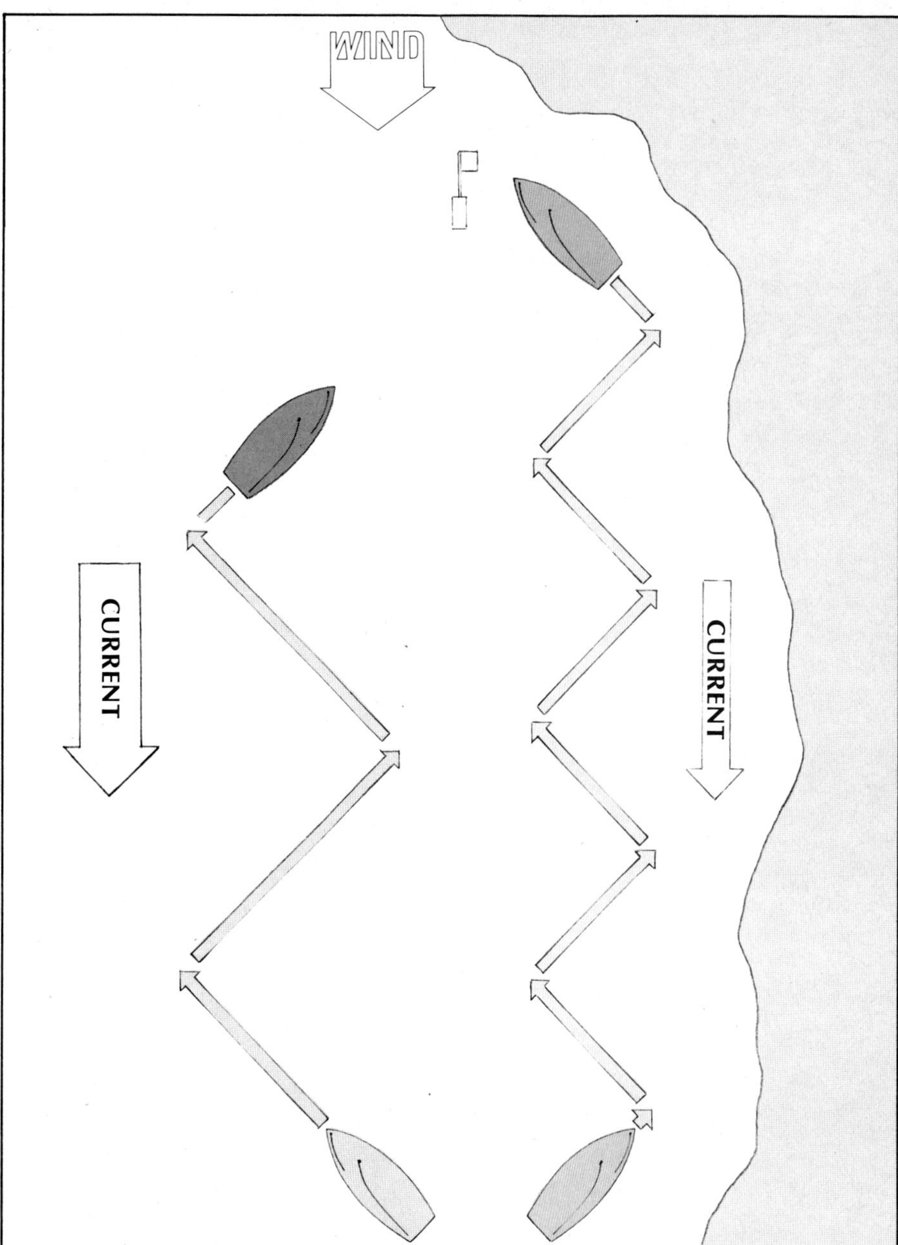

In light air, a skipper should seek a way out of an adverse current, even if he has to make numerous extra tacks to achieve this end. Here, the blue boat has sailed inshore, where the water is shallow and the current less strong; a series of short tacks maintains the advantageous position, bringing the boat to the mark ahead of a rival who has elected to make fewer tacks out in the current.

Upwind Helmsmanship

Throughout the windward leg of a race a skipper must remain alert to every change in wind or sea, and alter his course continually to compensate for the action of these forces. As illustrated on these pages, a skillful helmsman going to windward will typically alter course for four reasons: to stay on the best angle relative to the wind; to keep from getting knocked back by waves; to take advantage of lifts; and to avoid being set back by headers.

All such steering maneuvers should be done smoothly and gently, since strong, jerky movements of the tiller disrupt the flow of water over the rudder and slow the boat. Moreover, a well-balanced boat will often help the helmsman by steering itself, swinging back onto course after a sideways shove from a wave or easing to windward when heeled over in a puff.

While wind and waves may vary in unpredictable ways from moment to moment, both forces exert basic influences that are constant in determining how high a skipper should head on any given tack. A boat will usually point highest in a freshening breeze and a flat sea. In light winds or choppy seas, however, the helmsman should steer a bit below the normal heading to avoid losing way.

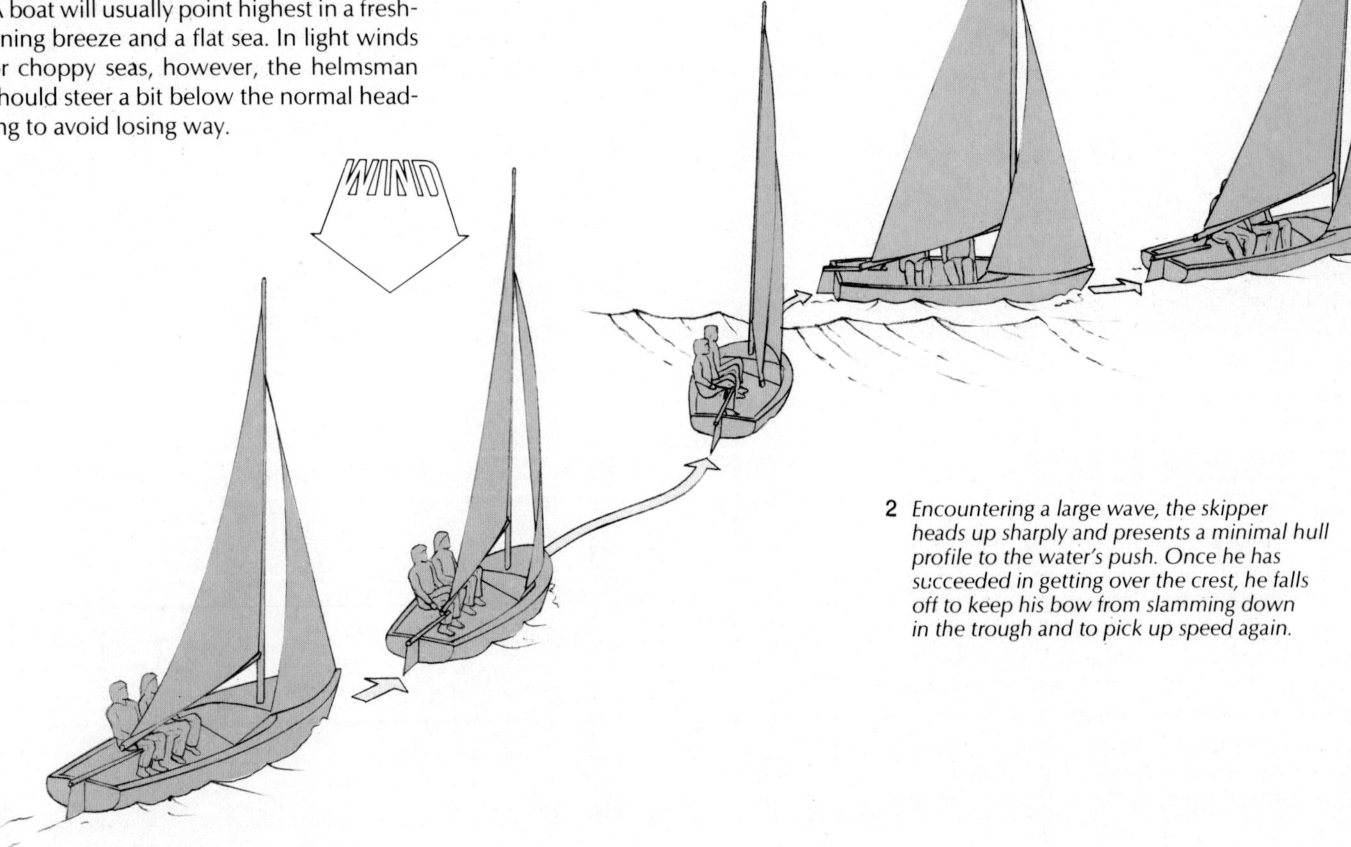

2 *Encountering a large wave, the skipper heads up sharply and presents a minimal hull profile to the water's push. Once he has succeeded in getting over the crest, he falls off to keep his bow from slamming down in the trough and to pick up speed again.*

1 *Starting out on his windward course, the skipper should periodically head up to test the wind for his optimum close-hauled sailing angle. By watching the telltales on his sails, feeling the pull of the tiller and sensing his changing angle of heel, he uses the boat itself as a sort of weather vane to detect each tiny change in the direction of the wind.*

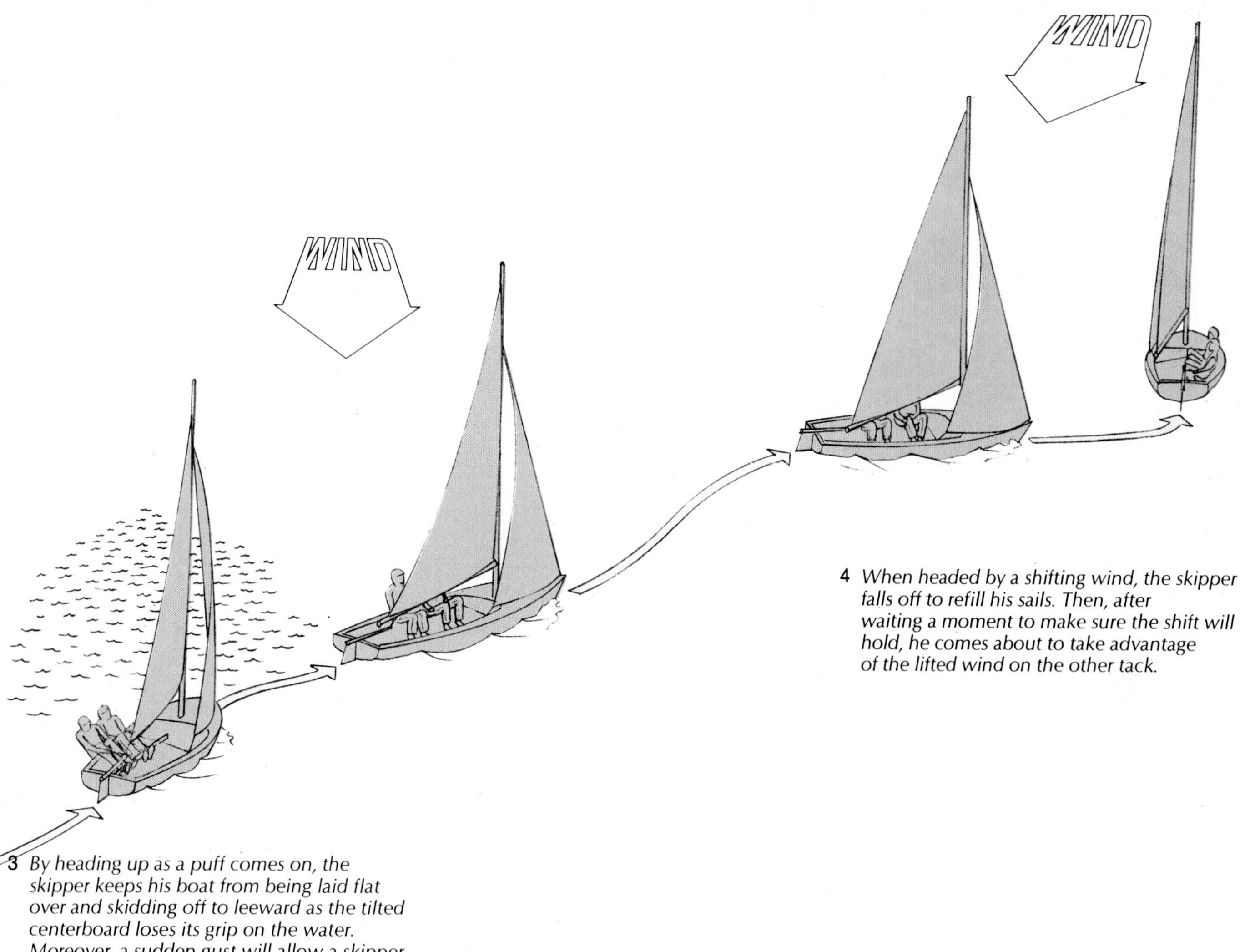

3 *By heading up as a puff comes on, the skipper keeps his boat from being laid flat over and skidding off to leeward as the tilted centerboard loses its grip on the water. Moreover, a sudden gust will allow a skipper to sail a slightly higher course because of a shift in the apparent wind (box, below).*

4 *When headed by a shifting wind, the skipper falls off to refill his sails. Then, after waiting a moment to make sure the shift will hold, he comes about to take advantage of the lifted wind on the other tack.*

apparent wind
true wind
apparent wind
true wind
boat-speed wind
boat-speed wind

A Better Slant in a Wind Puff

When the wind gusts, a boat receives a lift, enabling the craft to steer slightly closer to the mark even though the direction of the natural, or true, wind's flow over the water remains the same. This lift occurs because of a change in direction of the apparent wind —the one that the skipper feels and to which the sails are trimmed *(page 26)*. As shown in the diagrams at left, the apparent wind is a combination of two winds—the true wind, and a second breeze created by the boat's forward motion. In a sudden gust *(diagram at near left)*, the true wind's contribution to the mix suddenly increases. This changes the direction of the apparent wind, moving it aft on the boat and allowing the boat to sail a higher course. In a sudden lull, the opposite effect takes place: the true wind drops, the apparent wind moves forward and the boat is headed.

Hiking in perfect unison, this skipper and crew are holding their boat at its fastest sailing angle. Both sit with the backs of their thighs braced over the windward rail, extending their weight well outboard. By positioning themselves close together, they dampen the boat's tendency to "hobby horse," or pitch fore and aft with the waves. Also, their combined weight is slightly forward of the beam in order to keep the boat from squatting in its own wake and holding down speed.

Many racing boats use a compass to monitor wind shifts, and it is the job of the crew to keep track of key headings—which are often jotted directly onto the deck, as above. Before the start, the skipper luffs head to wind to establish the wind direction. The crew then calculates the close-hauled heading for each tack; this so-called standard heading (here noted as "std") turned out to be 180° on the starboard tack and 270° for port. A 10° margin of imprecision is then allowed for each tack. Thus when close-hauled on the starboard tack, the skipper knows the wind has given him a lift if his heading increases to 190° or above; and if he drops below 170°, he has been headed.

The Crewman's Key Role

In any race, an adroit crewman can mean the difference between victory and defeat. It is the crew s responsibility, as much as the skipper's, to keep the boat alive and driving. In a strong breeze a good crew stays in almost continuous motion, hiking out either by himself or with the skipper *(top left)* to hold the boat on its best sailing lines, and shifting his weight inboard the instant the wind drops or the skipper changes course. When sailing in light airs he crouches in the cockpit, keeping his body down low, whenever possible, to cut air resistance, and executes each motion with utmost care so as not to upset the boat's balance.

At the same time, the crew takes exclusive charge of the jib, sheeting it across during tacks and keeping it trimmed to each subtle change in wind strength or direction. If the centerboard needs raising or lowering, the crew does it. In addition, the crew usually operates the controls that modify the shape of both mainsail and jib: he adjusts the boom vang, outhaul, downhaul and Cunningham to alter the main, and positions the jib-sheet leads to reshape the jib and adjust the slot between the sails. And on downwind legs *(pages 114-131)*, the crew's deft touch on the spinnaker sheet is the single most important factor in keeping the boat moving smartly along.

In performing any of these functions, teamwork and timing of the crew and skipper together are vital. A boat that consistently comes about with a minimum of wasted motion, for example, or stays upright in gusts through concerted hiking by both sailors, gains steadily over its sloppier rivals. Indeed, a good crewman seems to anticipate the skipper's wishes and execute them in advance.

The complicated and hectic action at the start or when rounding marks calls for a further degree of cooperation. Here, perhaps more than at any other point in the race, the crew must anticipate what the skipper will do and be prepared—for instance, to luff the jib if the boat is early at the line, or ease the jib if the skipper must fall off quickly to pass astern of a boat with right of way.

Tactics are also part of the crew's responsibility. In fact, during a race, many skippers depend almost entirely on the crew for tactical information regarding possible current shifts, compass headings that may indicate a change in wind direction *(bottom left)*, the locations of marks and lay lines, and how the boat is doing against the competition.

This crew's-eye view of a windward leg is filled with critical information of the kind that a good crew would relay to his skipper. The helmsman ought to know, for example, that the boat immediately to windward has eased its mainsail and is therefore going faster (or slower). The next boat to windward seems to be pointing higher, which might indicate a change of wind direction to come. And farther ahead, two boats have tacked for the darker water that signals a stronger breeze—a maneuver the skipper may want to emulate.

Using the Flying Trapeze

On many high-performance racing craft—including virtually all catamarans—the boat-balancing chores of the crew are executed with the aid of a device called a trapeze, as demonstrated on these pages. Trapezing is not only more effective than ordinary hiking out but also calls for less strength and agility: instead of straining leg and stomach muscles to stay in position on a boat's windward rail, the crew is comfortably suspended in mid-air.

When donning the trapeze harness before a race *(right)*, some sailors put on a life jacket under the shoulder straps; others prefer their life jacket on the outside. Once the race is underway and the boat begins to tack for the windward mark, the crew hooks the harness to one of two wires strung from the mast (each tack requires a separate wire). Then, with feet on the gunwhale, the crew moves outboard. A bent-knee position *(opposite, far right)* may be sufficient to hold the boat flat in light to medium air, but if the wind picks up, the crew will have to straighten all the way out *(opposite, bottom)*. On some boats, the length of the wire can be adjusted to tailor the crew's body angle—hence leverage—to wind conditions.

Out on the wire, the crew must resist the tendency to fall forward each time the boat is slowed by a wave. One simple preventive is to brace a leg forward and bend the knee to absorb the shock; or the boat may have foot straps to hold the crew in place or special lines to grip.

Tacking presents no real difficulty for a practiced trapeze artist. The crew simply swings inboard, unhooks from the wire, ducks under the boom and hooks up to the wire on the other side.

To put on a trapeze harness, the crew steps into it, positions it around the middle of the hips and then tightens the laces in front. The harness should fit snugly for comfort during long periods out on the trapeze wire.

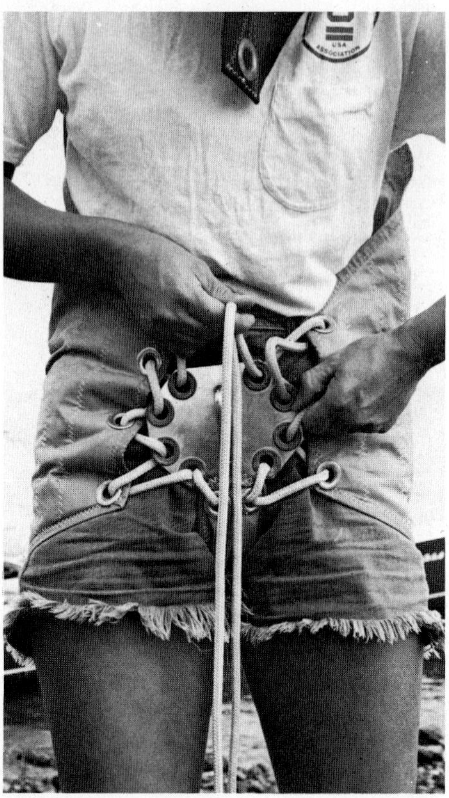

Next, the laces are run through the grommet in the shoulder straps and pulled tight enough to ensure firm support for the crew's back. The laces should then be tied with a square knot; additional square knots will keep the ends from whipping around in the wind.

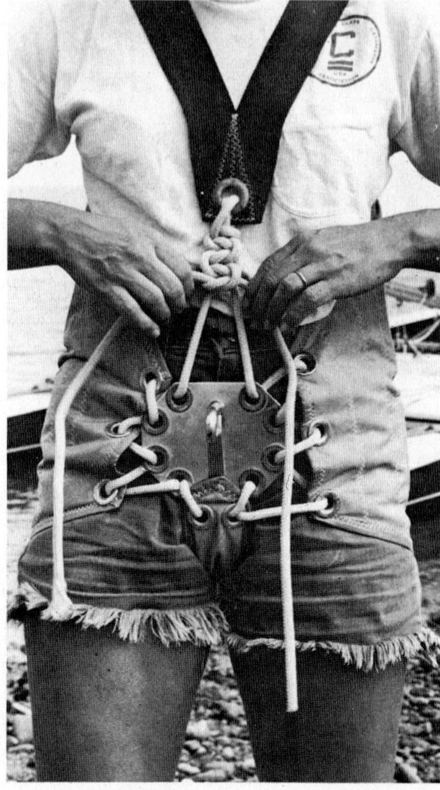

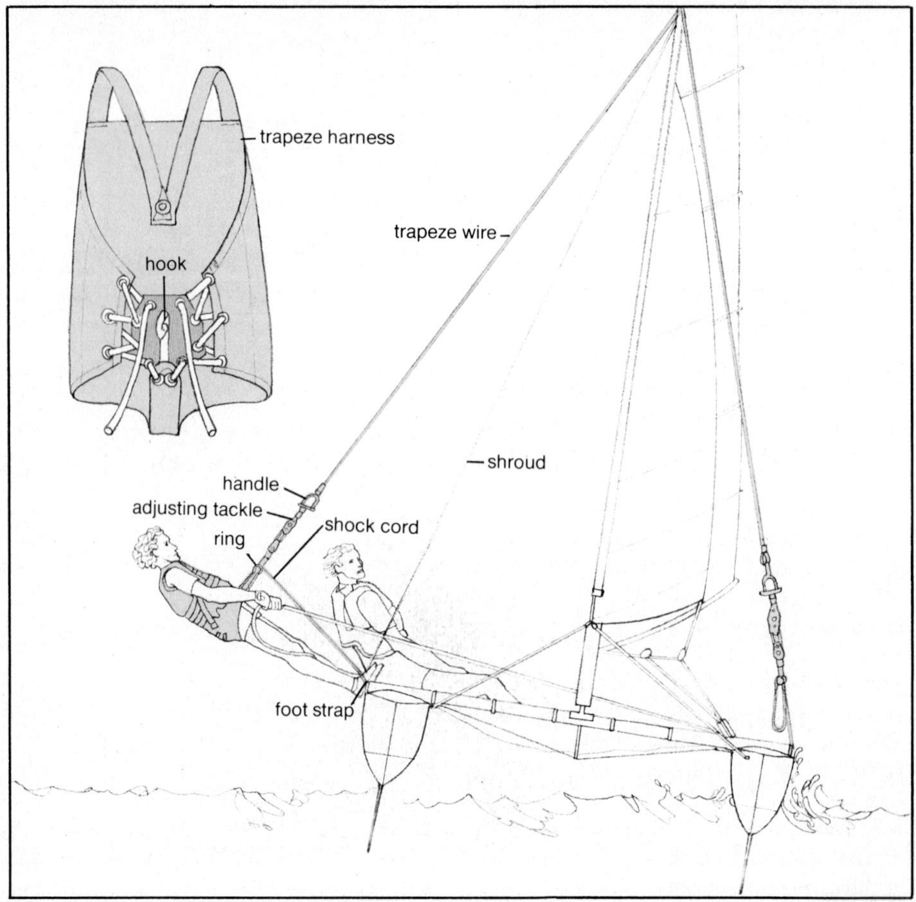

A typical trapeze includes a special harness and two wires rigged two thirds of the way up the mast, at the top of the shrouds. Near the bottom of each wire is a handle to help the crew swing out or in, and, in some cases, a tackle to adjust the wire's length. At the terminus of the wire is a metal ring that attaches to a downward-opening hook on the front of the trapeze harness. Shock cord links the wire to a point on deck near the base of the shroud. When the wire is in use, the shock cord stretches; when the crew hooks up on the opposite rail, the cord prevents the unused wire from flying free.

On board the boat, the crew hooks the harness to the windward trapeze wire. In this case, the attachment point—located below a tackle that adjusts the wire's length—is a double ring that permits two hook-up positions for crews of different heights.

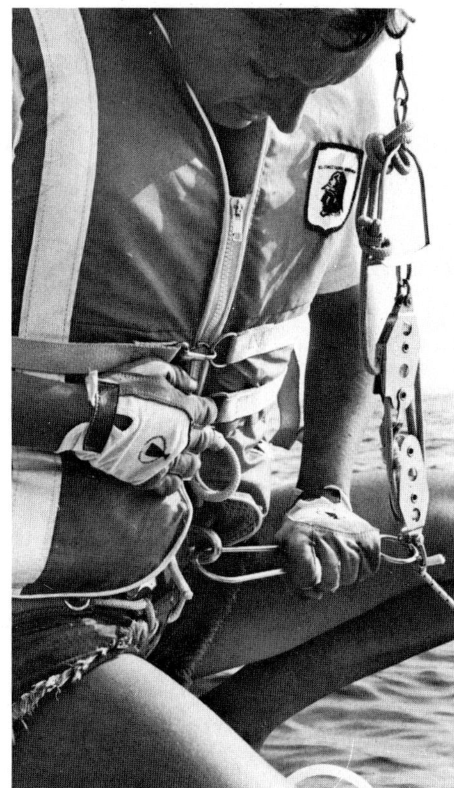

Holding the trapeze handle in one hand and the jib sheet in the other, the crew puts her weight on the wire and eases her way outboard. Her feet are tucked under straps that keep her from sliding forward or swinging up in the air when the boat pitches or slows.

In a puff, the crew straightens her legs and leans outboard for maximum leverage, balancing the boat so the windward hull skims the water.

A Quick-Tack Technique

When a sailboat tacks, its speed tends to drop and it may have to sacrifice anywhere from 15 to 100 feet of ground, depending on the type of boat and the conditions of the wind and sea. A winning skipper, therefore, generally tacks no more than he has to when working his way toward the mark on a weather leg.

Tacking is most costly in heavy seas, which can stop a boat dead when it is pointed head to wind. Very light air can also make tacking expensive, since a slowly moving boat will lose most of its momentum during the turn and is slow to gather way on the new tack. However, these losses can be cut if the boat is handled so as to maintain maximum momentum throughout the maneuver.

When tacking in a keelboat, avoid putting the helm hard over at the beginning of the turn; although the boat may pivot more quickly with the helm hard over, the rudder will act as a brake, offsetting any advantage of a fast turn. The correct method is to ease the helm gently until the vessel goes head to wind, then put the helm over the rest of the way, allowing the boat to pick up speed on the new tack before hardening up to close-hauled.

Lightweight centerboarders can be efficiently tacked by an altogether different technique, called the roll tack, depicted in the photographs at right. In this maneuver, the skipper and crew swivel the boat so deftly that it can even pick up speed as it turns.

The secret of the roll tack is a quick series of weight shifts that pivot the boat on its bilges, slew the stern around and force the sails so quickly across the centerline of the boat that the resistance of the air against their surface creates a false breeze. Often the sails stay full and pulling right through the eye of the wind. Some competitors have become so expert in using the roll tack to shoot the boat ahead, particularly in light air, that excessive use of the maneuver to gain ground has been branded by the racing rules as an unfair means of propulsion, and can result in a boat being expelled from the race.

About to begin a roll tack (1), the crew and skipper hike out only enough to hold their boat on its fastest sailing lines. Then the skipper eases the helm (2) and leans farther to windward, causing the boat to roll toward him. The crew, meanwhile, prepares to let go the leeward jib sheet. Banking into the turn, the boat shoots into the wind (3) while its sails, barely luffing, cross amidships. Skipper and crew move gingerly toward the new windward side. As the sails begin filling on the new tack (4), both hands reach the windward rail, and the crew sheets in the jib. Fully around (5), with the sails trimmed and the tiller pulled back amidships, the boat moves out on the new leg.

2

3

4

5

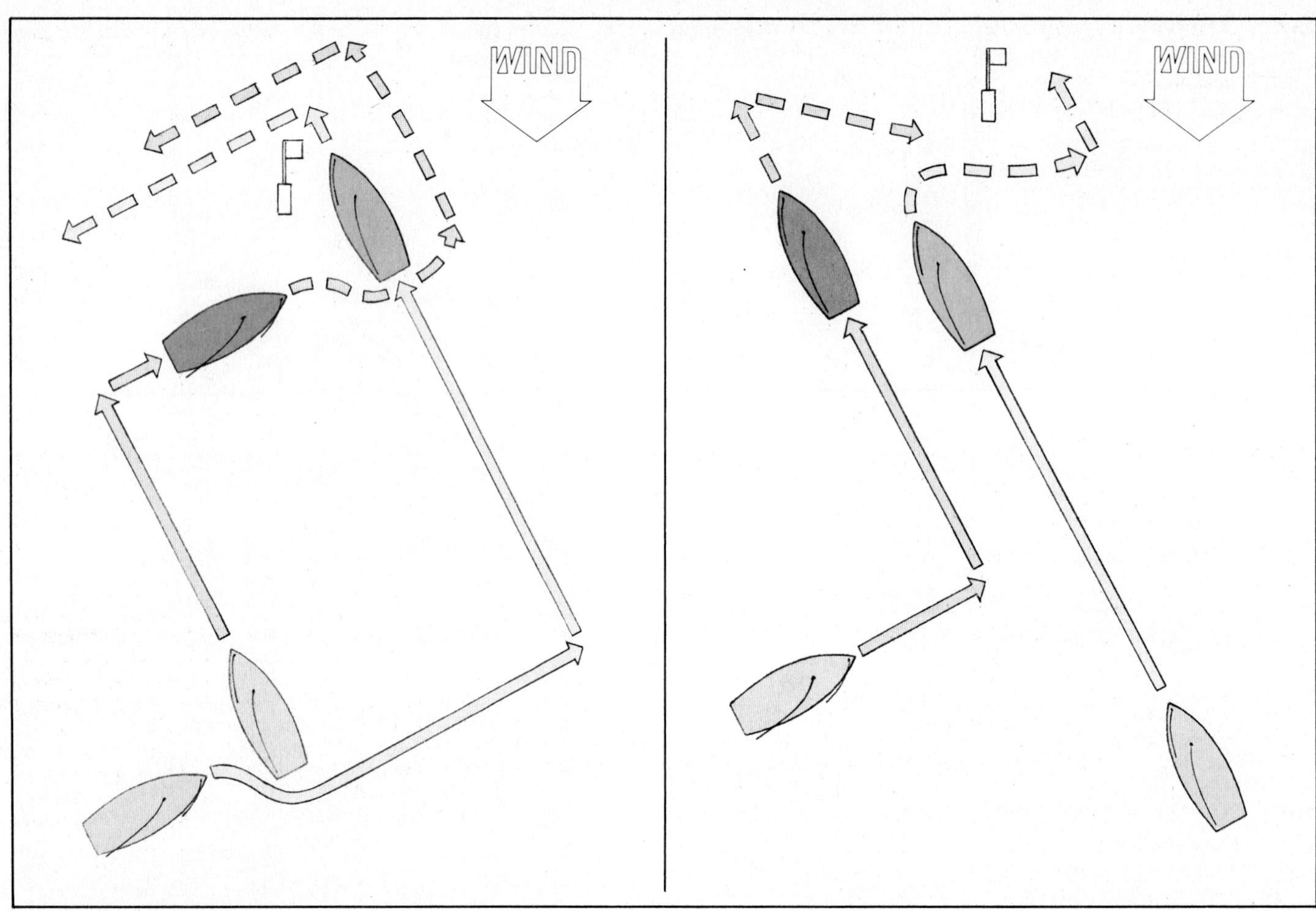

Nearing the windward mark, a port-tack boat that meets a boat on starboard has the choice of tacking or bearing off to cross astern. In the situation above, at left, the skipper on port tack (light blue), thinking ahead to the next time the two boats will meet, bears off, sails to the lay line and then tacks; with right of way (dark blue) at the mark, he rounds first. A starboard-tack skipper's best defense against this maneuver is to encourage the port tacker to tack under his bow (above, right) by waiting until the last minute before hailing loudly for right of way. With his rival unable to come about again, he continues on starboard, tacks at the last minute and rounds first.

A boat that is behind (light blue) as it nears the windward mark can either tack twice (dotted line) to join the parade of boats on the starboard-tack lay line, or can stay in clear air and risk an approach on port tack. Since the starboard-tack boats are giving each other backwind, they will tend to slow down and separate as they get closer to the mark. The port-tack boat may find a hole to tack into (dark blue), bringing him around the mark ahead of some of his opponents on starboard.

Maneuvers at the Mark

Any time boats in a fleet are close together, right of way becomes a crucial ingredient in the competition. One such phase of a race is at the windward mark, when the boats that dispersed after the start are again at close quarters. The skipper who prepares for this moment by making the right tactical decisions en route, then artfully negotiates his way around the mark, can dramatically improve his position.

The first vital decision involves choosing a tack for the final shot at the mark. Although there may be times when the risk of an approach on port is justified *(bottom left)*, most helmsmen prefer the security of having right of way on starboard, since it can mean the difference between crossing ahead of a cluster of boats or having to ease sheets and watch the opposition pass by. And the starboard tack is convenient for another reason. Since most courses are designed so that the marks are left to port, a starboard-tack boat can round simply by bearing off. But a port-tack boat has to come about in rounding —a maneuver that becomes particularly complex if the crew must simultaneously prepare to set a spinnaker.

Another crucial consideration is the length of the approach. A skipper who plans to sail on a long approach tack risks misjudging the lay line. Boats that sail at 45° should tack for the mark when it is directly abeam; but the farther away the mark is, the more difficult precise judgment of the lay line's location becomes.

If the skipper is not sailing right on the wind when he takes his sighting, he may find that he has tacked too soon, forcing him to make two additional tacks to fetch the mark. And if, in calculating where to make his tack, he attempts to allow for his boat's leeway on the approach, he may overstand the mark, throwing away distance to windward. Even if he judges correctly, a long approach compounds his exposure to the dangers of sailing on any lay line: a wind shift may create a new lay line and cost extra distance *(pages 98-99)*. Or a boat may find itself in a competitor's backwind, but be unable to tack away to get clear air without losing ground. To minimize these risks, the skipper should sail only the last 10 or 15 boat lengths to the mark on the lay line.

The success of the rounding maneuver itself depends on efficient teamwork by skipper and crew. While getting ready to set the spinnaker, they must keep the boat hiked flat, rapidly ease the main and jib sheets, and quickly locate the far-off mark that is their next goal.

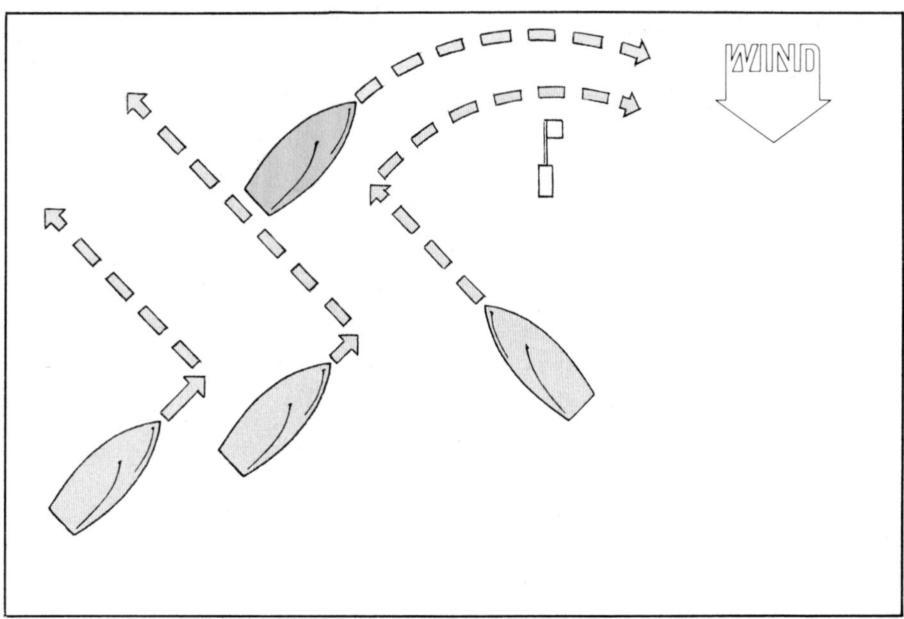

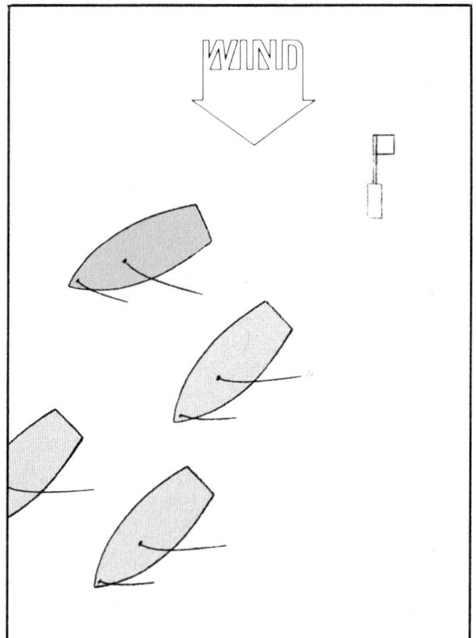

In those comparatively rare cases when the windward mark is to be left to starboard, a boat choosing to approach on port tack must realize that a boat on starboard may demand its rights at the mark. To minimize any loss from such a confrontation, the blue boat on port tack has sailed a little past the lay line, deliberately overstanding to allow room for a starboard-tack boat to tack inside and around the mark—with the blue boat close behind to windward. Two other port tackers on the lay line failed to foresee the danger and must tack to avoid hitting the boat on starboard.

Boats that are positioned well back in the fleet at the end of the windward leg can often pick up some ground immediately after rounding the mark. If the next leg is a reach, as at left, an aggressive helmsman who steers to windward of the fleet may be able to pass a few boats by taking their wind; but he must be careful not to lose too much ground by deviating far off course to the next mark.

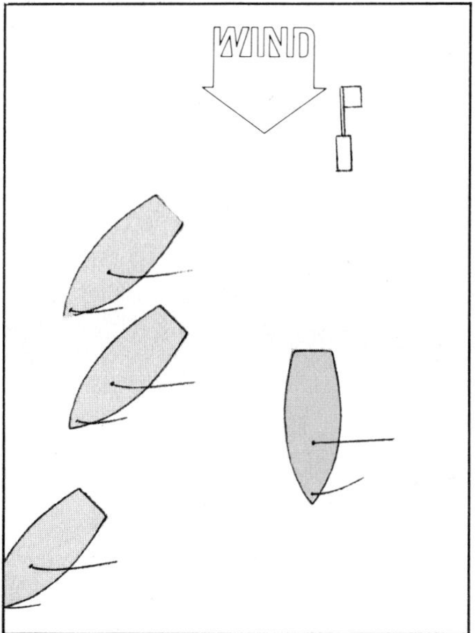

When the next leg is a run, the boats that go to windward to pass each other are in danger of sailing too far away from the mark. A skipper who rounds the mark and sails to leeward of the fleet will be in clear air, out of the fray and on course for the next mark.

Running the Leeward Legs

Flying Juniors with spinnakers up jockey for position on the leeward leg of a course. Although the chances of gaining tactical advantage are fewer on the leeward leg than when sailing to windward, a freshening breeze, which hits trailing boats first, can give an alert skipper an opportunity to catch up. In this instance, the helmsman of 3896 takes a ride on a puff of air and, thanks to his windward position, begins to blanket two downwind rivals and pass them.

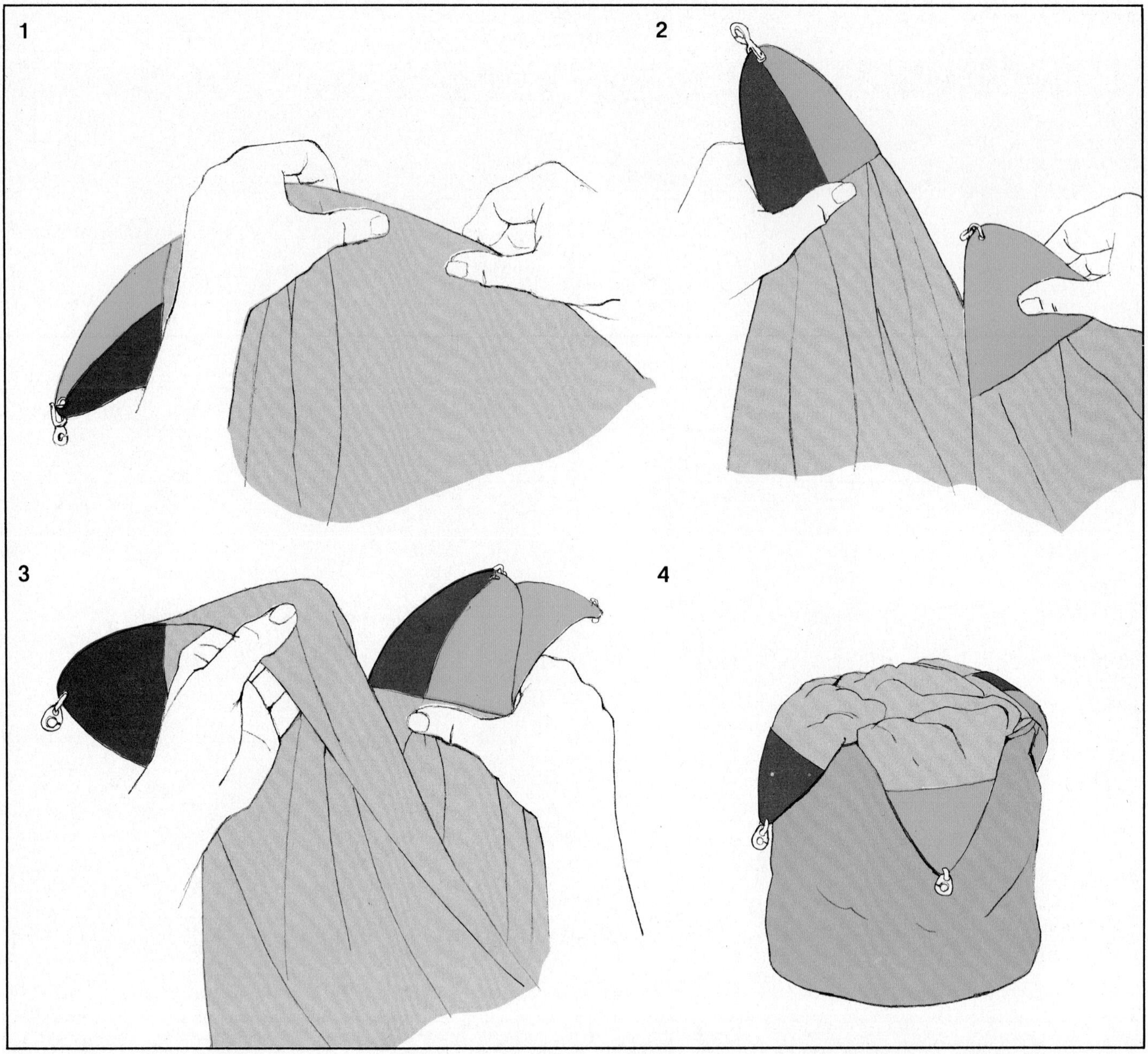

When bagging a spinnaker during a race, first find the sail's head—which, in this case, is fitted with a swatch of red (for port) and green (for starboard) fabric. Then, with your hands, follow along the starboard leech (1), untwisting any kinks. When the starboard clew (marked in green) is reached (2), bring it together with the green-coded side of the head. Now run your hand along the foot to the red port clew (3), again unfouling any twists. Loosely stuff the sail's body into the bag until only the head and clews are exposed (4), with the head out toward the bow, and each clew on its appropriate side.

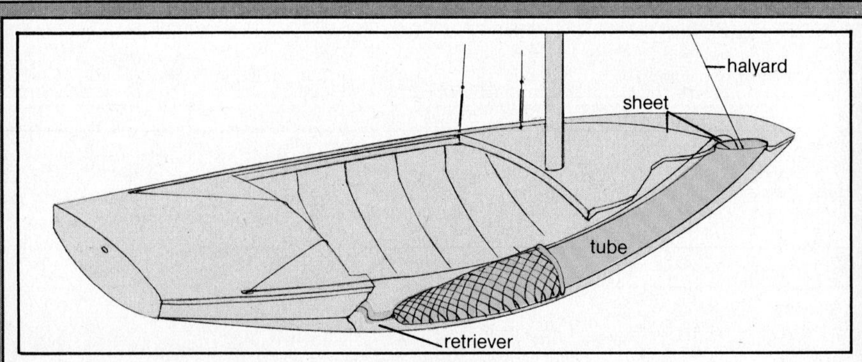

A Built-in Launcher for the Chute

In a number of one-design-class boats, spinnaker handling is speeded by a device called a launcher—a built-in container for the sail and lines. It consists of an entry port in the foredeck, a rigid fiberglass tube leading to the bulkhead, and a cloth extension of the tube with a retriever line threaded through its end. Before a race, the halyard and sheets are attached to the chute, and the retriever is tied to a cloth ring at the sail's center. A pull on the retriever stows the sail inside the length of the tube; hauling on the halyard sends it airborne.

Handling the Spinnaker

On the leeward leg the spinnaker is the racing boat's work horse, and no other sail demands more careful attention. Before leaving the dock, the chute should be methodically arranged in a container, with all three corners left exposed so that lines and fittings can be attached easily when the time comes. Some skippers pack the sail in a cardboard carton, but many racers prefer using a bag or—whenever class regulations permit—a spinnaker launcher *(below, left).*

On the way out to the starting line the crew must check that the chute's topping lift and halyard are clear; then he rigs the sheets and makes sure the mast fitting for the spinnaker pole is set at the proper height *(pages 38-39)* for the expected wind strength. After the start, as the boat is approaching the windward mark, the skipper determines on which side he will set his spinnaker. The crew then attaches the halyard and sheets to the sail, fixes the pole to the mast, and sees that all lines and fittings are properly set up. Thus, at the right moment, the sail can be taken up quickly and cleanly, without any twists in the fabric or tangles in the rigging.

In rigging the chute, conventional practice has been to position the sail, still in its bag, on the leeward side. From there it can be hauled up by the crew with a minimum of effort in the lee of the main and jib, and then pulled around to windward, where it fills. But recently, racers have discovered they can gain seconds by rigging the sail to windward initially, so that it starts drawing the instant the crew has it up. This racing set also has the advantage of keeping the crew's weight on the windward side during the preparatory stage. On some modern racing craft, such as the Flying Juniors at right, the halyard is led aft to the cockpit, where it can be hauled up by the helmsman, leaving the crew free to concentrate on the guy and sheet.

The spinnaker, in most situations, is raised the instant that the boat rounds the mark and the main sheet has been slacked. But occasionally, as when much of the fleet is bunched and running just after the mark, the spinnaker should be delayed a minute or two to allow the boat to maneuver clear of the traffic jam. The jib remains up until the chute is set; then the jib comes down to rest on the foredeck throughout the spinnaker run.

In some races the spinnaker has to be set more than once. If this is the case, the crew must repack the sail in its bag, guarding against twists by the technique shown in the diagrams at left, above.

A Flying Junior leading two competitors around the windward mark breaks out its spinnaker. As the helmsman takes up the halyard —which is led aft along the centerboard housing—the crew hauls back on the guy with one hand while pushing the spinnaker pole forward with the other. The crew will then take charge of the sheet. Because the Flying Junior's spinnaker is small and leaves considerable space between the sail's foot and the deck, these sailors will continue to keep the jib up and trimmed for extra thrust.

Reaching for the mark on a leeward leg, the skipper of a racing boat most often takes the direct rhumb-line course, aiming his craft precisely (light blue boat) at the mark. But if, as here, he encounters a crosscurrent, to compensate for the current's effect he points slightly above (dark blue boat) the rhumb line and thus avoids being set.

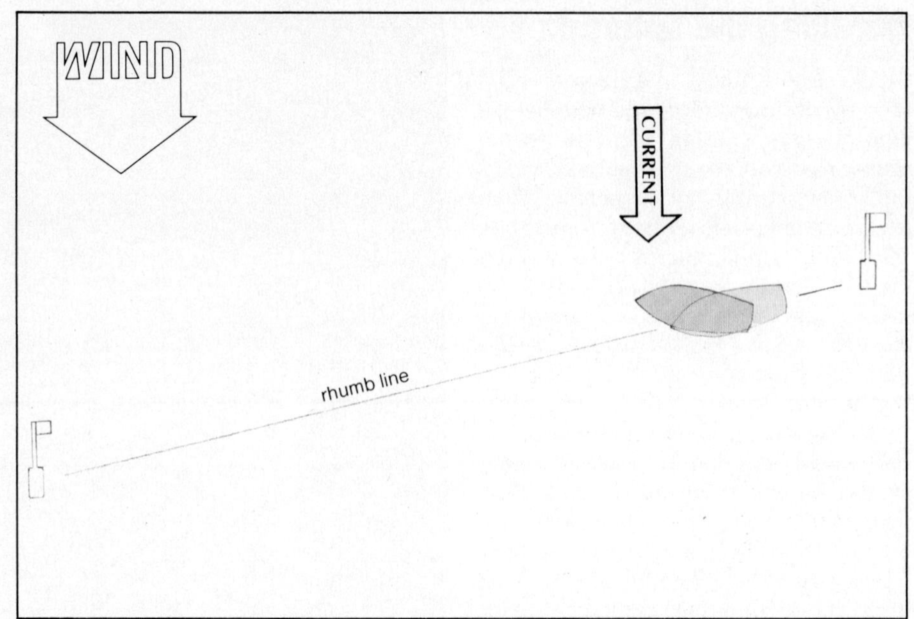

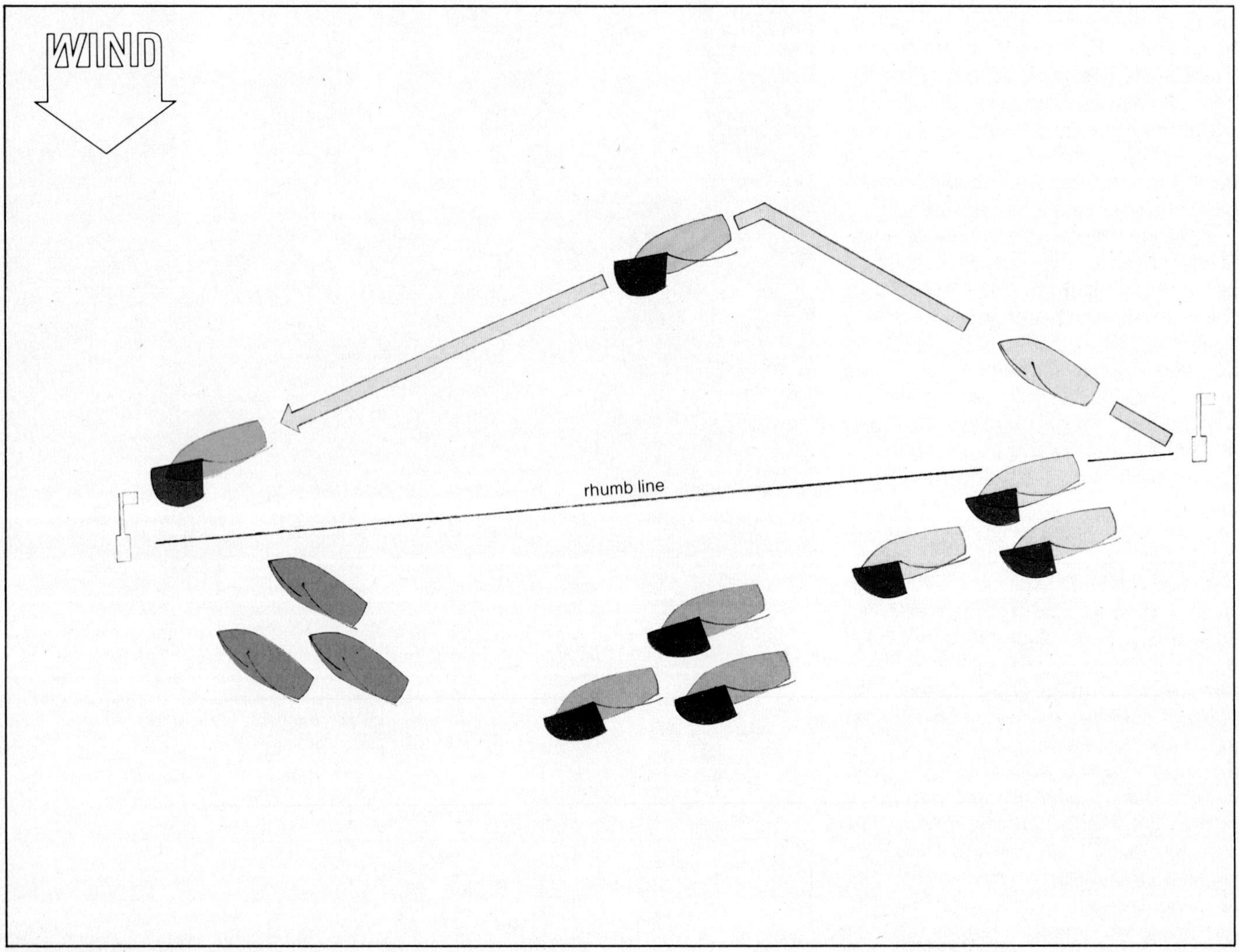

Beam-reaching in a strong wind, the main fleet has started (light gray boats) down the rhumb line with chutes set (red). This is a mistake; because of the extra sail, the boats are forced downwind (medium gray) until they must douse their spinnakers to fetch the mark (dark gray). Noting this error, a trailing boat can close reach (light blue) to get a better slant of wind (medium blue) in carrying his chute; this speeds him to the mark well ahead (dark blue) of his rivals.

Tactics on a Reach

Given a fair current and a steady breeze, the fastest course when reaching along a leeward leg is generally a straight line, or rhumb line, from the last mark to the next one. A skipper with clear wind and a reasonably good position in the fleet simply sails along it, keeping a constant eye on the trim of his sails and the balance of his boat to maintain maximum speed. If he must move through a crosscurrent, the skipper will naturally have to modify his heading *(top left)*—but his boat sails the rhumb line nonetheless, as shown.

There are certain circumstances, however, when a skipper has a better chance of winning if he abandons the rhumb line for a more roundabout path. For example, a boat caught in the middle of the fleet, where its sails are blanketed by nearby craft, should head for open water and clear wind. And any skipper who finds himself toward the rear as he turns his boat into the leeward leg may want to take a flier, bearing deliberately away from the straight-line course in a gamble for stronger wind or, as in the diagram at bottom left, to capitalize on tactical errors made by the boats ahead.

Indeed, there can sometimes be a certain paradoxical advantage to starting a leeward leg slightly behind the leaders, particularly on a broad reach. Not only does the trailing boat catch each wind puff first, but he avoids passing duels that tend to pull the leaders high above the optimum course *(right)*, where they may have to complete the final stretch on a dead run, the slowest point of sail *(page 122)*. The leading boat in a fleet, meanwhile, must keep a close eye on the goings on behind and maneuver so as to stay directly between its competitors and the mark, even when this tactic leads it away from the rhumb line; then, should the trailing craft gain ground because of an unexpected increase in wind strength, the lead skipper is still reasonably sure of staying out ahead.

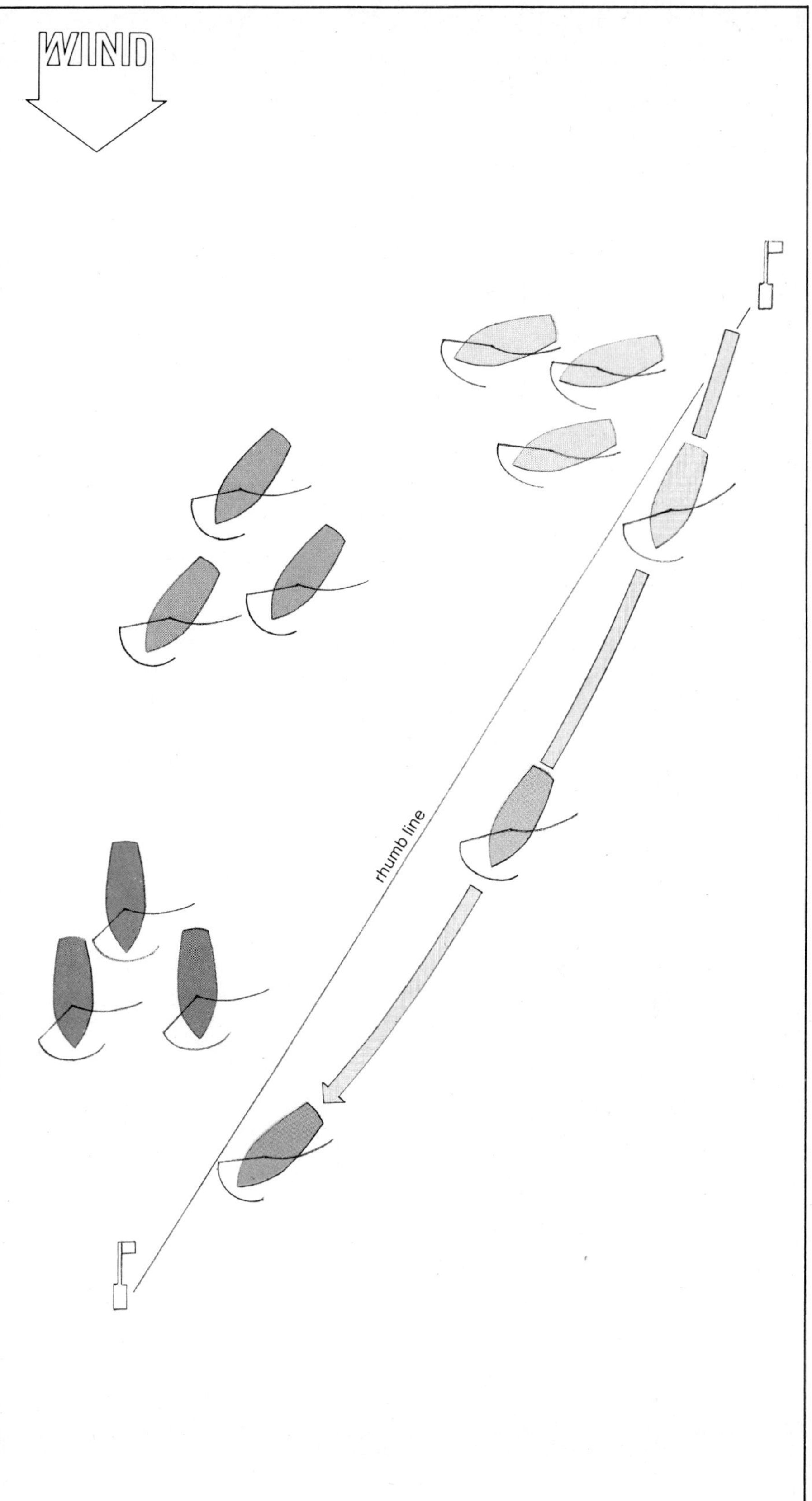

On a broad reach, the fleet has headed upwind (light gray boats) of the rhumb line—an error that often occurs when trailing vessels try to overtake the leader by passing him to windward. The fleet will soon have to bear off (medium gray), and may end up on a slow dead run (dark gray). A smart maverick gains ground by sailing slightly below the line (light blue boat), covering a shorter distance (medium blue) and arriving first at the mark on a faster point of sail (dark blue).

For maximum speed on a reach, skipper and crew constantly adjust the sails to wind shifts, while using their weight to trim ship. The skipper, here sitting to leeward, holds the helm steady and plays the mainsail, letting it out to the verge of a luff, and hauling it in when the sail begins to soften. The crew balances on the windward rail where she can watch the spinnaker; with the guy cleated, she fine-tunes the sail with the sheet, keeping a hint of curl in the sail's luff.

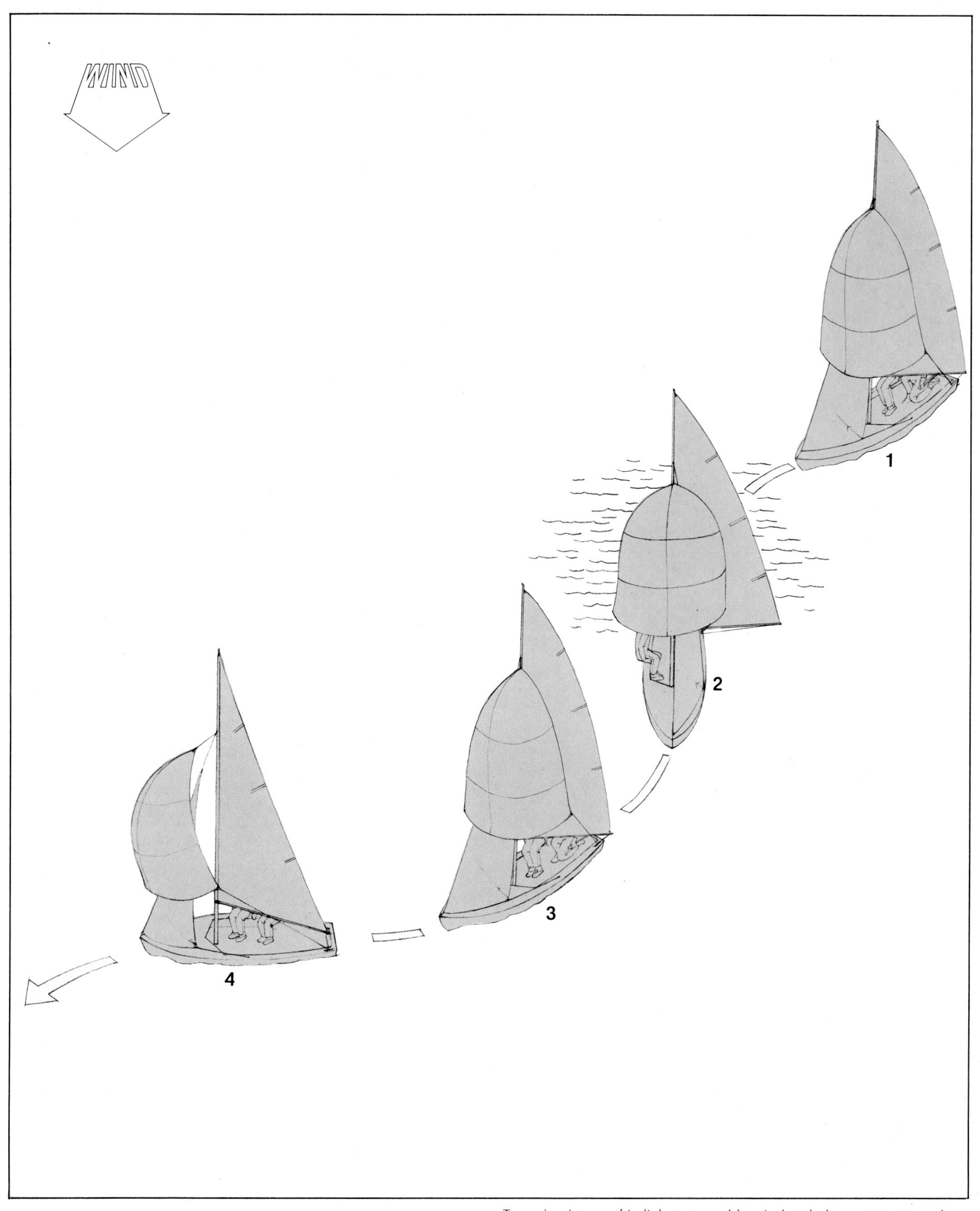

To maintain speed in light or unstable winds, a helmsman on a reach can make small detours that help carry him through the lulls; but these digressions should cancel one another out to keep the boat near the rhumb line. On a course just high of the mark (1) he hits a cat's-paw and turns downwind with it (2). When the puff dies, he hardens up to his original course (3). Then, in a lull (4), he heads higher to gain speed, but is ready to return quickly to the rhumb line.

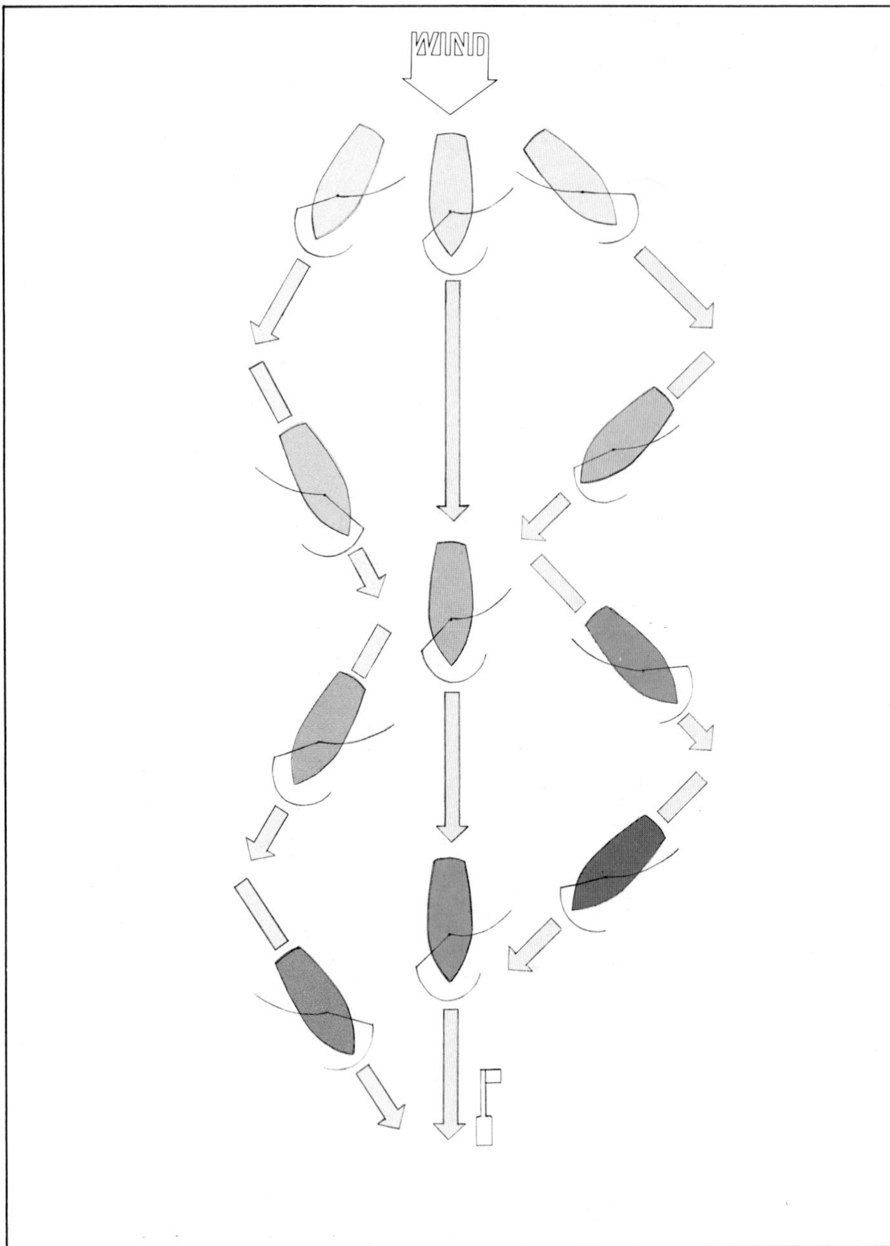

On a course to a downwind mark, a boat (blue) that avoids a dead run and opts instead for a series of faster broad reaches can often outdistance a vessel (gray, center) plodding straight down the rhumb line, even though the tacking boat covers more ground. But the exact heading on each reach must be carefully assessed: a boat (gray, right) that sails at too great an angle to the rhumb line squanders whatever advantage it gains in speed by sailing an excessively long course.

Tacking Downwind

When the next mark is directly downwind, most racing skippers will raise centerboards, ease sheets and make straight for their goal on a run—even though this is a relatively inefficient point of sail *(page 27)*. In strong winds, this may be the best tactic for everyone, since the sacrifice in speed will be slight. But in light airs, and particularly when sailing a high-performance planing boat *(pages 126-127)*, a skipper may be wiser "tacking downwind," i.e., making a series of broad reaches on alternate tacks to increase his boat's speed *(left)*. If the knots gained exceed the extra distance sailed (and his crew has had plenty of experience jibing the spinnaker), then he will have improved his racing position.

Every boat will have its own optimum sailing angle for tacking downwind, and this angle will usually vary according to the wind's strength. As a general rule, a heading that puts the wind at roughly 15° to 30° to port or starboard of the transom (as demonstrated by the blue boat shown at left) will produce a favorable speed-to-distance ratio, but the exact angle for any particular wind condition can be found only by experimentation.

This tactic can be equally effective on a day when there are wind shifts. In that case the helmsman should plan his various headings to take advantage of any such shift. Usually, the most productive strategy is to sail a relatively short initial reach away from the direction of a beginning wind shift *(blue boat, near right)*, then jibe back for a longer reach to the mark; if the shift continues in the same direction, the boat will sail at an increasingly faster angle as it closes on the mark. But a boat *(gray)* that heads first in the direction of the shift will find itself sailing most of the leg on a dead run.

When the wind does not shift permanently in one direction or the other but oscillates back and forth, the skipper can counter each fluctuation with a jibe onto the opposite broad-reaching tack *(far right)*. Thus, while avoiding a direct run, he can still stay close to the rhumb line.

Anticipating a gradual clockwise wind shift, the skipper of the blue boat heads away from the shift on a short starboard-tack reach. If the shift continues, he jibes onto port tack and sails for the mark on a long broad reach. The gray boat makes the mistake of starting out toward the shift and, upon turning for the mark, must finish the leg on a slow run.

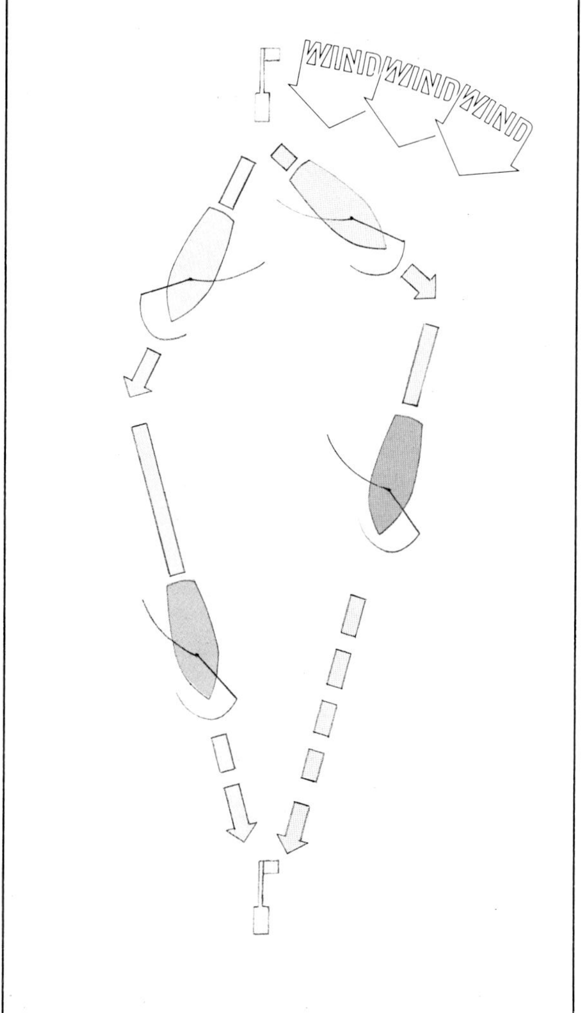

With the wind oscillating across the rhumb line, the blue boat sails directly toward the mark, while still taking the wind in a series of broad reaches. Whenever the wind shifts, he jibes onto the opposite tack. Although in jibing he may alter course slightly, moving from one side of the rhumb line to the other, his general heading stays constant.

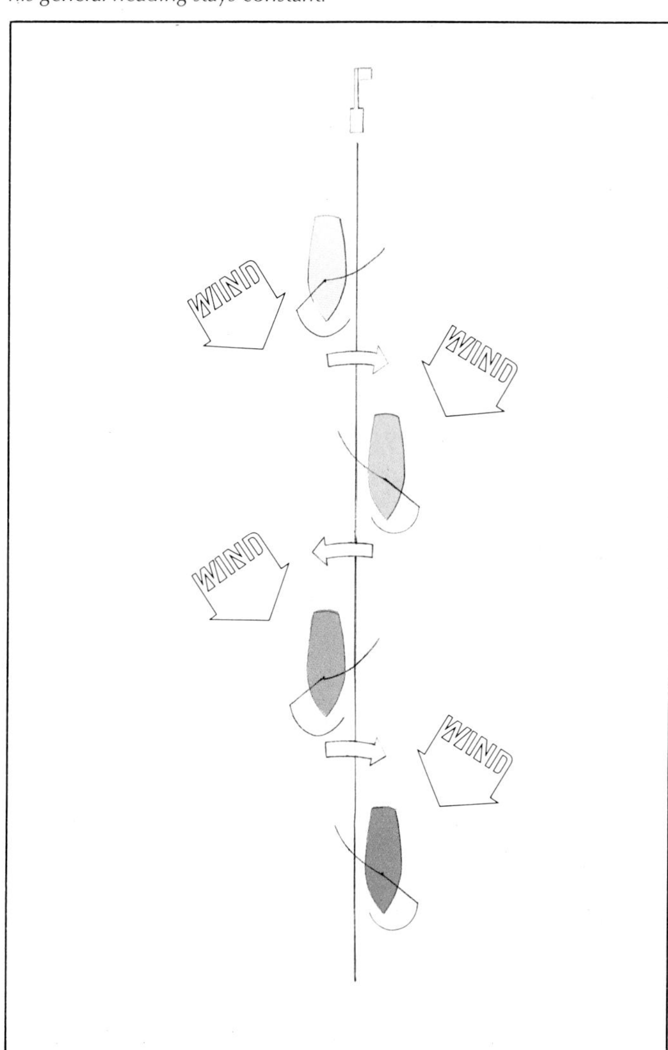

Better Balance on a Run

When a vessel heads downwind with its mainsail eased way out, the force of the wind in the sail, acting outboard of the hull, tends to lever the boat's bow to windward. This weather helm *(page 46)* can often be countered by rigging a spinnaker on the boat's upwind side. But in boats that have undersized chutes—or no headsail at all—the skipper and crew use their weight to heel the boat to windward *(right),* thus tilting the mainsail upward into a more efficient position *(page 48)* and reducing its sideways leverage. In addition, most sailboats have a tendency to turn in a direction opposite to the one in which they are tipped; thus heeling to windward produces a leeward turning force *(arrow)* that helps to counterbalance the vessel's weather helm.

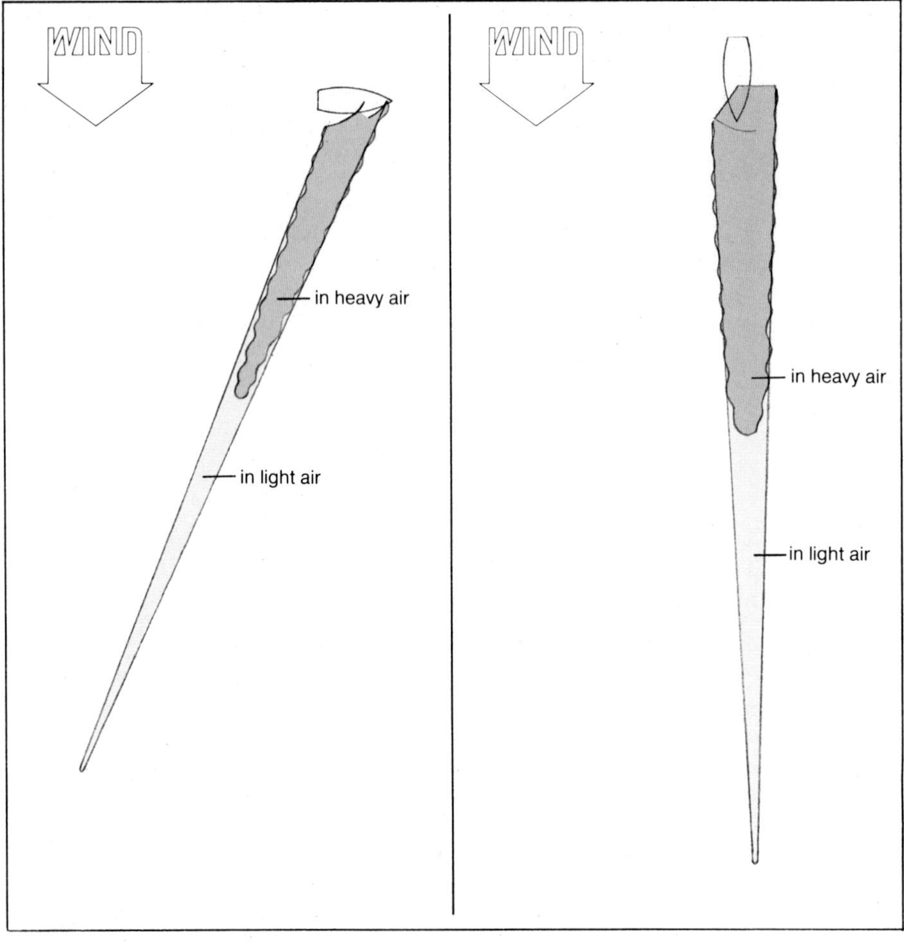

On a reach or a run, a boat's wind shadow extends anywhere from about four to 10 boat lengths off its lee rail, depending on the strength of the wind. Heavy winds, being more turbulent, will fill in behind a sail in a shorter span (dark blue). Light winds are slower to resume their normal course, and thus create a longer but smoother cone of dead air (light blue). The shadow is cast in the same direction as the apparent wind. Thus, with the true wind blowing broadside to the reaching boat at left above and the apparent wind coming from slightly forward, the wind shadow will be angled slightly abaft the beam. The shadow of the boat on a run (right) extends directly ahead.

Passing Techniques

Downwind legs—running and reaching—are the great levelers of a race: they give a skipper who has fallen behind during the windward stretches a good chance to catch up, and to overtake the boats ahead. Not only do the trailing craft receive each puff of breeze first but, being upwind, they are strategically positioned to cut off the leaders' air.

Just as a boat sailing into the wind casts an umbra of disturbed air over the surrounding water *(pages 96-97)*, so a vessel on a reach or a run generates a wind shadow that affects the area to leeward of it *(left)*. This blanket zone is roughly conical in shape, and varies in length in inverse proportion to the strength of the wind. In winds of any velocity, however, the skipper should remember that the axis of his blanket zone in effect follows the path of the apparent wind aboard his boat *(pages 26-27)*, rather than the direction of the wind blowing over the race course.

A skipper's wind shadow also provides him with a valuable aid in passing another boat. By heading up slightly and sailing to windward of the lead boat *(top right)*, he can effectively block his opponent's wind, slowing him down sufficiently to pull ahead. The lead skipper, when thus challenged, may try to cut off the overtaking vessel by heading up to windward himself *(center right)*. But the resulting luffing match can put both vessels in jeopardy by allowing the rest of the fleet to slip by to leeward *(bottom right)*. To avoid this, the overtaking skipper can break off the match, turning downwind in an attempt to pass the lead boat to leeward. In doing so he sacrifices his blanketing ability, and must be prepared to give the lead vessel a wide enough berth so as not to be blanketed himself.

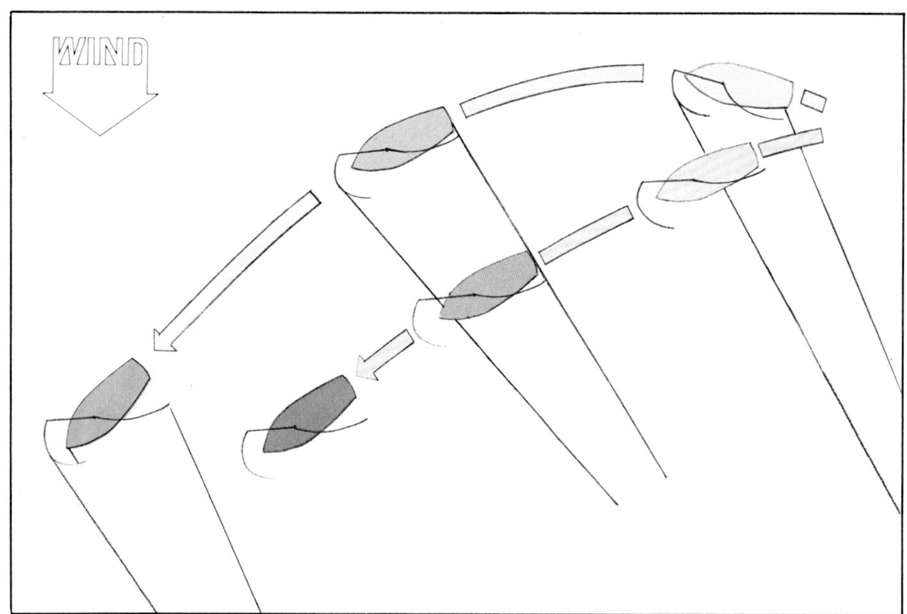

In a basic passing maneuver, an overtaking boat (light blue) has edged to windward of its opponent (gray), gaining speed as it moves closer to the wind. As the challenger pulls abeam (medium blue), his wind shadow engulfs the rival craft, slowing it down. Turning back on course, the challenger then surges into the lead (dark blue). To ensure success, the overtaking skipper should begin the maneuver early, heading up when he is approximately 10 boat lengths astern of the lead vessel; and he should keep far enough to windward of his competitor to avoid being caught in a luffing match (bottom).

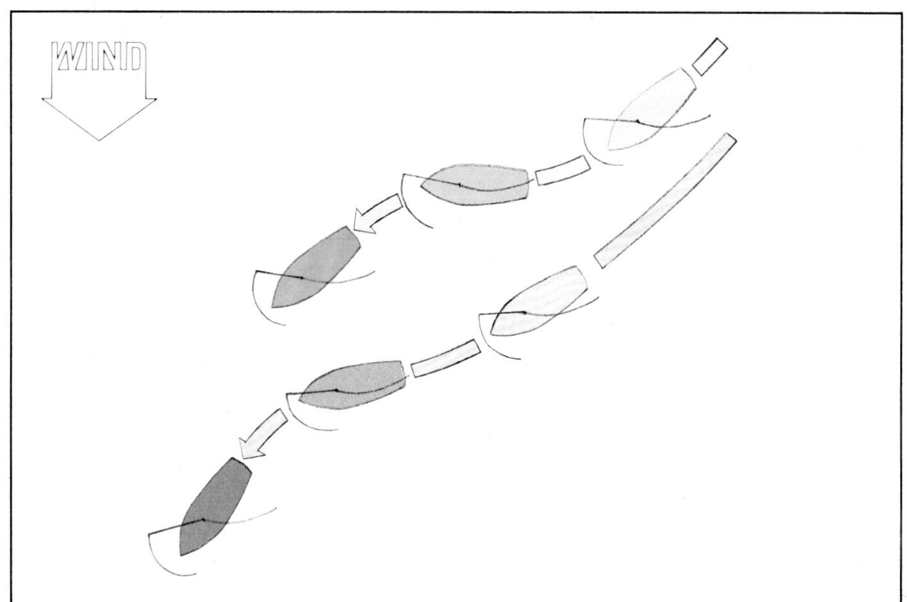

Attempting to pass upwind, an overtaking boat (light blue) is effectively blocked by an alert lead skipper (light gray). The moment the challenger heads up to secure the windward slot (medium blue), the leader heads up himself (medium gray), thereby countering the challenger's upwind drive. The challenger then gives up the attempt (dark blue) and allows the lead vessel to head back on course, still clearly ahead.

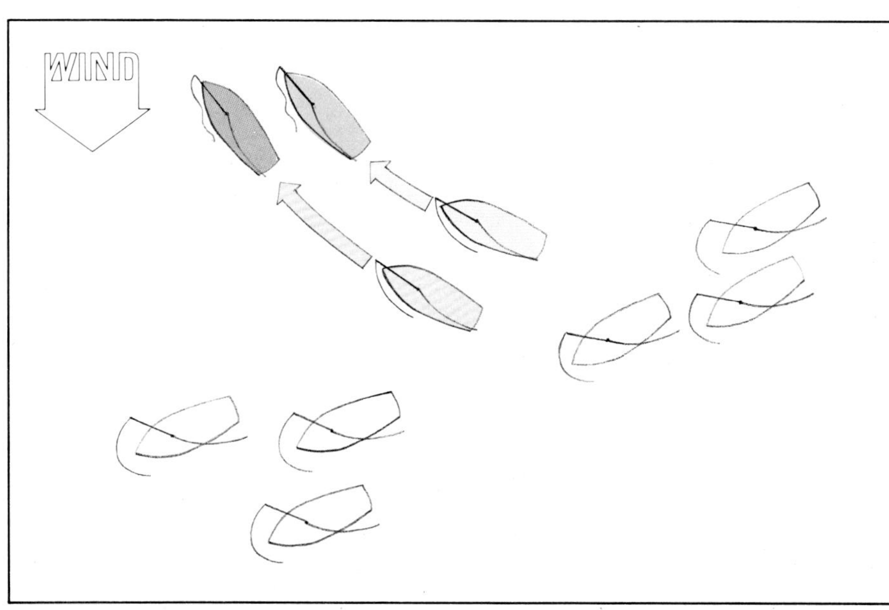

The hazards of a prolonged luffing match are shown here: an overtaking skipper (light blue) attempts to pass to windward, but the lead boat (light gray) turns upwind, forcing the challenger to head even higher to secure an upwind passage. Eventually, both boats stray far above the rhumb line, chutes luffing, while the rest of the fleet sails on ahead. The wiser course for the skipper of the blue boat might be to break off the match and try to pass to leeward. And the skipper of the gray boat, if a brief luffing contest fails to stop his rival, should simply let the challenger pass, in hopes that he can overtake him later.

Planing and Surfing

Both the speed and challenge of a downwind leg increase dramatically for a skipper who races in a planing boat, such as a Great Lakes scow, a Finn or the Flying Junior illustrated at right. These craft, characterized by a lightweight hull, a flat bottom, a sharp trailing edge at the transom and a generous amount of canvas relative to the hull size, can sometimes be made to skim over the water at a pace unattainable on nonplaning vessels.

In light winds and on windward legs in general, planing boats are sailed very much like heavier, nonplaning craft, except that they are more tender and frisky. But in moderate to strong winds the planing boat will, with the special handling techniques described at right, move at nearly double its normal velocity. This increase comes from the planing craft's downwind ability to free itself from its bow and stern waves, which act as a drag on conventional hulls. A planing boat will accelerate to the normal hull-speed limit, then break out of the trough between the two waves and ride up on top of its bow wave, leaving the trailing wave astern.

To stay up on the bow wave, skipper and crew must maintain boat speed by subtle weight shifts, sail adjustments and course changes. Even so, the boat is almost certain to fall back into its trough from time to time, and the planing technique must be initiated again.

In addition to bona fide planing boats, a number of light-displacement boats, such as Lightnings and Stars, can also be made to skim the water with expert coaxing in a strong wind. Although their increase in speed is less dramatic than that of the true planers, the two or three extra knots gained over a nonplaning rival can give them a winning advantage.

Heavy-displacement craft—most keelboats, ocean racers and virtually all cruising vessels—are normally incapable of planing. But they can add substantially to their normal speed downwind by getting a lift from a following sea. The trick is to get the boat on the leading edge of a good-sized wave and keep it there, as described in the box opposite.

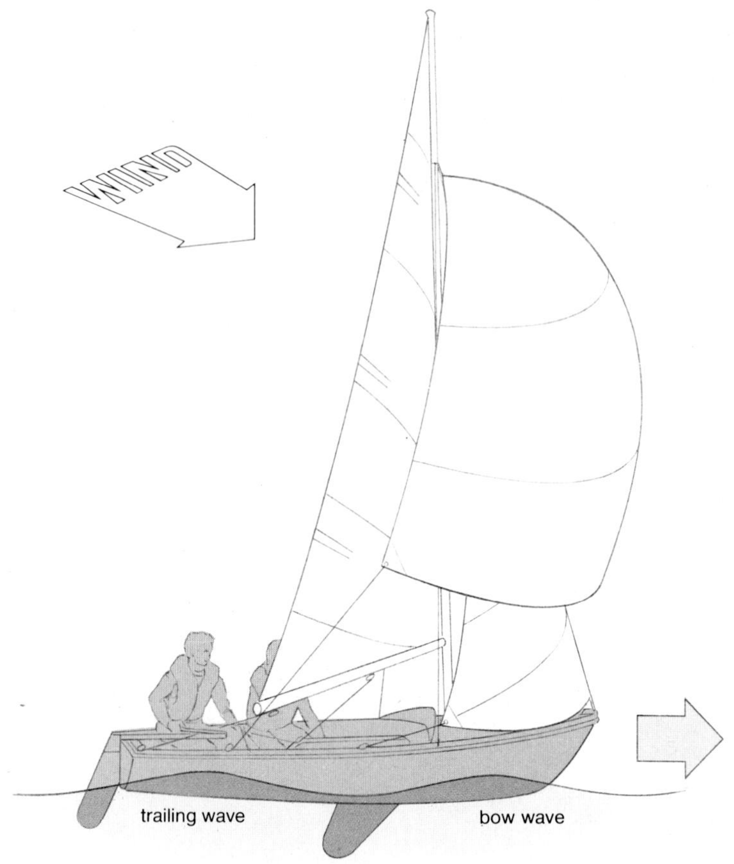

On a broad reach but not yet planing, this Flying Junior rides in the trough between its bow wave and trailing wave. The skipper looks to windward for a ruffled patch of breeze on the water, hoping to find the extra propulsive force he needs to lift his boat up onto a plane.

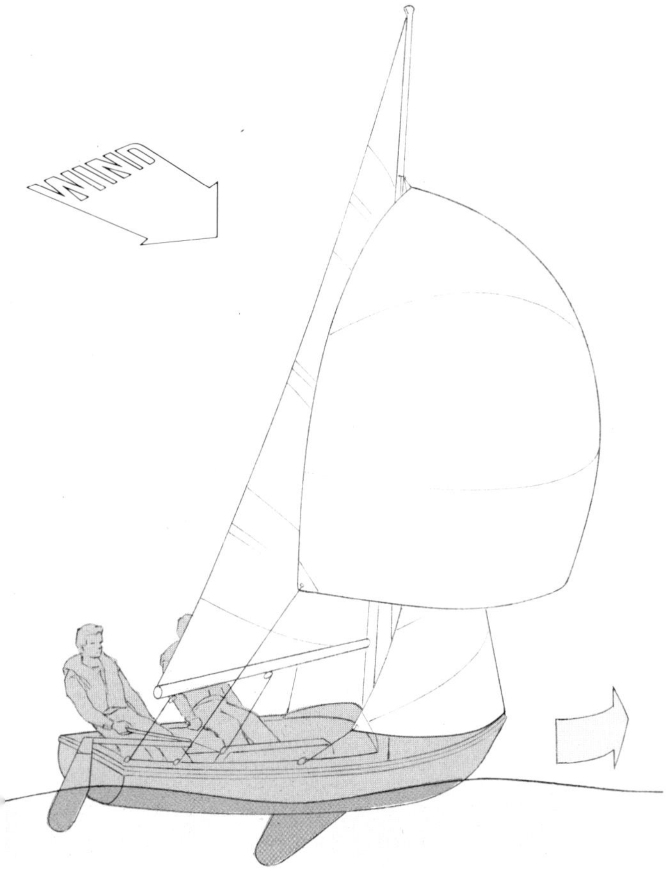

To pick up speed, the skipper heads up toward an approaching puff and quickly hauls in the mainsail, while the crew trims the jib and spinnaker. At the same time, both sailors hike out, taking care that every motion is done smoothly so as not to upset the craft's delicate balance. When the puff hits, the velocity increase is usually sufficient to lift the bow, boosting the boat up and over the bow wave.

Now riding on its bow wave, the Flying Junior's hull not only presents less wetted surface to the water but also skims along continually on the wave's crest, where it can move at speeds up to 10 knots. To keep the boat planing, skipper and crew must adjust the boat's heading and the trim of its sails to each fluctuation in wind strength, heading up to gain speed in the lulls and turning back on course in the puffs —all the while deploying their weight to keep the boat perfectly level in the water, the best possible attitude for successful planing.

Hitching a Ride on a Crest

Just as a surfer is able to ride for hundreds of yards on the face of a large wave, so a displacement craft can catch a lift from a following sea—thereby boosting its velocity well above the natural hull speed. In effect, the boat coasts downhill on the wave's face. To achieve this free ride, the boat must be steered with exquisite timing onto the leading edge of the wave, then held in position just forward of the crest for as long as possible. The helmsman catches the wave by heading up momentarily to gain speed. Just before the wave arrives, he heads down so his transom is roughly perpendicular to the surge and receives the maximum forward thrust. Once on the wave, he rides it for the few seconds before it passes. Then he heads up, watching for the next wave.

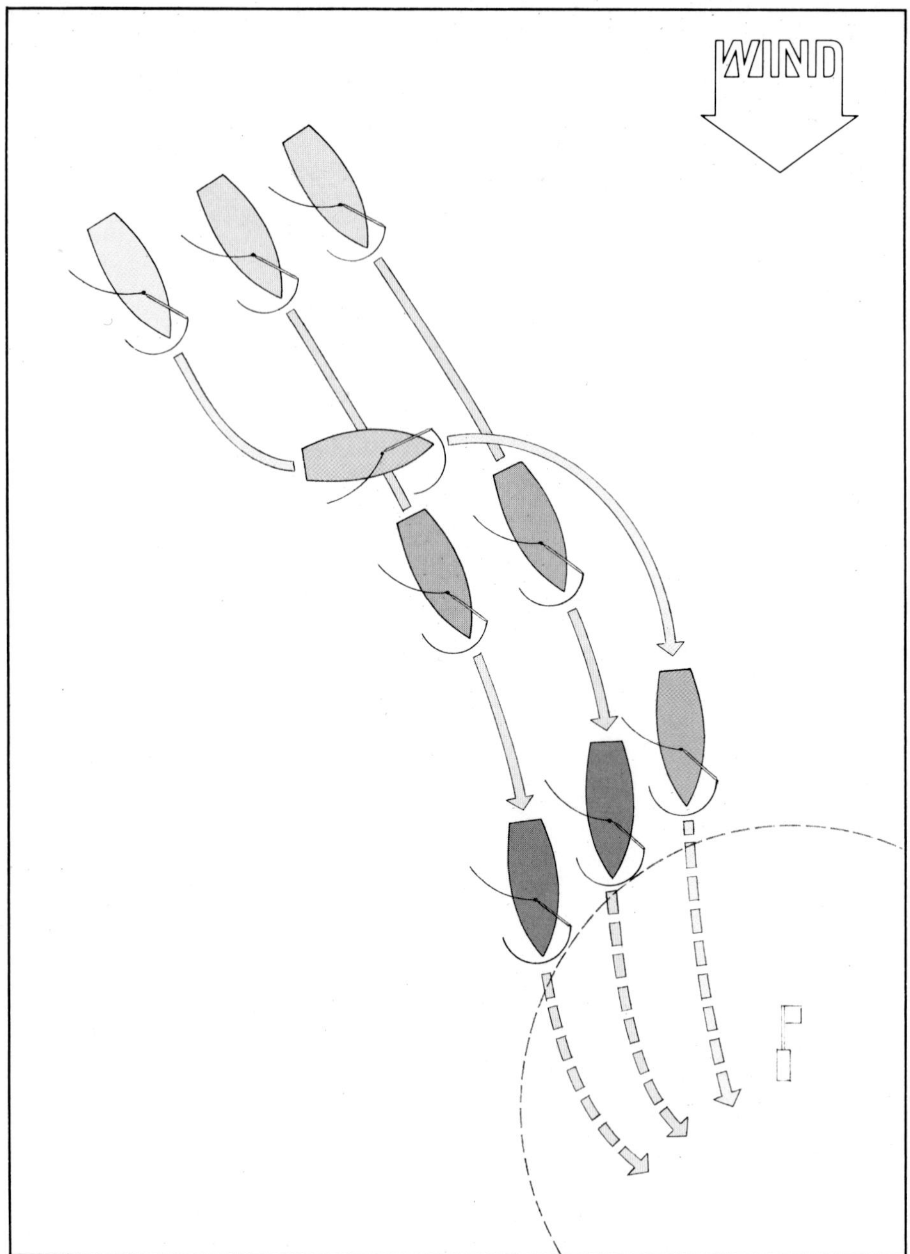

With three boats broad reaching neck and neck for the mark, the outside vessel (blue) makes a successful bid for an inside position. As the maneuver begins, the favored slot is held by the gray boat on the right. But the blue boat hardens up, scooting across the sterns of its adversaries. The new point of sail increases its speed and cuts that of the other craft, since it passes upwind of them and momentarily steals their air. The burst of speed allows the blue boat to secure an inside overlap on its rivals just before reaching the two-boat-length circle (dotted line). With the overlap established as the boats enter the circle, the blue boat receives its right to demand buoy room.

The Inside Track

Any small competitive edge that a skipper manages to pick up during a downwind leg is subject to severe challenge as the fleet closes in on a leeward mark. The skipper must plan his rounding tactics well in advance, being ready when necessary to invoke key articles of the racing rules to maintain his position at the mark —or even to improve it.

The optimum place to be during the approach is on the inside of the fleet, where the skipper will be able to round close enough to the mark to emerge from the turning maneuver in clear air, upwind of the other boats *(page 130)*. Knowing the general superiority of this inside slot, a skipper caught on the periphery will usually try either to cut inside *(left)* or to crowd ahead of the inside vessel. But the racing rules extend a degree of anti-crowding protection to the inside skipper: provided he can establish an overlap *(page 74)*, he must be given sufficient room to maneuver around the mark.

There is one key proviso to this rule, however: the overlap must exist at the moment the contending vessels enter an imaginary circle—shown in the diagrams here by a dotted line—with a radius of two boat lengths from the mark. If this condition is met, the inside skipper retains his rights to buoy room even though he may lose the overlap once within the circle.

While an inside skipper fights to gain an overlap before reaching the protective circle, an outside skipper will do his utmost to shake his rival before entering the circle. He can do this either by luffing him up *(top right)* or by executing a sudden turn that momentarily breaks the overlap *(bottom right)*.

In addition to the tactical moves a skipper employs when rounding the mark, he must also get ready to make any sail changes required by the new heading. If the next leg is to be a reach, he will probably have to jibe his spinnaker; if it is a beat, he will have to drop the chute entirely. Even a skipper who finds himself entirely alone at the downwind mark must coordinate these maneuvers and plot his track around the turn with utmost care *(overleaf)*, or risk losing valuable ground.

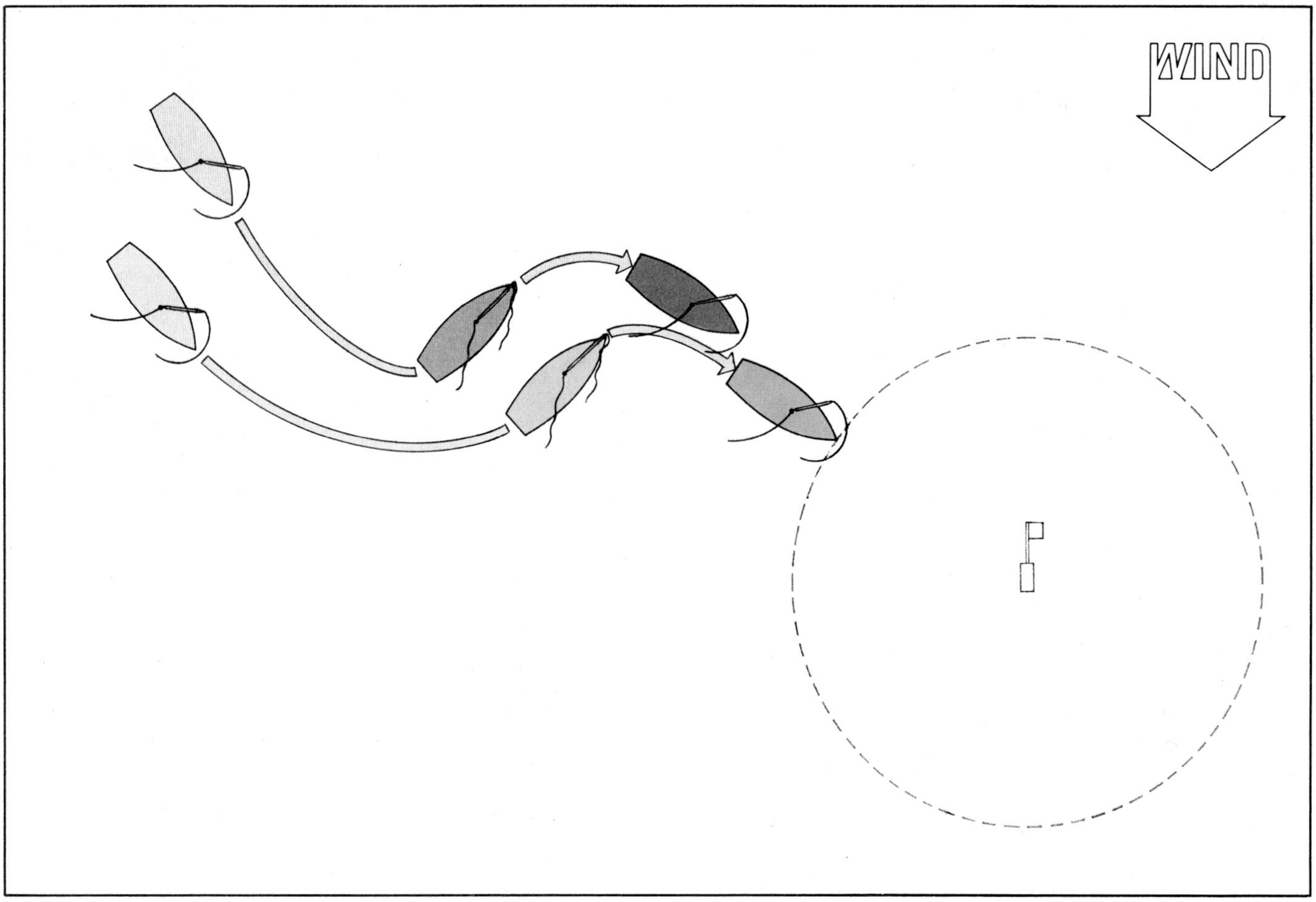

If a leeward boat approaching a mark finds a windward boat trying to seize the inside slot, it must break any overlap before the protective circle is reached. In the situation shown above, the blue boat shakes free of an overtaking vessel (gray) by luffing up just long enough to interrupt its drive for the inside, then drops back to a course that will carry it safely around the mark. Even if the gray boat then reestablishes the overlap, it will have lost its rights to room at the mark, since the blue boat will have already entered the two-boat-length safety zone.

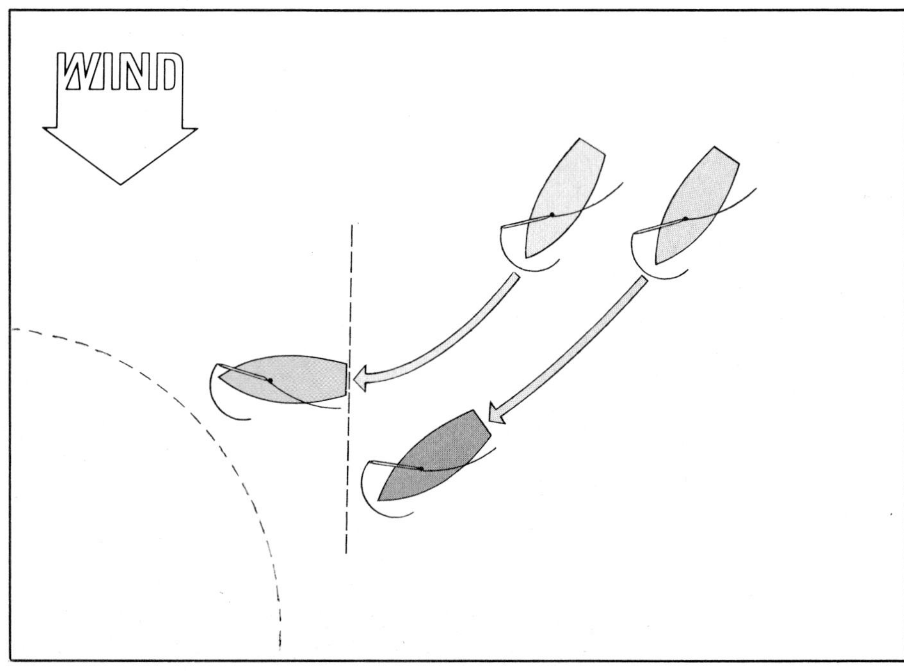

An alternative method for breaking an overlap is the last-minute gambit shown here. The skipper of the leading boat (blue) waits until his bow is very close to the two-boat perimeter, then makes a sharp turn upwind. This maneuver swings his transom at an oblique angle to the overlapping boat (gray). Since an overlap exists only when the trailing boat has nosed across an imaginary line running perpendicular to the lead boat's stern, the blue boat has now broken clear. Seconds later it enters the protective circle and then swings back onto its original course; though the gray boat may once again be overlapping, it can no longer claim buoy room—and must yield.

When going around a mark from one spinnaker reach to another, the helmsman should approach as wide as is tactically safe, giving himself ample room to jibe smoothly (medium blue) before rounding up close to the mark. In that way he can end up shaving past the mark under full way (dark blue), with sails already trimmed on the new tack, and in less danger of having a rival slide in to windward (below). During the jibe the crew must bring the spinnaker across without spilling the wind and losing pulling power.

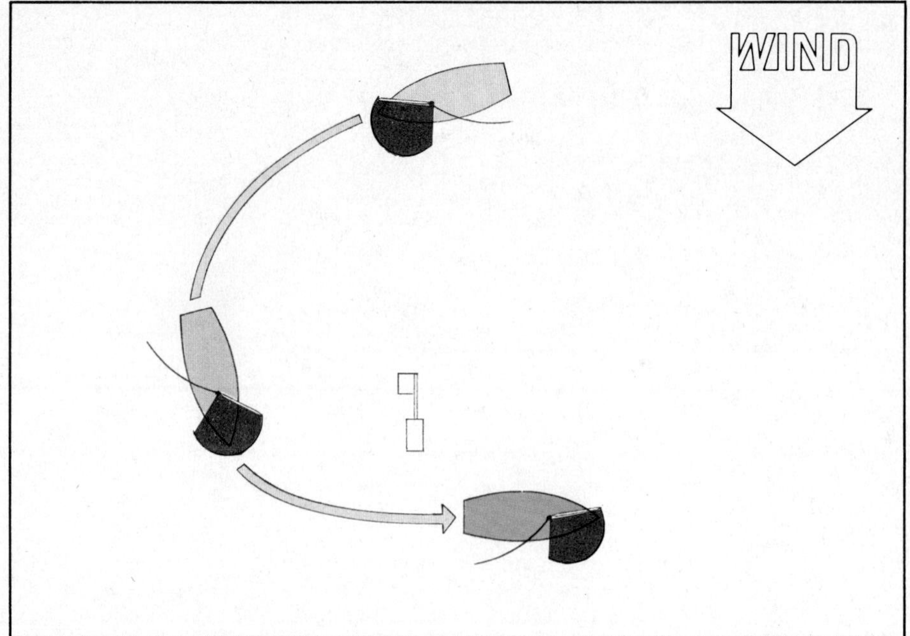

When two or more boats are in close contention at the end of a leeward leg, the boat that succeeds in getting the inside position during the rounding maneuver gains the upper hand. In the situation shown here, the leading boat (gray) has been slow in rounding up for the windward leg. Its rival (blue) seizes the opportunity to drive for the inside—a maneuver that pays off in clear air and a slight windward advantage as the boats head for the next mark. Since the new leg is a beat, both boats take down their spinnakers before rounding.

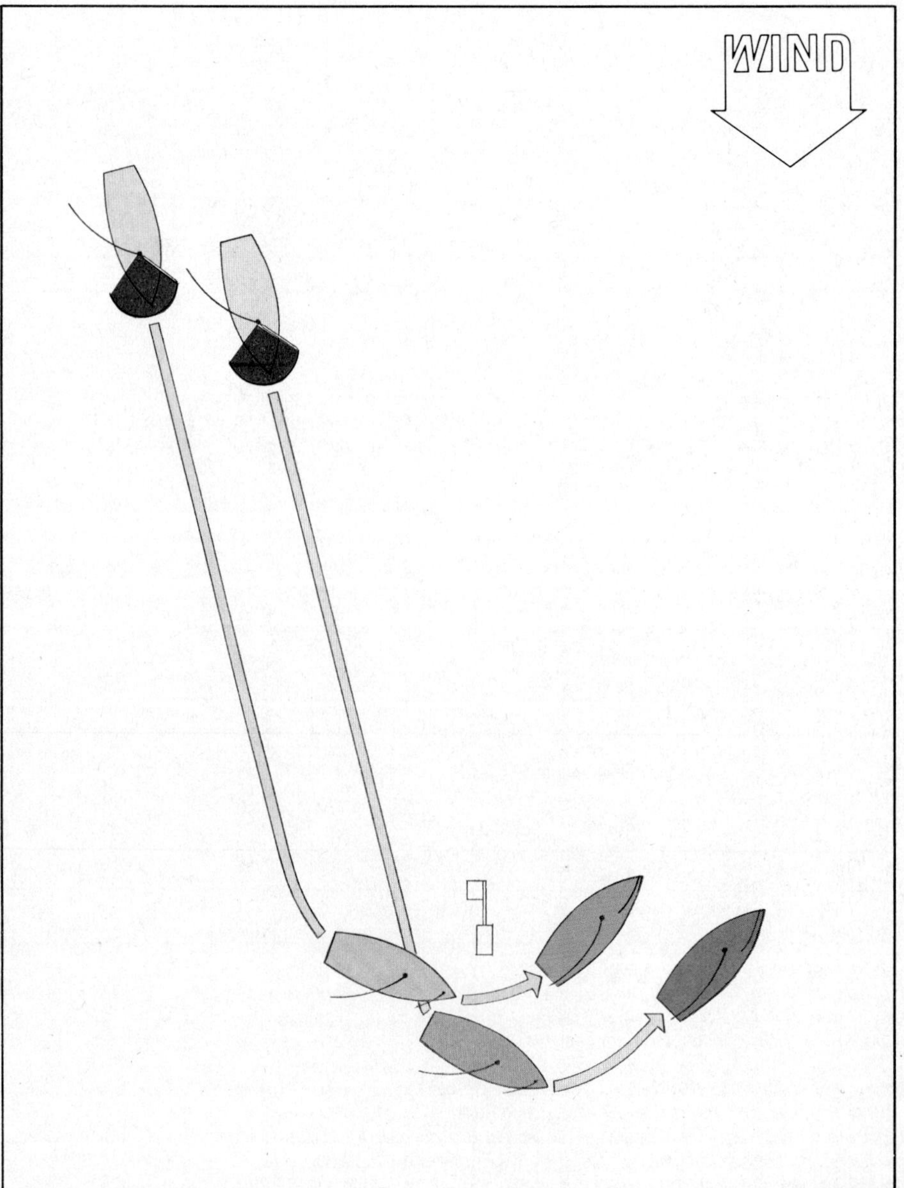

Anticipating an upwind leg, crews of two Flying Juniors prepare to douse their chutes, using a technique called a windward takedown. In it, the sail is kept full until the last minute, and then brought down on the boat's windward side—rather than in the lee of the mainsail as is conventionally done. The crew of the boat in the foreground starts the maneuver by taking in the spinnaker pole, while the skipper controls the halyard. With the sheet eased off, the halyard then will be lowered and the guy hauled in to bring down the sail. The skipper of the second boat has decided to carry his spinnaker a few seconds longer, hoping to gain extra ground before reaching the mark.

The Sprint to the Finish

After turning the leeward mark, two close competitors trim sail for the final leg of the race—a beat to the finish line. Although the boat at right is almost two lengths ahead of his nearest rival and giving him a large dose of backwind, his position is not entirely secure. Boat 3194, by shaving closer to the mark, has squeezed slightly to windward of the lead boat. Furthermore, by tacking quickly he will be able to clear his air and launch a strong bid to overtake.

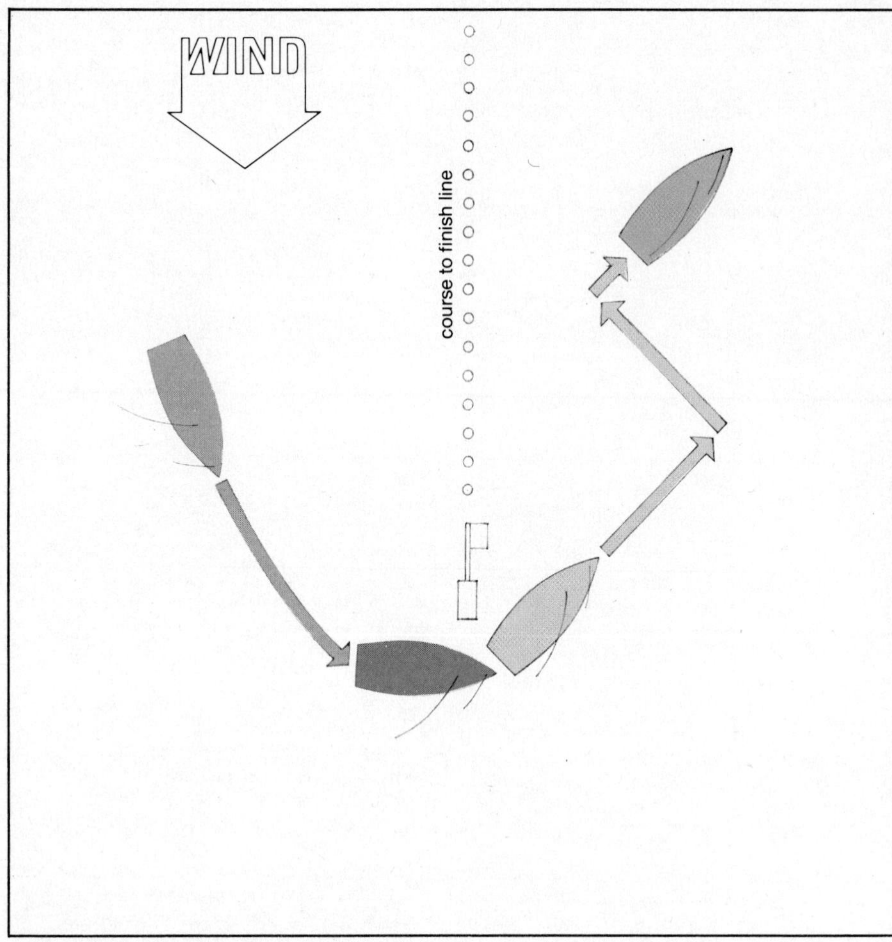

Rounding the final mark onto a windward finish, a skipper with a reasonably secure lead (blue boat) moves quickly to put himself in the optimum covering position. Right after rounding, he sails approximately half his lead distance on one tack, then comes about and sails the remaining half on a second tack. As his rival (gray) turns the mark, the leader comes about once again, putting himself in a solid covering position well upwind.

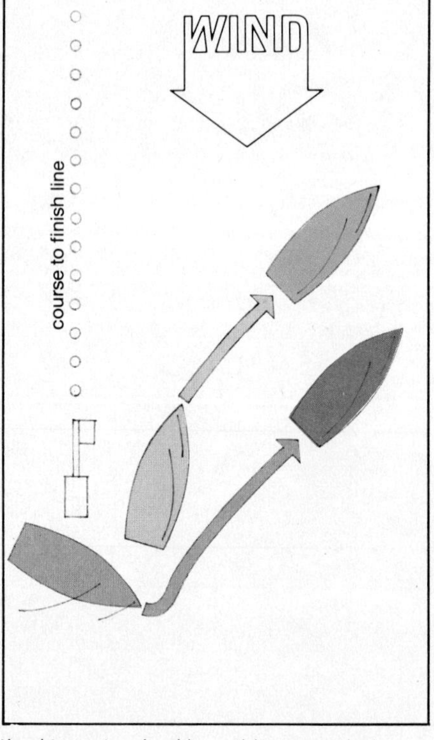

If a skipper in a lead boat (blue) rounds the last mark immediately in front of another vessel (gray), he can keep his opponent from nosing in to windward by pinching up, as here. This forces the second boat to fall off under his stern to avoid collision, leaving the leader in a covering position to windward.

Covering a Challenger

As a racing fleet rounds the last mark, the competing boats usually have become strung out, leaving several craft clearly out in front. The skippers in this extremely competitive vanguard, who may have spent most of their time thus far concentrating on pure speed rather than on one another, now turn their attention to direct boat-to-boat competition to be sure they are not passed.

To protect a lead, a skipper often employs the classic offensive tactic called covering: he makes certain to keep between his opponent and the finish. On an upwind leg, like the one shown here, he covers by staying ahead and to windward of his competitor, matching him move for move in order to maintain that position. Any fluctuation of wind or current that might otherwise allow the trailing boat to slip past will thus benefit the leading skipper as well.

A skipper with a lead of several boat lengths *(blue boat at top left)* can frequently set up an effective cover as he rounds the leeward mark: he makes a quick pair of tacks to ensure that he will be upwind and in position. If the trailing boat is right at his heels, however, the skipper may have to pinch slightly, heading momentarily above his normal close-hauled sailing angle as he rounds *(bottom left)*, in order to be sure his rival does not slip in to windward.

As the skipper sets up his cover—either at the mark or elsewhere on the course—he may be close enough to his opponent to block the flow of wind with his sails. This so-called tight cover not only gives the lead skipper an advantage in boat speed, but it can be used as a device to manipulate the trailing vessel. For example, if the lead skipper needs to cover more than one boat, he must first herd both competitors onto the same tack. By interfering with his nearest rival's wind, and forcing him to come about for clear air, he brings him onto the same tack as the other boat *(opposite)*. If, however, one of his two rivals is heading off for a less advantageous side of the course, the lead skipper should ignore him and concentrate on covering the remaining boat.

In a covering situation, the front-runner should be wary of following his rivals willy-nilly. It may be wiser for a skipper who is well ahead to sail his own race—especially in shifty and unpredictable winds. And for anyone not clearly well up in the fleet, the objective on this last stretch should be to catch up with the leaders, not cover the followers.

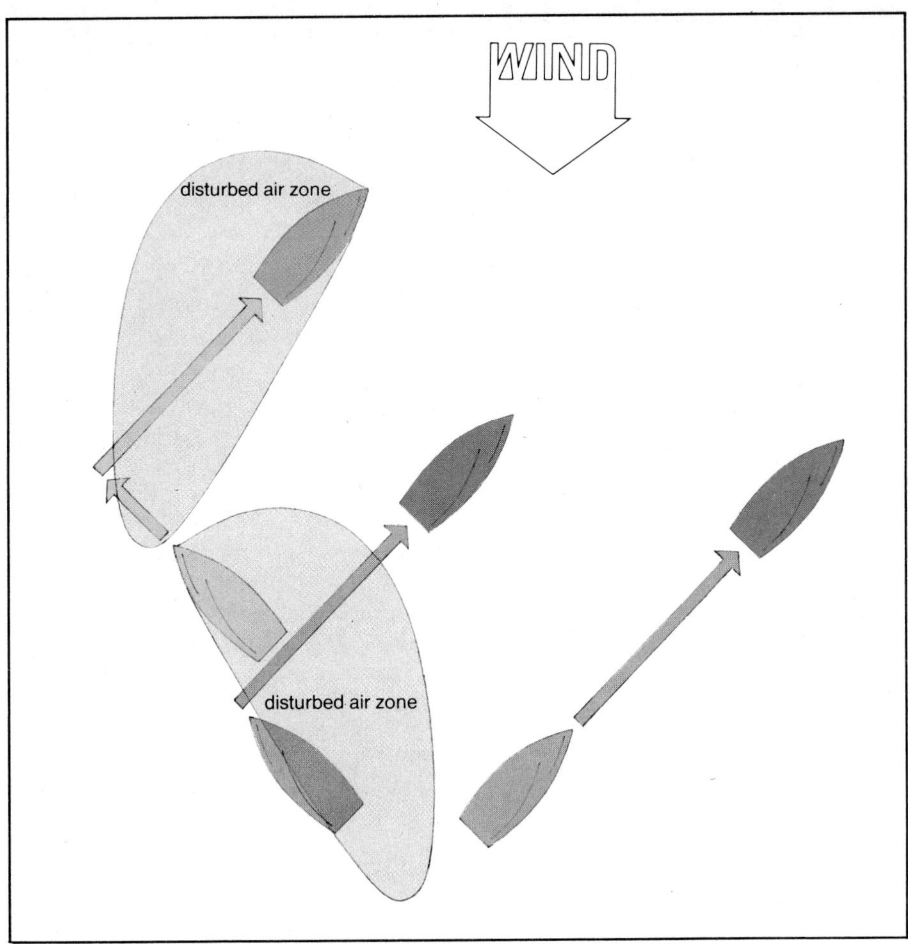

Challenged by two boats or more—and with the trailing craft (light gray) on opposite tacks —the leading skipper (light blue) coaxes his rivals onto the same tack. He does so by momentarily holding a close cover over his nearest rival, which must come about to escape the leader's disturbed air zone —outlined in simplified form here and shown in detail on pages 96-97. The lead skipper then relaxes his cover by delaying his own tack until he is far enough to windward (dark blue) to avoid disturbing the wind of either challenger—thus encouraging them to continue sailing the new tack.

Herding two boats onto the same tack when neither one is under a tight cover is slightly more complicated and involves an extra step. In order to convince one of his two opponents to tack, the covering skipper (light blue) bears off and sails down (medium blue) on his nearest rival (gray, at bottom), trapping him in his disturbed air zone. When his opponent tacks to clear his air, the lead skipper again delays his own tack and loosens his cover (dark blue), thus tempting his competitor to let well enough alone and stay on the new tack (dark gray) along with the other downwind boat (below, far left).

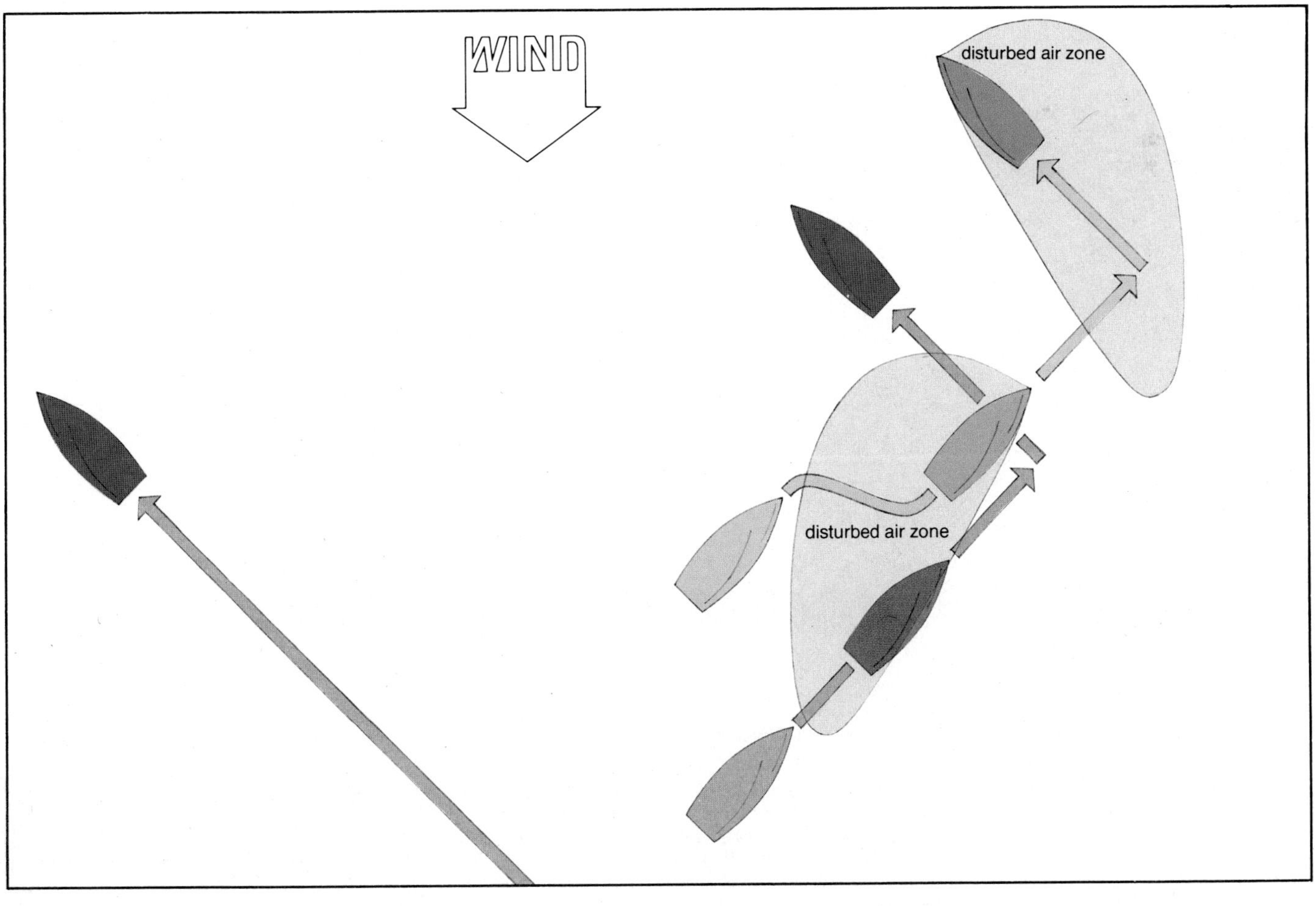

Caught in the disturbed air zone of a tight cover, a trailing skipper (light blue) tries to break away by engaging the covering skipper (light gray) in a tacking duel. He starts the duel by coming about, forcing the lead skipper to come about as well, or else abandon the cover. As the trailing skipper repeats the maneuver, his split-second head start on each tack gives him a slight but telling advantage. After repeated tacking he has gained a boat length (dark blue). Now abeam of his opponent (dark gray), he is free of the wind shadow and even backwinds his rival from a safe leeward position.

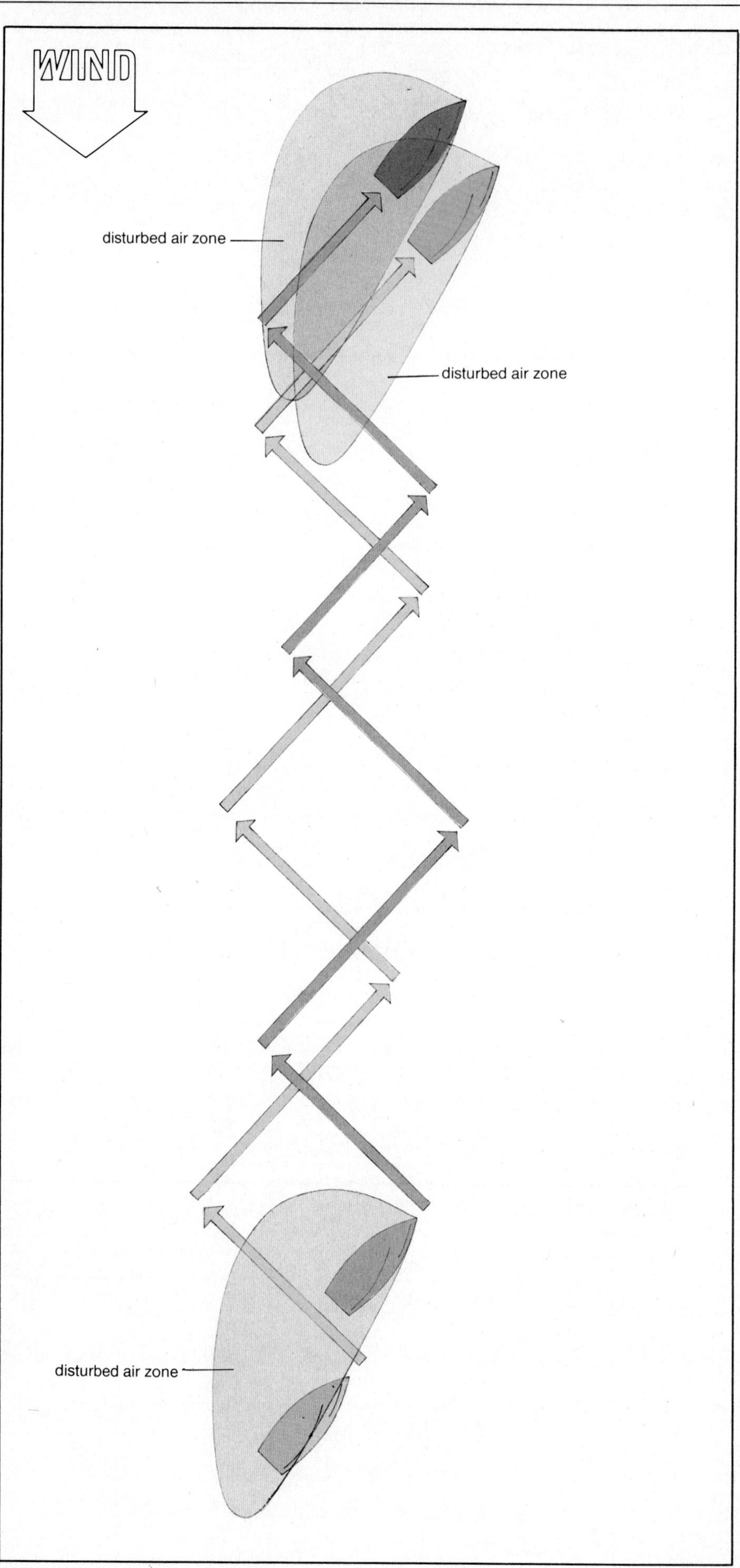

Breaking a Cover

While a skipper who is out ahead engages in a series of covering tactics to prevent other boats from passing him, the helmsman of a trailing boat can execute certain maneuvers of his own to break through the blockade and establish a lead himself. If the front-running vessel holds a substantial lead—approximately eight or 10 boat lengths—the cover will be fairly loose, and the challenger simply sails his own race in an effort to catch up. But as he closes the gap, the challenger may find the lead skipper bearing down to set up a close cover. If this happens, he must respond quickly, or else find himself caught in the wind shadow of his rival's disturbed air zone *(pages 96-97)*.

The basic ploy is for the challenger to switch tacks in order to clear his air: by getting on the opposite tack from his opponent, he banks on a shift in wind or current to put him ahead. But the lead skipper will usually tack as well, in order to maintain the cover. The challenger can then make several more quick tacks—hoping, since he takes the initiative on each tack, to catch his opponent off stride. By thus engaging in a so-called tacking duel, the challenger may be able to work his way out of the cover *(left)*.

Occasionally the lead skipper, either because he has an inherently faster boat or because he comes about more quickly and efficiently than the challenger, will manage to maintain his lead throughout the tacking duel. The challenger must then turn to other tactics. He can sometimes trick a tenacious opponent into inadvertently breaking the cover himself with a foxy maneuver called a fake tack *(top right)*. Or he can take advantage of other boats on the course to dispatch a troublesome adversary—particularly just after he rounds a mark and starts sailing back through stragglers who have not yet turned the buoy *(bottom right)*.

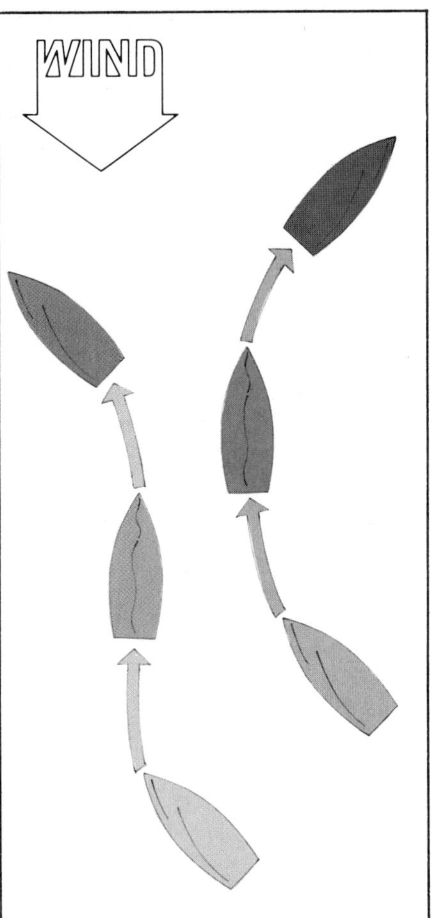

A trailing skipper, taking advantage of his rival's reflex to cover promptly during a tacking duel, can sometimes break cover with a false tack. Loudly calling "Ready about," the challenger (blue boat) turns head to wind —just as though he were tacking. The covering skipper (gray) unsuspectingly heads up also, and comes about as quickly as he can to maintain cover. But instead of passing head to wind, the challenger bears off on his original tack—leaving his opponent badly outfoxed and no longer in charge.

Having turned a leeward mark, a crafty challenger (light blue) uses oncoming vessels as interference to break cover. As the maneuver begins, both the challenger and the boat covering him (light gray) are on starboard tack and to leeward of the approaching craft, and so have right of way. Just in front of the trailing boats, the challenger flops onto port tack (dark blue); though he sacrifices right of way, he still has room to stay clear. But the defending skipper does not; to avoid fouling the oncoming boats, he must continue on starboard tack (dark gray), letting the challenger escape.

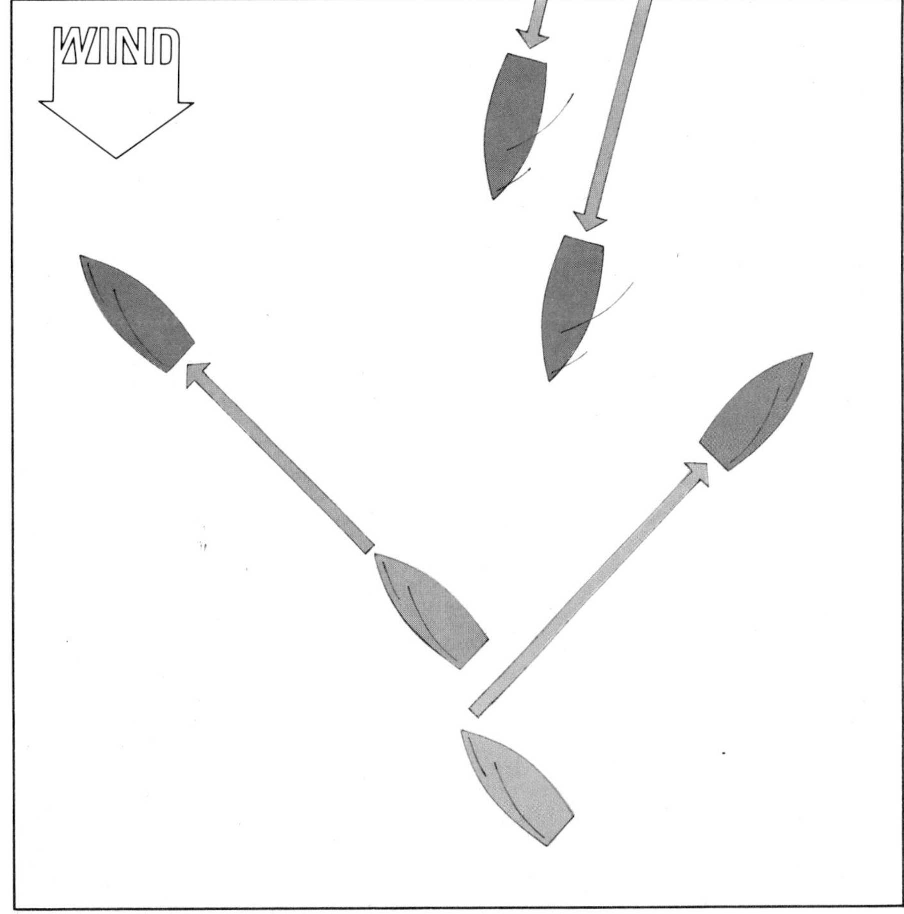

A skipper closing in on a windward finish line can determine the favored, downwind end of the finish line by judging his angle to the line as he makes his last few tacks. The tack that is more perpendicular to the line (blue tint) will point toward the favored end, and by taking it the skipper will then sail a shorter course to the finish line.

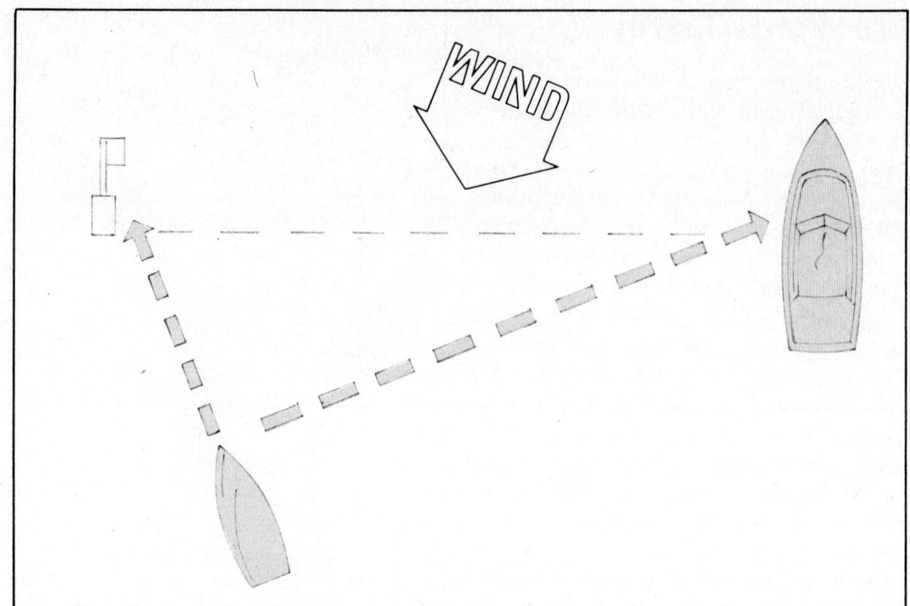

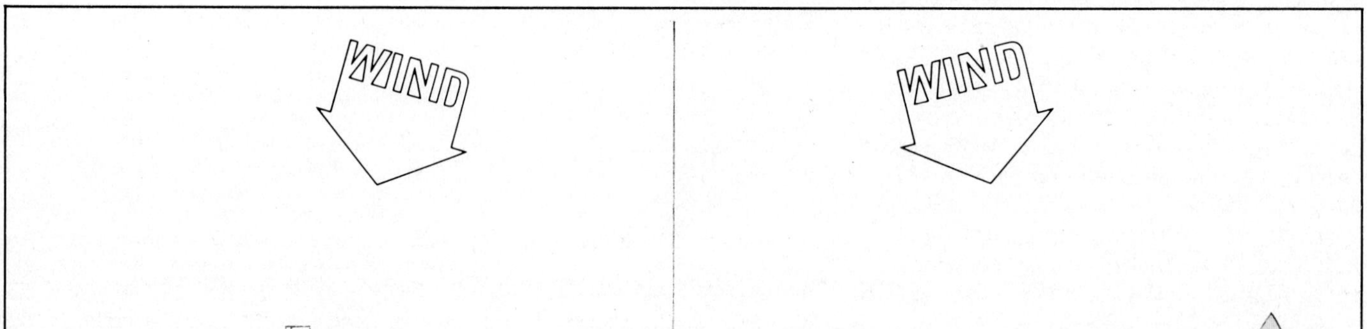

In trying to beat out a close rival at the finish, a skipper can often exercise a right-of-way privilege in conjunction with his drive toward the downwind end of the line. When a portside finish is favored (above, left), a boat on the privileged starboard tack (blue) aims directly for the mark, thus forcing a port-tack opponent (gray) to sail under his stern to avoid fouling him. But when the wind favors a finish at the starboard end of the line (above, right), a boat on the port tack (blue) may hold the advantage. Even though he must make room for a starboard tacker (gray), if he ducks quickly under the other boat's stern and then hardens up, he can cross the line ahead.

Tactics at the Finish Line

As a skipper nears the finish, whether he is in close contention with other boats or comfortably out front, he must turn his attention to a final tactical consideration: deciding which sector of the line to cross. If the final leg is a reach or a run, the skipper simply sails a direct course to the line marker that is closest to him. But on a windward finish, his choice will depend on the same key element that governed his start—finding which end of the line is favored. As at the start, the favored end is determined by the direction of the wind *(pages 88-89)*.

On the finish line, the favored end is downwind (at the start it lies upwind). Therefore, on a course where the start and the finish are at the same line, the skipper can usually assume the end of the line that was unfavored at the start will be the favored at the finish. However, this rule will apply only if the wind has not shifted toward the opposite side of the course in the interim. When there is doubt, the skipper can determine the favored, downwind end by the method described in the top diagram at left.

Unless the skipper has outsailed his competition earlier in the race and approaches the finish line comfortably in the lead, he may encounter a rival also heading for the favored end. If the two boats approach on opposite tacks, right of way may well be the decisive factor in crossing first *(bottom left)*. When the two boats are sailing on the same tack, the skipper with a windward advantage can sometimes foil his competitor by keeping him from tacking, thus forcing him to overstand the end of the line *(top right)*. Or, if there is so much room between the leeward boat and the mark that this gambit will not work, the windward skipper can use a trick called shooting the line *(bottom right)* to finish first.

An aggressive skipper can sometimes crowd a leeward rival out at the finish line by forcing him to overstand the mark at one end. As the two boats near the finish, the windward skipper (blue boat) sits on the leeward boat's (gray) quarter, preventing him from tacking for the line. The windward skipper then tacks at the last possible moment (dark blue), leaving his rival no choice but to follow in his wake.

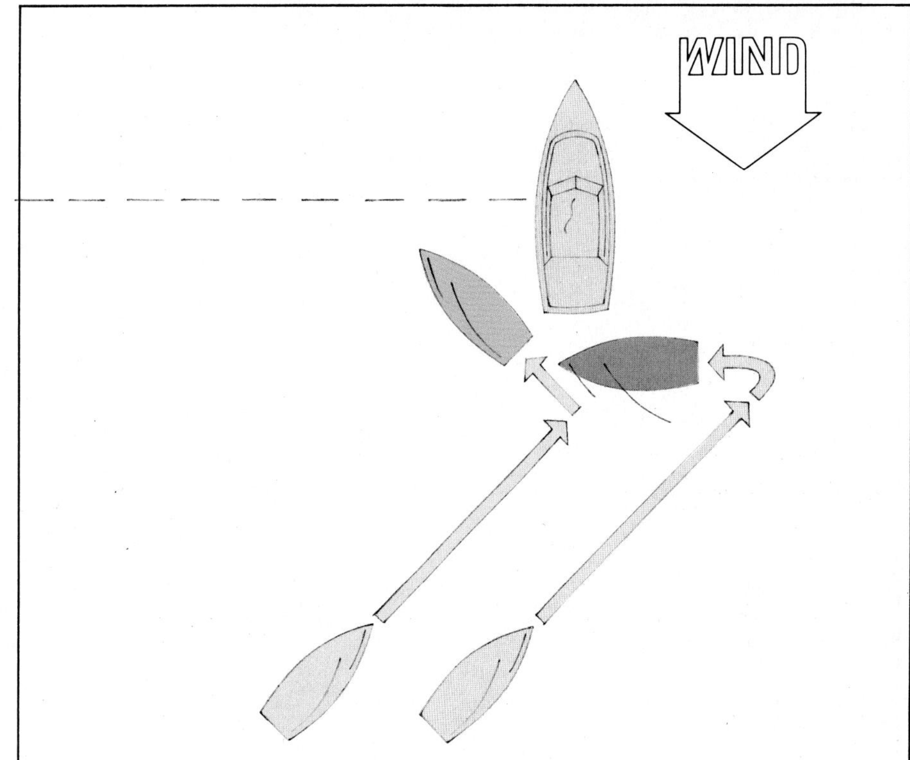

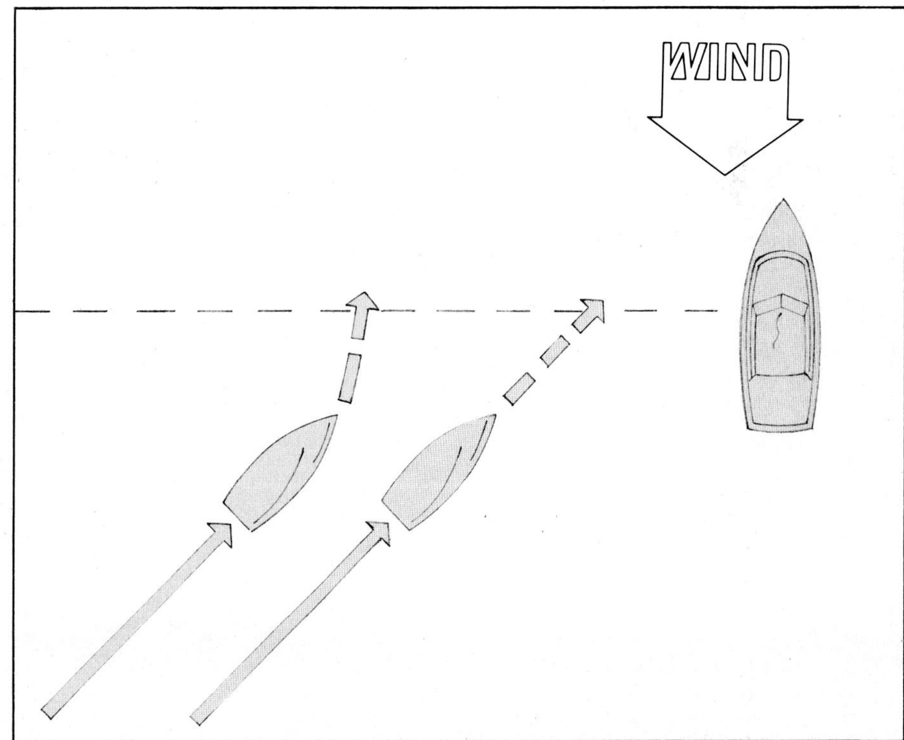

Even if the windward skipper is unable to force his competitor to overstand the line, he can increase his chances of winning with a last-ditch maneuver called shooting the line. As the windward skipper (blue)—sailing neck and neck with his rival (gray)—comes within a couple of boat lengths of the finish, he turns head to wind. Although his sails are no longer pulling, he has shortened his path by as much as a boat length and his own momentum should carry him across.

5

When boats are propelled by motors instead of sails, the gusto of racing takes on an altogether different dimension. Tactical subtleties fade in importance; weather plays a secondary role; and the consistency of a finely tuned engine becomes paramount as skippers skim around an oval course on a lake, slash through offshore swells at 75 miles per hour, or roar down a quarter-mile drag-racing run at speeds more than twice as great.

One major similarity holds, however. In high-performance powerboat races, as with sailboats, most contests are arranged so that the entrants are closely matched in design. Powerboats of various engine sizes and hull con-

THE CHALLENGES OF POWER

figurations are grouped into more than 150 classes by the American Power Boat Association, a national body organized in 1903 to promote and regulate powerboat racing. The classes range in size from tiny outboard-driven runabouts to unlimited hydroplanes, whose supercharged aircraft engines burn about seven gallons of highly volatile methanol every mile while hurtling down the race course in a fury of noise and spray that one driver likens to a "wet earthquake" *(pages 160-167)*.

But class races between specially designed speed machines are only part of the story of powerboat rivalry. Pleasure cruisers also have a long competitive history dating back to match races between steam-powered yachts at the turn of the century *(pages 152-155)*. In the early days of powerboating, sporting skippers made several attempts to devise handicapping systems so that a single contest could accommodate vessels that might range from a 30-foot mahogany day cruiser to a 60-foot yacht with a crew of six. One simple system adjusted the results according to the horsepower of the entries. Another, similiar to the method used by amateur golfers, rated boats according to their past performances. Still another system gave luck a part in the proceedings: winners were determined by drawing lots among the top finishers.

Today, however, the most popular and exacting type of pleasure-boat competition is an ingenious trial known as a predicted-log contest *(pages 142-151)*, which tests the skill of the skipper rather than the power of his boat or the luck of the draw. Pioneered in the 1930s, these events are loosely fashioned after automobile road-rally races, in which the objective is to reach checkpoints at specific times. Scoring is based on the accuracy of a skipper's predictions as compared with the actual time he takes to complete each leg of the course; victory in a three-hour contest is usually a matter of seconds. Hundreds of predicted-log contests are now sanctioned each year by the American Power Boat Association and the U.S. Power Squadron, an organization devoted to fostering boat-handling skills. Despite their leisurely pace, these matches generate fully as much competitive spirit as high-speed races. One demanding skipper, striving to match his prediction of the time he would take to run the course, went so far as to refuse to permit his passengers to go to the head during a contest because he feared that the shift in weight would alter his boat's trim and throw off its carefully calibrated speed.

In ordinary duels of speed, as well—from long-distance powerboat races offshore to drag races on lakes and reservoirs—boat-handling skill is often the winner's edge. The velocities of the larger powerboat racers may vastly magnify problems that a sailboat skipper could handle effortlessly: a mere six-inch chop, for example, can send a mighty hydroplane skittering out of control. In one such incident on Lake Washington, near Seattle, the hydro rocketed skyward, coming to rest in the rose garden of a lakeside home, a few feet from a badly frightened lawn party. The driver, miraculously unscathed, walked away, apologizing profusely as he brushed off the rose petals.

Bow to bow, three power cruisers in a predicted-log contest run the final leg of a course on Long Island Sound—all of them attempting to cross the finish line at a specified time.

A circular announcing a predicted-log contest sponsored by the Huguenot Yacht Club of New Rochelle, New York, details the course, finishing time and other information needed by prospective skippers. Five navigational buoys are designated as control points over a 31.7-mile course, and the finish is scheduled for 1500 hours—3 p.m. This sheet waives a handicap factor—a carefully calculated mathematical adjustment used in some competitions to assist slower boats, which are subjected to the complicating forces of wind and current for a longer period of time.

H U G U E N O T Y A C H T C L U B
Eighteenth Annual Predicted Log Contest
E A S T E R N C R U I S E R A S S O C I A T I O N
Commodore's Contest

DATE: August 2

CONTROL POINTS	DESCRIPTION
START - Can #1	North of Execution Light
CONTROL - Bell #32	Cows, Stamford
CONTROL - Bell #15	Lloyds Point
CONTROL - Can #19	Oak Neck Point
CONTROL - Whistle 32A	South of Stamford
FINISH - Can #1	North of Execution Light
APPROXIMATE DISTANCE	31.7 MILES
FINISH TIME	1500 E.D.S.T.
MINIMUM SPEED	6 knots over the bottom, each leg
MEMBERSHIP	ECA mandatory - except for Huguenot Yacht Club entrants competing for the Huguenot Grog Bowl

GENERAL NOTES

1. The amendments to the ECA rules, adopted in 1968, will govern this contest.
2. Entries must be in by Tuesday, July 29.
3. The Handicap factor will not be used for this contest.
4. Briefing at Huguenot Yacht Club, 2100, Friday, August 1. Predicted Log forms must be delivered to Contest Chairman by 2300, August 1.
5. Completed Log forms to be turned into the Contest Committee by 1600, August 2, by the Observer, at the Club Office.

PRIZES AND TROPHIES
EASTERN CRUISER ASSOCIATION COMMODORE'S TROPHY AND HUGUENOT TROPHY will be awarded to the winning contestant for one year, plus a permanent trophy. A Second and Third trophy will also be awarded.

NAVIGATOR'S TROPHY to be awarded for one year to Navigator turning in lowest score and finishing closest to official finish time. COMMODORE'S TEAM TROPHY awarded to the best team.

HUGUENOT GROG BOWL for Huguenot Yacht Club Members only.

At the briefing meeting commonly held before such contests, navigator Virginia Moore arrives to get any last-minute instructions, inspect the prizes and meet an official observer who will be stationed on board her boat during the run over the course. The observer, whose role is to serve as impartial witness, computes any difference between elasped and predicted times.

Plotting for Victory

In the frequently raucous world of powerboat competition, a predicted-log contest seems almost preternaturally sedate. And indeed the thrills and satisfactions of predicted-log contests are generally low-key. However, there is no more precise test of a power skipper's boat-handling and navigational skills.

For one of these events, contestants first predict how much time they expect their boats will take to run successive legs of a designated course. Then they attempt to match performance to prediction—without the aid of any time-related instruments, either a clock or a speedometer. Courses range from 15 to 100 miles in length and usually include four or five legs around buoys or other control points selected by the host yacht club. Starting times are selected by the contestants themselves, but the host club sets the common finishing time to be aimed at by all entrants.

As an initial step toward making a prediction, a contestant must learn precisely how fast his boat travels when the engine is running at a given level of revolutions per minute, or rpm's. This information is gained with the aid of a simple arithmetical formula: distance divided by time yields speed. Using a stop watch, he makes a series of timed runs between objects separated by a known distance, maintaining his engine's rpm's—hence his speed—at a level that will be matched during the actual contest. Dividing the stop-watch readings into the known distance gives the boat's speed.

Later on, the fundamental arithmetical formula will be used in reverse: the known distance of the course legs will be divided by the speed to yield time predictions. To these predictions will be added the time the boat takes to round the course marks—a computational ingredient that is also determined by tests made before the day of the contest. Lastly, the predictions will be adjusted to account for the effects of the tide.

The tasks of working out a prediction and piloting the boat are generally shared by two people, such as the sister-and-brother team of Virginia Moore (navigator) and Jim Moore (helmsman), whose progress through a race is analyzed here and on the following pages.

Running a series of time trials in the waters where the race is to be held, the Moores clock their boat over a measured distance—starting at red bell buoy #6—to establish the boat's speed for a specified engine-rpm rate. Many coastal areas offer the convenience of measured miles—sets of ranges indicated on nautical charts. For accuracy in a speed trial, the helmsman must keep an absolutely straight course.

SPEED RUNS
#1: 6 MIN. 09 SEC.
#2: 5 MIN. 57 SEC.
#3: 6 MIN. 12 SEC.
#4: 5 MIN. 54 SEC.

AVERAGE RUN
6 MIN. 03 SEC.
SPEED 9.9 KNOTS
TURN TIME [360°]
87 SEC.

After four test runs back and forth over the same course, navigator Moore draws up this list of times. Then she derives an average, which compensates for the effects of wind and current. She has also recorded the time needed to complete a 360° circuit around a buoy at a distance of about 150 feet. This figure will enable her to predict turning times around course marks by simple ratios: for example, a 180° turn will take 43.5 seconds.

Establishing the precise lengths of the individual legs of the course, Virginia Moore uses dividers to span two of the control points on a chart of Long Island Sound; a scale on the chart translates that span into nautical miles. As required by the rules, she then makes travel-time estimates for each leg. Next she will use the course protractor at her left to determine the compass heading of each leg.

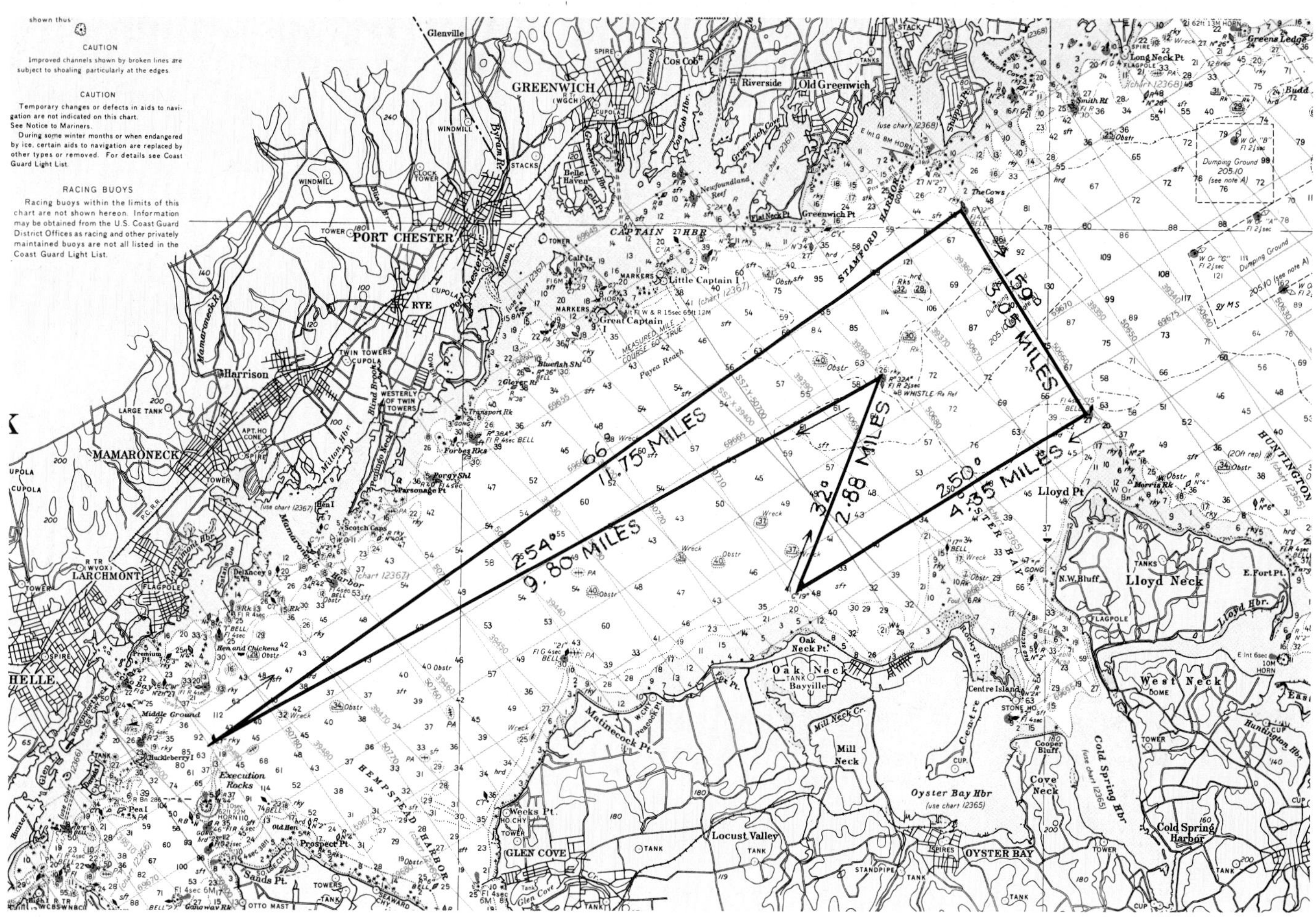

As a visual aid to her computations, Virginia Moore draws the course legs on her chart and labels each one with a directional arrow, the estimated distance and the compass heading. The zigzag route of this contest challenges competitors with several tight turns and two legs so long that the pilot will have to steer by compass rather than sight.

POINTS	DISTANCE	COURSE (CHARTED)	TURN (DEGREES)
BELL #32	11.75	66°	–
BELL #15	3.05	159°	93
CAN #19	4.35	250°	91
WHISTLE #32A	2.88	32°	38
CAN #1	9.80	254°	42
TOTALS	31.83	–	–

A preliminary work sheet incorporates the basic data navigator Moore will use—along with information on the tides—in working out her predictions. Her estimate of the total course length is slightly higher than the 31.7-mile figure given in the yacht-club circular, a result of her decision to calculate the distances in hundredths of miles rather than rounding them off to the nearest tenth.

THE RACE, LONG ISLAND SOUND, AUGUST

F-FLOOD, DIR. 295° TRUE E-EBB, DIR. 100° TRUE

DAY	SLACK WATER TIME H.M.	MAXIMUM CURRENT TIME H.M.	MAXIMUM CURRENT VEL. KNOTS	DAY	SLACK WATER TIME H.M.	MAXIMUM CURRENT TIME H.M.	MAXIMUM CURRENT VEL. KNOTS
1	0009	0235	1.9F	16	0116	0411	2.7F
F	0538	0908	2.2E	SA	0702	1015	3.1E
	1204	1456	2.3F		1331	1632	2.9F
	1802	2145	2.8E		1924	2247	3.7E
2	0106	0336	2.0F	17	0216	0516	2.8F
SA	0637	1005	2.3E	SU	0804	1115	3.2E
	1302	1551	2.4F		1430	1735	2.9F
	1858	2237	3.0E		2022	2344	3.7E
3	0159	0431	2.3F	18	0310	0609	2.9F
SU	0735	1059	2.6E	M	0900	1208	3.3E
	1357	1647	2.7F		1524	1827	3.0F
	1953	2329	3.4E		2114		
4	0248	0522	2.6F	19		0033	3.7E
M	0829	1151	3.0E	TU	0358	0658	3.0F
	1451	1740	3.0F		0947	1257	3.4E
	2046				1612	1912	3.0F
					2159		

Allowing for Current

As a final step in computing her vessel's anticipated time in a predicted-log contest, a navigator like Virginia Moore must allow for the influence of tidal currents—a task greatly simplified by tables and charts issued by the National Ocean Survey. First she consults the tidal current tables *(left)* for ebb and flood times of local currents for the day of the contest—in this case August 2. Then she turns to a series of 12 charts, called tidal current charts, that show—by hourly intervals—the direction and velocity of the tidal current during its 12-hour cycle.

Data gleaned from the tables enables her to choose the correct tidal chart for any stage of the contest. For example, on this particular day slack water before maximum flood current is scheduled to occur at 1302, or 1402 daylight time. Since she has estimated that she will be running the last leg for roughly an hour prior to the designated finishing time of 1500, she selects the chart labeled "one hour after slack; flood begins." Thus she can see the precise current her boat will encounter on that leg. The current velocity on the chart *(below)* is then factored into the basic boat-speed figure, yielding a net speed that reflects actual progress.

Tidal currents in Long Island Sound for Saturday, August 2 (blue tint), the day of the contest, are forecast in this portion of a page from the Atlantic Coast tidal current tables. These forecasts are based on tidal behavior at a key point known as the local reference station—in this case a relatively narrow inlet called The Race, at the eastern end of the Sound. Times of slack water and of maximum ebb and flood are listed in hours and minutes—abbreviated as H.M. Peak current velocity, initialed E or F for ebb and flood, is noted in knots. Days of the week are abbreviated—as F (Friday), SA (Saturday), etc.

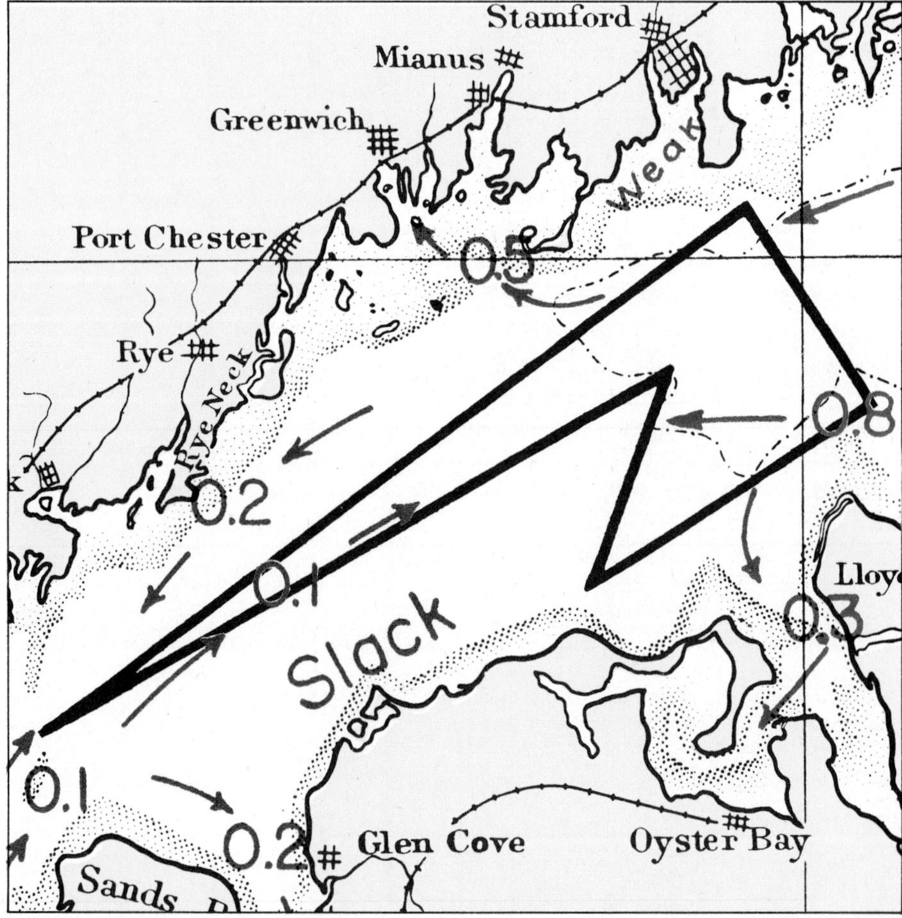

After using the current tables to find the right tidal current chart, navigator Moore pencils onto it her predicted-log course. The chart she has chosen, describing tidal conditions prevailing during the hour before the finish, shows that a boat proceeding along the last leg of the course will be set by an 0.1-knot current. To predict the boat's net speed over the bottom, the current velocity is subtracted from the normal boat speed, since the current will be flowing directly against the bow. If the current were flowing at an angle to the course, then a fraction of its velocity proportionate to that angle would be figured.

LAST LEG WHISTLE 32A TO CAN 1

ELAPSED TIME = $\frac{\text{DISTANCE} \times 3600}{\text{NET SPEED}}$

DISTANCE = 9.80 NAUTICAL MILES
NET SPEED = BOAT SPEED ± CURRENT
BOAT SPEED = 9.9 KNOTS

NET SPEED = (9.90 −.16)
NET SPEED = 9.74 KNOTS
ELAPSED TIME = $\frac{9.80 \times 3600}{9.74}$

TOTAL ELAPSED TIME = 3622 SEC.
(+15 SEC. TURN)
OR 1 HR. 00 MIN. 37 SEC.

TIME AT CAN 1 (FINISH) = 15:00:00
− 01:00:37
TIME AT WHISTLE 32A = 13:59:23

A series of calculations yields a schedule for running the final leg. First, navigator Moore figures the net boat speed by combining speed and tidal-current computations. Secondly, she determines the elapsed time by multiplying the measured distance by 3,600 (thus converting hours into seconds) and dividing the product by the net boat speed. She next adds 15 seconds to allow for the 42° turn around the final mark. Then she subtracts the predicted elapsed time from the finish time, giving the actual time the last leg should begin. Using the same formula for the other legs, she will decide her starting time.

To be completed by **CONTESTANT**

CONTROL POINTS	(1) PREDICTED TIME			(2) ELAPSED TIME BETWEEN CHECK POINTS		
	HRS.	MIN.	SEC.	HRS.	MIN.	SEC.
START Can #1 No. of Execution Rocks	11	46	30			
Control - Bell #32 Cows, Stamford (Port)	12	56	02	1	09	32
Control - Bell #15 - Lloyds Point	13	14	41		18	39
Control - Can #19 - Oak Neck Point	13	41	54		27	13
Control - Whistle #32A - Mid Sound	13	59	23		17	29
				1	00	37
FINISH Can #1 No. of Execution Rocks	15	00	00			
PREDICTED STARTING TIME	11	46	36	2	71	150
ELAPSED TIME (FINISH Less START)	3	13	30			
PROOF - That columns 1 and 2 are correct: Convert hours and minutes of elapsed time from column 1 to seconds. (Use Conversion Table, entering seconds in spaces at right, and total.) In column 2 convert to seconds and add. These Totals (A) in each column must be identical.	3 HRS	10800 SEC		2 HRS	7200 SEC	
	13 MIN	780 SEC		71 MIN	4260 SEC	
		30 SEC			150 SEC	
		11610 SEC			11610 SEC	
		TOTAL (A)			TOTAL (A)	

Total distance of course given by Committee 31.7 Miles.

Predicted Average Speed = $\frac{\text{COMMITTEE DISTANCE} \times 3600}{\text{TOTAL (A)}}$ = 9.9 Knots.

Handicap Factor - see back of this Form = NONE (HF)

I hereby certify that no part of this Predicted Log is based on any test run over any portion of the course. My measurement of the distance for the entire course is 31.8 miles.

I agree to abide by the E.C.A. Predicted Log Contests Official Rules and modifications set forth hereon.

James B Moore
CONTESTANT

On an official form submitted by the Moores to the host Huguenot Yacht Club, elapsed-time predictions for each leg of the course appear in the right-hand column. The left-hand column lists the actual clock times at which the boat is scheduled to pass the control points in order to finish at precisely 1500 hours. To prove that the calculations are consistent, the elapsed times between start and finish (column 1) and the total elapsed time (column 2) are converted into seconds and compared. The entry also includes the navigator's predicted boat speed and her own estimates of the total distance.

Jim Moore throttles up his 50-foot twin-screw powerboat to stipulated cruising rpm's—3,100 for the first leg—as his sister counts off the last seconds before their chosen starting time. Her clock will be turned over to the official observer as soon as they pass the starting mark. All other time-related instruments on the dashboard have been taped over.

A slow-moving barge looms ahead as the Moores traverse the fourth leg. Having been forced to deviate from the planned course, Jim Moore will later accelerate for a few seconds to make up for the slight increase in the distance the boat must travel.

The Test at Sea

A course run so carefully on paper seems unlikely to hold any major surprises for experts like the Moores when they put their predictions to the test of the official observer's timepiece in the actual contest. But happenstance always plays at least a minor role in any sea passage.

In predicted-log contests, weather is the great unknown: both wind and waves can drastically alter their speed. And the helmsman, in this case Jim Moore, has no way of combating these influences other than by intuitively increasing or reducing the engine's rpm's. Happily, this day is one of light air and calm seas, and his work is mainly limited to closely watching the tachometer and the compass. His sister, meanwhile, surveys the water ahead for any obstacle—another boat, or even a lobster pot—that could force them from their designated path and call for a brief compensatory change of speed.

Each leg amounts to a separate contest —crucial in scoring—of a team's ability to match the actual times at the checkpoints with their predictions. The time differences, due to slowness or excess speed, accumulate from leg to leg, and by the rules cannot be made up; to do so would increase a contestant's total net error.

Swinging smoothly around whistle 32A in the wake of the Moores' boat, a rival follows them toward the finish. Contest rules state that the boats must pass within 200 feet of a control point. In so doing, the skippers attempt to round the buoys with turns of exactly the same radii as in their trial runs.

Hearing the helmsman call, "Mark," as the boat passes a control point, the official observer aboard the Moores' boat notes the amount of time taken to complete the leg and computes the difference between prediction and actual performance.

While her brother holds the boat steady on his compass heading for the last leg of the course, navigator Virginia Moore scans the water through binoculars for any obstructions —and the earliest possible glimpse of the buoy marking the finish of the contest.

HUGUENOT YACHT CLUB
PREDICTED LOG CONTEST
AUGUST 2, 1975

ACTUAL LOG

BOAT GINJIM-E V
CONTEST No. E99 FINISH No. ______
LENGTH 48' SPEED 9.9 Knots
CONTESTANT James B. Moore
RADIO CALL WN 4554
BOATING ORGANIZATION N.Y.A.C.
OBSERVER Erwin Blair
TEAM N.Y.A.C. Yacht Club.

To be completed by OBSERVER

ERRORS: DIFFERENCE BETWEEN COLS. 2 AND 4 IN SECONDS — SLOW COL. 4 LARGER	FAST COL. 4 SMALLER	(4) ACTUAL ELAPSED TIME — HRS.	MIN.	SEC.	(3) ACTUAL WATCH TIME — HRS.*	MIN.*	SEC.*	CONTROL POINTS
					11	46	30	START Can #1 No. of Execution Rocks
	-180	1	06	32	12	53	02	Control - Bell #32 Cows, Stamford (Port)
	83		17	16	13	10	18	Control - Bell #15 - Lloyds Point
03			27	16	13	37	34	Control - Can #19 - Oak Neck Point
	08		17	21	13	54	55	Control - Whistle #32A - Mid Sound
78		1	01	55	14	56	50	FINISH Can #1 No. of Execution Rocks
81	271				11	46	30	PREDICTED STARTING TIME
ADD Slow	81	2	68	140	3	10	20	ELAPSED TIME (Finish Less Start)
+ Fast,	271							
Total Error (E)	352							

(4)		(3)	
2 HRS	7200 SEC	3 HRS	10800 SEC
68 MIN	4080 SEC	10 MIN	600 SEC
	140 SEC		20 SEC
TOTAL (B)	11420 SEC	TOTAL (B)	11420 SEC

ACTUAL STARTING TIME HRS. 11 MIN. 46 SEC. 30

PROOF - Convert hours and minutes to seconds. Totals (B) in columns 3 and 4 must be identical.

PROOF
That error columns are correct:

	Difference between slow & fast	Difference between totals (A) and (B)
Larger	271	11610
Smaller	81	11420
Net Error	190	190

If Net Errors are identical in each column above, then the errors have been correctly figured.

I hereby certify that this Actual Log is acurate within the limits imposed by the watch used. To the best of my knowledge no unauthorized person has had access to the time of day or elapsed time during this event.

Erwin Blair
OBSERVER

Actual % Error = TOTAL (E) X 100 / TOTAL (A) = 352 X 100 / 11610 = 3.0318 % (AE)

Corrected % ERROR (AE) X (HF) = ______ X NONE = ______ %.

CALCULATIONS APPROVED James B Moore
CONTESTANT SCORER

*NOTE: Use predicted starting time

CONVERSION TABLE

Hours to Seconds	Hours to Minutes	Minutes to Seconds
3,600	1	60
7,200	2	120
10,800	3	180
14,400	4	240
18,000	5	300
21,600	6	360
25,200	7	420
28,800	8	480
32,400	9	540
36,000	10	600

The log completed by the observer for the Moores' boat notes the time each control point was passed and compares the actual elapsed time for the course legs with the predictions. Slow and fast errors are separately totaled (light blue), then added to give a total computed error. This total, in turn, is expressed as a percentage of the total predicted running time (dark blue). The Moores' percentage of error was a mere 3.03; but it turned out to be not good enough (right).

Rocking in one another's wakes, four cruisers descend on the black can marking the finish at intervals only fractionally off the target hour of 1500 hours. When the performances of the day were finally tabulated and judged, the boat second from left proved to be the winner. It finished with a total error of only 51 seconds, making its predicted log 99.54 per cent accurate. Despite their own skilled calculations, the Moores wound up 13th in the crack fleet of 20.

A fleet of outboard hydroplanes hurtles down the Hudson River in an early running of the 132-mile Albany-to-New York marathon. Such long-distance races, first popularized in the 1920's, were grueling challenges of endurace and skill. Only 22 of the 88 starting boats finished this race: in addition to the toll from fatigue, mechanical problems and hidden shoals, several of the drivers capsized after hitting the wakes of the ferry boats that were crossing the Hudson.

Historical photographs by Morris Rosenfeld

A SUDDEN SURGE OF POWER

Just after World War I, the rivers, lakes and coastal waters of America began to rumble to the sound of competing powerboats. Elegant mahogany speedboats, snarling outboards like those at left and queenly cruisers proliferated as engineers developed efficient, reliable engines to run them. Also, the hull designs became sleeker and faster—partially because of a heavy demand from Prohibition's rumrunners for swift craft to smuggle liquor past federal patrol boats in coastal waters.

Inevitably, the owners of these new power craft began to challenge one another to race. A few of the competitions, notably those between rumrunners and revenuers, were deadly. Others, like those that are shown overleaf, represented the epitome of dilettantism, more *concours d'élégance* than combat. But most were straightforward speed trials among daring drivers who often designed and built the hulls and engines they piloted.

By far the most successful figure in this giddy surge of powerboat racing was a millionaire-sportsman named Garfield Arthur Wood. Inventor of the hydraulic-lift dump truck, Gar Wood devoted his profits to building the fastest boats the world had ever seen. In a Michigan boatyard he fitted out a series of radical, surface-skimming hydroplanes with airplane engines that could push them at the unheard of speed of 100 miles per hour. Wood himself did the driving, always with a pair of goggled and helmeted Teddy bears at his side for good luck.

Wood won a score of major races between his debut in 1917 and his retirement in 1933, including eight victories in the Harmsworth Trophy, emblematic of the world speedboat championship. At one point he ran out of marine competition and began taking on trains—first the Havana Express from Miami to New York, then the Twentieth Century Limited from Albany to New York. Naturally, Wood won both times.

Aboard the flagship of the Columbia Yacht Club, a swank group of guests and members cluster about the seated commodore to watch the club's 1919 Fall Regatta in New York Harbor. Eleven splendid cruising craft, from 33 to 41 feet in length, turned out for the feature contest, a handicap event covering 10 miles. One of the slowest and shortest boats, aptly named Turtle, won —thanks to a fat boost from her handicap— after completing the course at 9 mph.

Flag-bedecked cruisers—one carrying a passenger swathed in furs—purr past the starting line in a charmingly uncontentious event called a chance race, staged at Palm Beach, Florida, in 1927. In these cheerful regattas, the winner was chosen by lot, with the number of draws based on the order of finish: the first of five boats getting five chances, the second four, and so on.

A quintet of gleaming Chris-Craft speedboats hurtles down the Detroit River in a special class race at the city's 10th Annual Regatta in 1926. Although they were capable of reaching a top speed of about 35 miles an hour, these mahogany beauties were designed primarily for family pleasure boating.

Spectators massed in front of the Municipal Club House of Oshkosh, Wisconsin, look on as the drivers of a small-inboard class make last-minute preparations for an event in the Mississippi Valley Powerboat Association's 17th Annual Regatta, held on July 4, 1924. Between races, the crowd of more than 80,000 was treated to band music and vaudeville acts. That night, fireworks and a banquet capped off what one reporter called "a regular good ol' Valley meet."

A3

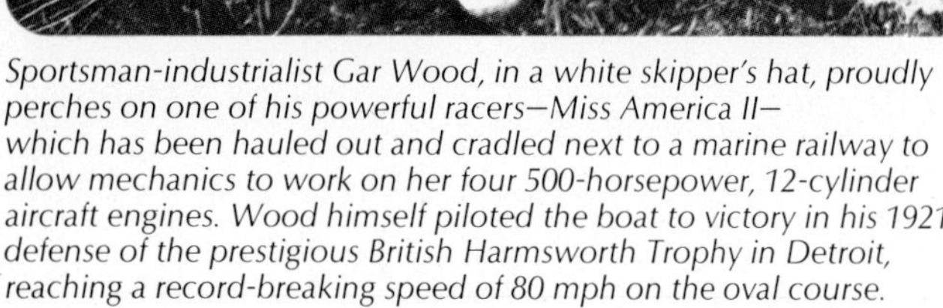

Sportsman-industrialist Gar Wood, in a white skipper's hat, proudly perches on one of his powerful racers—Miss America II—which has been hauled out and cradled next to a marine railway to allow mechanics to work on her four 500-horsepower, 12-cylinder aircraft engines. Wood himself piloted the boat to victory in his 1921 defense of the prestigious British Harmsworth Trophy in Detroit, reaching a record-breaking speed of 80 mph on the oval course.

In a one-two finish in the 1929 Harmsworth Trophy competition, two of Gar Wood's racing machines thunder down an avenue of flag-bedecked spectators and past a grandstand along the Detroit River. In this photograph Miss America VIII, driven by Wood, leads, closely trailed by Miss America VII, with his brother Phil at the wheel. Big brother eventually won, causing a commentator to muse: "As far as any real competition is concerned, the event was a failure."

THE EXCITEMENT OF SPEED ON WATER

The spectacle of high-speed powerboat racing today shatters most traditional notions about the shape of boats and how they move through water. Modern racing craft combine superlight construction materials and the latest hydrodynamic design theories with massive doses of horsepower to blast over the surface at speeds that seem more suited to sports cars.

Three very specialized powerboat competitions—offshore, closed course and drag racing—attract modern racers. Each requires unique handling skills and a carefully bred high-performance boat. Offshore ocean racers *(right)* are often powered by twin 600-horsepower engines, hooked up to rugged inboard-outboard drives. Their deep-V hulls, usually 35 to 40 feet long, are designed to slash through ocean swells rather than bounce haphazardly off—or over—them. The courses covered may take them from 175 to 250 miles over unsheltered waters.

On inland waters a spectrum of craft, ranging upward in size from outboard runabouts *(overleaf)* with engines as tiny as seven horsepower, run laps on closed oval courses. These boats are raced in regattas, organized mainly by the American Powerboat Association, for trophies, cash prizes—and national standings. The most powerful, radically shaped and costly boats are those in the unlimited inboard hydroplane class *(page 166)*. As the name implies, these heavyweights operate under no restrictions in size or engine horsepower. They are driven by surplus World War II fighter-aircraft engines with more than 3,000 horsepower. Mounted on flat fragile hulls, the engines rocket a hydroplane around a three-mile course at speeds averaging 120 miles per hour.

But even these do not represent the ultimate in competitive boat speed. The fastest craft are drag boats, which harness supercharged, converted truck engines to catapult them down straightaway courses at upwards of 200 miles per hour.

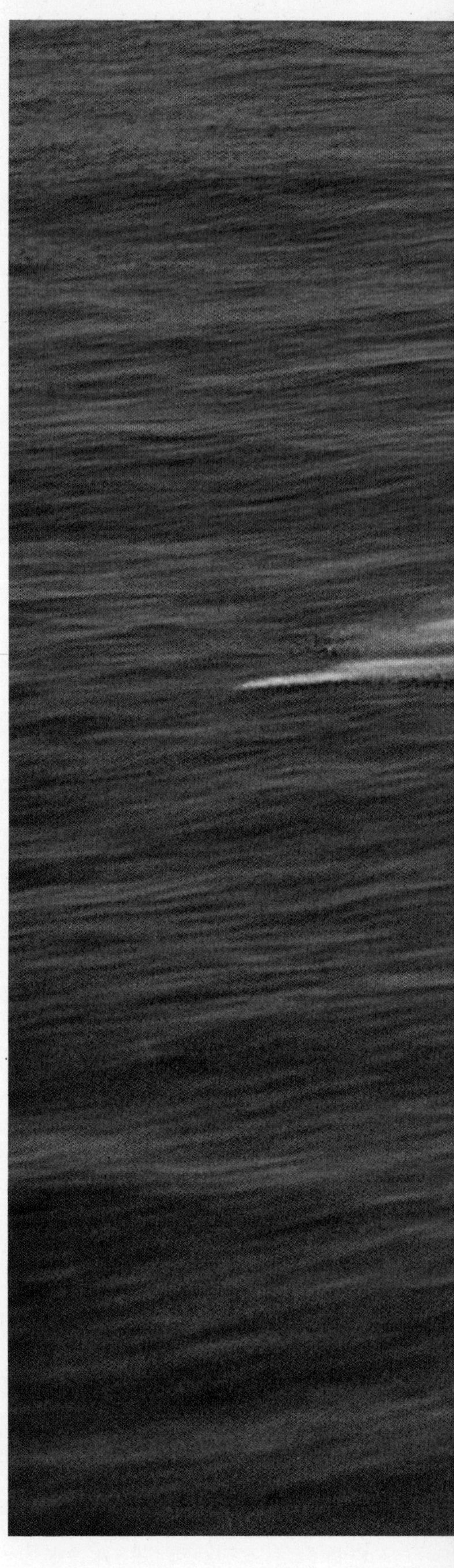

A 19,000 pound, 38-foot-long offshore racer slices across the blue Atlantic at more than 70 mph in a 180-mile race from New Jersey to Long Island and back. Steering through one of these events requires such strength and concentration that the skipper never tries to touch the gas; his crew operates the throttle, speeding up and slowing down as the racer hurtles through the endless succession of swells.

Outboard Classes

Racing teams on the banks of the Cooper River in Collingswood, New Jersey, prepare to launch their outboard runabouts for one of the final heats of the National Marathon Championship races for stock outboards, i.e., boats whose engines are basically unaltered after purchase from a regular dealer. To prevent their wooden racing hulls from absorbing any water, most drivers pull their craft from the water between heats.

Steadying his lacquered hydroplane in the water, a racer makes final adjustments on the outboard's carburetor. Ceaseless fine tuning, particularly of the fuel-air mixture, and fastidious maintenance are key factors in getting top performance from racing engines.

Three racing outboard runabouts skid around a buoy on New Jersey's Cooper River as their helmeted drivers lean forward to keep their craft at optimal trim. The leading boat, at right, has earned the designation 2-US by winning the previous year's five-mile Short Course National Championship. The symbol 1-US is reserved for the National High Point Champion, the driver with the highest average of points (based on his finishing positions) in a season of 15 or more races.

Kneeling in his cramped cockpit, the driver of a small outboard hydroplane cruises slowly toward the starting line. The boat's compact outboard packs enough power to drive the light craft to a top speed of 57 mph.

Drag Boats

A drag racer inches his boat beneath a restraining line to join competitors waiting to make solitary runs against the clock at Marine Stadium in Oakland, California. Timed by an electronic-eye apparatus, the boats blast down a quarter-mile course with such speed that they must be stopped by parachutes when their run is finished.

Given the green light signaling the start, a drag racer hits the throttle of his 400-horsepower supercharged engine. The initial thrust from its propeller has made the craft squat momentarily in the water, before surging up and forward on its run. Eight separate air-intake pipes on top of the engine are part of a special fuel-injection system that develops extra power in each cylinder.

A dazzling drag boat beached between races serves as an exotic grandstand for its owners, who watch a competitor speeding across the water. Flamboyant decorations, typified by the pink elephant on this craft's bow, the chrome engine exhaust pipes and color-coordinated trailer, are all part of the swashbuckling sport of drag racing.

Unlimited Hydroplanes

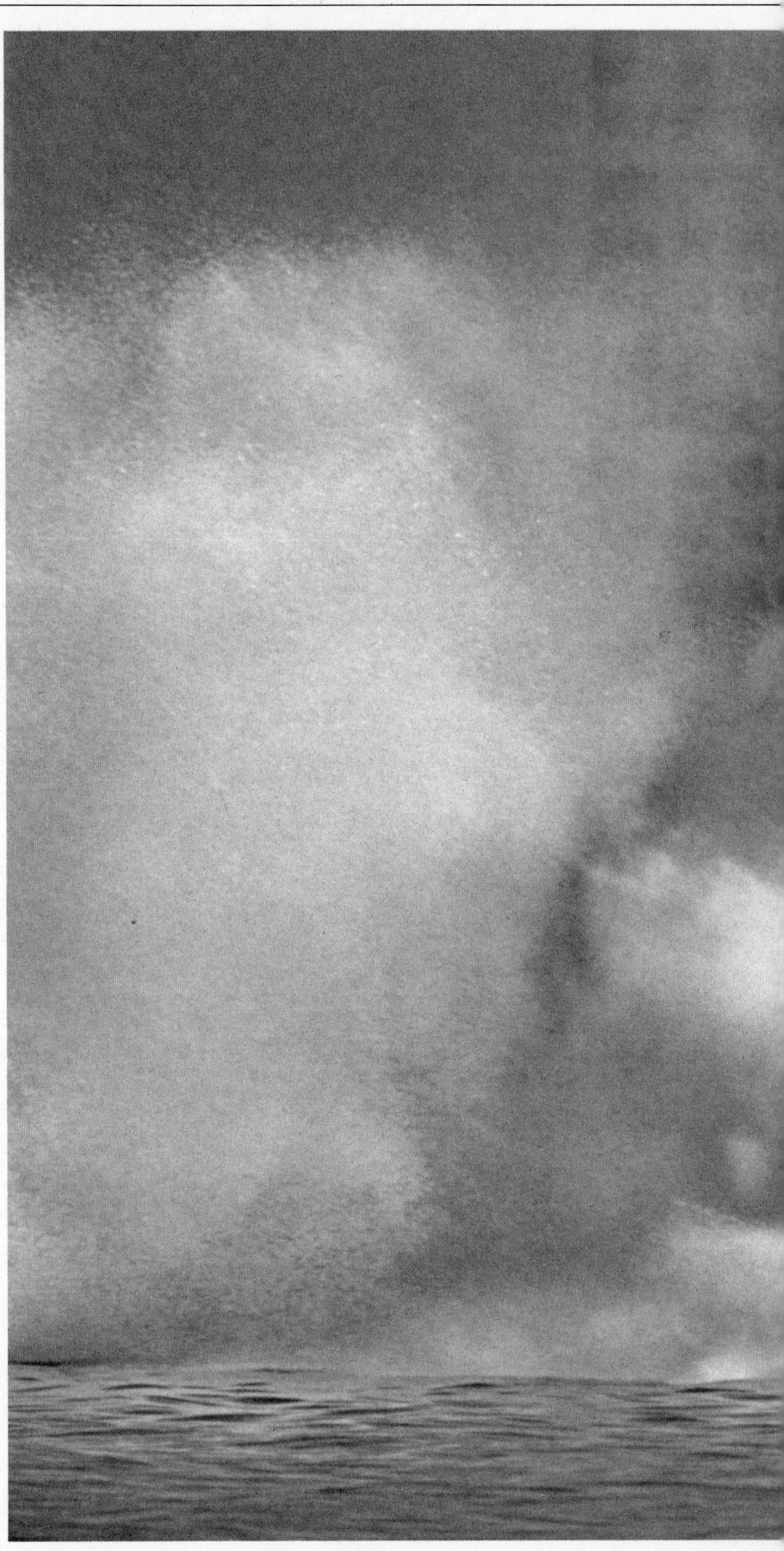

Throwing a 50-foot rooster-tail wake behind, an unlimited hydro thunders down a raceway in Miami Beach, Florida, during the Champion Spark Plug Regatta. Such speed machines, which cost upwards of $100,000, touch the water only with their propellers and two small planing surfaces on either side of their hulls—and have a special wing configuration at the sterns to counteract their tendency to become airborne.

Atlas
Van
Lines

Glossary

Apparent wind A combination of the natural wind and the breeze created by the boat's forward motion.

Backwind The wind deflected from one sail onto the leeward side of another, or deflected from the sails of one boat onto those of a boat that is behind or to windward.

Barber haul A device for adjusting the athwartships trim of a jib sheet.

Barging At the start of a race, illegally forcing one's way between the starting mark and boats to leeward.

Battens Flexible strips of wood or fiberglass placed in the leech of a sail to help the sail's trailing edge retain its proper shape.

Bear off To turn a boat away from the direction of the wind.

Beat To go to windward in a sailboat by sailing close-hauled, tacking so that the wind is first on one side and then on the other.

Blanket To obstruct the wind's flow to another boat's sails by passing or holding a position on its weather side.

Boom vang A block and tackle used to hold down the boom while reaching or running.

Broach To swing out of control when running, so that the boat turns broadside to wind and sea, in danger of capsizing.

Buoy room The amount of space needed for a boat to round or pass a mark.

Camber The horizontal curves described by the sectional shapes of a working sail.

Cat rig A small-boat rig in which a mast mounted near the bow carries a single fore-and-aft sail.

Cat's-paw A patch of rippled water resulting from a localized gust of wind.

Center of effort (CE) A theoretical point on a boat's sail plan that represents the focus or center of the total forces of wind on the sails.

Center of lateral resistance (CLR) A point below a boat's waterline representing the focus or pivot point of the total hydrodynamic forces on the hull.

Chord A hypothetical straight horizontal line from the luff to the leech of a sail; the base line of an aerodynamic shape.

Clear air Wind undisturbed by obstructions, such as the sails of boats.

Clew The lower after corner of a sail, where the foot meets the leech.

Closed course A race course specifically designed to include various points of sail and whose start and finish lines are in approximately the same place.

Close-hauled A boat is close-hauled when its sails are trimmed in tight and it is heading as close to the wind as it can while still keeping its speed.

Continuing shift A wind that shifts sequentially a few degrees at a time in one direction.

Cover To keep between an opponent and the next mark; a tactic used by a leading boat in a race to prevent a trailing boat from passing.

Cunningham A line run through an eye in the luff of a sail and tightened or released to flatten the sail or make it more full.

Disturbed air Wind that has been affected by the presence of a boat's sails or some other obstruction.

Downhaul A length of wire or line that pulls down the tack of a sail or the foremost end of the boom to tighten the luff.

Draft The depth a vessel extends below the waterline; the position, and amount, of maximum camber in a sail.

Drag The forces acting on the hull of a boat that retard its forward progress through the water.

Drive The forces exerted by the wind on a sail that propel a boat forward.

Ease To let up, slack off, reduce tension —as on the helm, a sheet or a halyard.

Ebb tide A tidal current that occurs when the sea-water level is dropping.

Fairlead An eye or block—usually attached to a deck—that guides a line in a desired direction.

Feather To steer intermittently just above a close-hauled course, in order to avoid excessive heeling in heavy weather.

Fetch To head toward or achieve a desired destination under sail, particularly with an adverse wind or tide.

Flood tide A tidal current that occurs when the sea-water level is rising.

Foot The bottom edge of a sail; also, to make speed in a sailboat.

Foreguy A line running from the middle or outboard end of a spinnaker pole to a block on the foredeck, used to keep the spinnaker pole from rising.

Frostbite dinghy Any small, one-design boat, usually cat-rigged, and raced in cold weather.

Gooseneck The fitting, connecting boom to mast, that allows the boom to swing laterally and vertically.

Guy The windward spinnaker sheet, used to control the spinnaker pole.

Halyard A line used to hoist or lower a sail, or to place tension on the sail's luff.

Harden up To sail closer to the wind.

Head The uppermost corner of a triangular sail.

Head down To steer a boat away from the direction of the wind.

Head up To steer a boat in the direction of the wind.

Header A shift in the wind's direction toward a sailboat's bow, forcing the boat to head down or the crew to trim sail. A boat receiving a header is said to have been headed.

Heading The direction in which a moving boat's bow is pointing.

Heel A sideways leaning of a boat caused by the wind's force on the sails.

Hike out To sit on the windward rail and lean out over the water to counteract a sailboat's tendency to heel.

Hiking strap A strap under which a crew member can hook his feet to secure himself when hiking out.

Hull speed The limit of speed imposed on a displacement hull by the resistance of its own wave systems.

Hydroplane A hull shape, specially designed for high-performance powerboat racing, that allows boats to plane at high speed with little frictional resistance from water.

Incidence The angle—sometimes called the angle of attack—at which a sail is trimmed to the wind.

Jibe To turn a sailboat's stern through the wind so that the sails swing from one side of the boat to the other, putting the boat on another tack. In technical racing terminology, a jibe is defined by the rule book as beginning at the moment the foot of the mainsail crosses the centerline; it lasts until the mainsail has filled on the other tack.

Lay line An imaginary line on which a boat, sailing close-hauled, can fetch a mark without further tacks.

Lee helm The tendency of a sailboat to steer off or away from the wind, usually due to imbalance between the sails and hull.

Leech The after edge of a sail.

Leech line A line that controls the tension on the trailing edge of the sail.

Leeward In the direction away from the wind (pronounced LOO-ard).

Leeway The lateral movement of a boat caused by the force of the wind.

Leg One of the segments of a race course, designated by marks at either end.

Lift A shift in the wind's direction away from a sailboat's bow, allowing the boat to point higher than it could previously; also, a force developed by water flowing over the hull and keel, in a direction generally perpendicular to the centerline, and typically acting in opposition to the side force on the sails.

Luff The leading edge of the sail; also, the fluttering of a sail when the boat is pointed too close to the wind, or the sail is let out too far; also, to head up.

Mark Any object—such as a flag, government navigation aid or anchored committee boat—used to designate the start, finish and the various legs of a race.

Mast abeam A situation in a race in which the helmsman of a windward boat, sighting directly abeam, is abreast or ahead of the mast of another vessel sailing parallel to leeward.

Multihull Any vessel, such as a catamaran, with more than one hull.

One-design boat A boat built to uniform specifications and measurements so that it is in effect identical to all the other vessels in its competitive class.

Oscillating shift Wind that shifts first in one direction and then in the other.

Outhaul A fitting on the after end of the boom to which the sail's clew is attached, and which can be tightened or loosened to adjust the tension and shape of the sail's foot.

Overlap A situation in which part of a boat's hull or equipment projects ahead of the transom of another boat immediately adjacent to it.

Overstand To sail past the lay line for a mark, usually inadvertently.

Pinch To head closer to the wind than a sailboat's optimum close-hauled course.

Planing The action of a boat that is riding atop its own bow wave, an attitude that permits it to exceed its normal hull speed.

Plumb bow A bow that is straight up and down, with no overhang.

Point To sail close to the wind; also, the start and finish of a race from one venue to another, as in point-to-point racing (as differentiated from closed-course racing).

Point of sail The heading of a boat in relation to the apparent wind. The three basic points are running, reaching and beating.

Port tack A sailboat is said to be on port tack when the wind is coming over its port side.

Pram A small rowboat or sailing dinghy with a squared-off bow.

Predicted-log contest A competitive event for powerboat cruisers, similar to an automobile road rally, in which each skipper must reach various checkpoints on a course at specified times, based on his own prior computations of estimated speed.

Proper course In the racing rules, the course a boat would normally sail after the starting signal, in the absence of any competitors, to round the prescribed course as quickly as possible.

Protest A declaration by a skipper to the racing committee to the effect that, in his opinion, a competing boat has violated one of the racing rules.

Rake The inclination from the perpendicular (usually aft) of a sailboat's mast.

Reach A course sailed between a beat and a run, with the wind coming more or less at right angles over the boat's side. On a close reach the wind is farther forward; on a broad reach, farther aft.

Rhumb line The straight line between two marks on a racecourse.

Right of way The authority that entitles one boat to hold its direction while other vessels in the vicinity must give way.

Rudder angle The angle between the rudder blade and the boat's fore-and-aft line; or between the rudder and the flow of water passing over it.

Run To sail before the wind.

Runabout A small, lightweight motorboat with an open cockpit.

Sailing instructions A supplement to the racing rules that lists the specific regulations and arrangements for a given race.

Set The direction in which a current is moving, expressed in compass degrees; also, the direction in which a boat is pushed by current or wind.

Sheet A line used to adjust the trim and shape of a sail.

Shoot the line On an upwind finish to a race, to head a sailboat into the wind and coast across the line on momentum.

Shrouds Ropes or wires led from the mast to chain plates at deck level on either side of the mast, which prevent the mast from falling or bending sideways.

Side force The lateral force exerted by wind on a sail, causing leeway or heel.

Slack A term used to describe a line that is not taut; the amount or degree of easement in a line; a command to ease a line.

Slack water The period of little or no current about halfway between maximum flood and maximum ebb currents.

Slot The opening between two adjacent sails that are set and filled, as between a jib and mainsail.

Spreaders Horizontal struts attached to each side of the mast and used to hold the shrouds away from the mast, thus giving them a wider purchase.

Stall Loss of flow of wind or water, caused by too abrupt a curve in the shape of a sail or too large an angle of attack by either a sail, keel, centerboard or rudder.

Starboard tack A sailboat is said to be on starboard tack when the wind is coming over its starboard side.

Stay A rope or wire supporting the mast and running forward or aft. The headstay is foremost, on which the jib is set; backstays lead aft from the masthead.

Surfing Traveling down the forward face of a wave so as to increase a boat's speed.

Tack The lower forward corner of a sail; also, to alter a boat's course through the eye of the wind. As defined by the racing rules, a boat is said to be tacking from the moment it is beyond head to wind until it has borne away on its new course with its mainsail filled.

Tacking downwind Making a series of broad reaches on alternate tacks to increase speed.

Tacking duel A racing maneuver, usually initiated by a trailing skipper, designed to help break away from a lead skipper's cover.

Telltale A piece of yarn tied to shrouds or sails to indicate the direction of the apparent wind.

Tidal current The horizontal movement of water caused by the ebbing and flooding of the tide.

Topping lift A line attached to the spinnaker pole that is raised or lowered to keep the spinnaker properly trimmed; also, a line from the masthead to the end of the main boom to support the boom.

Track A metal strip attached to a spar or a deck to accommodate one or more movable blocks or slides.

Trapeze A wire from a sailboat's mast attached to a harness worn by a crew member, allowing him to hike out with his entire weight suspended over the water.

Traveler A bar or track secured athwartships to a sailboat's deck so that the sheet of a sail, attached to the traveler by a block and slide, can move back and forth across it.

Trim To adjust the set of a sail relative to the wind; also, to adjust a boat's load so that the craft rides at the desired attitude.

True wind The wind as it blows freely across the water or land without regard to the movement of the boat.

Tune To alter or adjust a boat, its sails, rigging or engines, in order to improve its performance.

Turnbuckle A threaded, adjustable fastening that attaches a boat's shrouds and stays to fittings on the hull, and allows the tension of stays and shrouds to be adjusted.

Twist The difference in trim between the head of a sail and its foot due to the variance of wind speed and direction at different elevations on the sail.

Weather helm The tendency of a sailboat to head up toward the wind.

Wind shadow A zone of reduced wind speed and force on a sail's leeward side.

Yaw The angle between a boat's heading and its actual path through the water; also, the side-to-side deviation of a boat from its course caused by bad steering or by heavy seas.

Bibliography

General

Blanchard, Fessenden S., *The Sailboat Classes of North America.* Doubleday & Company, Inc., 1968.

Budd, Rhonda, ed., *Sailing Boats of the World, a Guide to Classes.* Prentice-Hall, 1974.

Colgate, Stephen, *Colgate's Basic Sailing Theory.* Van Nostrand Reinhold Company, 1973.

Henderson, Richard, *Sail and Power.* Naval Institute Press, 1973.

One-Design and Offshore Yachtsman editors, *Encyclopedia of Sailing.* Harper & Row, Publishers, 1971.

Rae, Rusty, *Speed and Spray.* The Stackpole Company, 1975.

Robinson, William, *Bill Robinson's Book of Expert Sailing.* Charles Scribner's Sons, 1965.

Scharff, Robert, *One-design Class Sailboat Handbook.* G. P. Putnam's Sons, 1961.

Sailing Theory

Howard-Williams, Jeremy, *Sails.* John de Graff Inc., 1967.

Marchaj, A. J., *Sailing Theory and Practice.* Dodd, Mead & Company, 1964.

Ross, Wallace, *Sail Power, the Complete Guide to Sails and Sail Handling.* Alfred A. Knopf Inc., 1975.

Racing Rules

A.P.B.A. Rule Book. American Power Boat Association, 1975.

Aymar, Gordon C., *Yacht Racing Rules and Tactics.* Van Nostrand Reinhold Company, 1970.

North American Yacht Racing Union, *The Yacht Racing Rules Including Team Racing Rules of the International Yacht Racing Union as Adopted by the North American Yacht Racing Union,* 1973.

United States Yacht Racing Union:
U.S.Y.R.U. Year Book, 1975.
Race Committee Manual, 1975.

Sailboat Racing Techniques

Bavier, Robert N., Jr., *Sailing To Win.* Dodd, Mead & Company, 1973.

Colgate, Steve, *Manual of Racing Techniques.* Offshore Sailing School, Ltd., 1975.

Elvström, Paul, *Expert Dinghy and Keelboat Racing.* Quadrangle Books, 1967.

Gülcher, Conrad, *Racing Techniques.* John de Graff Inc., 1968.

Hall, R. L., Jr., *Competitive Sailing.* American Design Industries, 1974.

Knapp, Arthur, Jr., *Race Your Boat Right.* Grosset & Dunlap, 1973.

Pinaud, Yves-Louis, *Sailing from Start to Finish.* Stein and Day, 1971.

Twiname, Eric, *Start to Win.* W. W. Norton & Company, Inc., 1974.

Walker, Stuart H., *The Tactics of Small Boat Racing.* W. W. Norton & Company, Inc., 1966.

Walker, Stuart H., ed., *The Techniques of Small Boat Racing.* W. W. Norton & Company, Inc., 1960.

Wells, Ted, *Scientific Sailboat Racing.* Dodd, Mead & Company, 1958.

History

Brown, C. Pennington, "The North Haven Dinghies." *Downeast,* August 1974.

Chapelle, Howard, *A History of American Sailing Ships.* W. W. Norton & Company, Inc., 1935.

Day, Thomas Fleming, ed., "The Half-Raters." *Rudder,* November 1895.

Ebb, W. J. and Robert W. Carrick, *The Pictorial History of Outboard Motors.* Renaissance Editions, Inc., 1967.

Elder, George W., *Forty Years among the Stars.* Schanen and Jacque, 1955.

Leavens, John, ed., *The Catboat Book.* International Marine Publishing Company, 1973.

Lipscomb, F. W., *A Hundred Years of the America's Cup.* New York Graphic Society, 1972.

Manley, Atwood, *Rushton and His Times in American Canoeing.* Syracuse University Press, 1968.

Paddlefast, "How to Build Cheap Boats, No. VIII." *Scientific American Supplement No. 42,* October 14, 1876.

Parkinson, John, Jr., *Seawanhaka Corinthian Yacht Club, The Early Twentieth Century 1897-1940.* New York, 1965.

Phillips-Birt, Douglas, *The History of Yachting.* Stein and Day, 1974.

Rosenfeld, Stanley and William H. Taylor, *The Story of American Yachting.* Appleton-Century-Crofts, Inc., 1958.

Slaughter, Sam C.:
"Age Before Beauty." *Yachting,* July 1952.
"Three Score and Ten." *Yachting,* April 1959.

Stephens, William P.:
Seawanhaka Corinthian Yacht Club, Origins and Early History 1871-1896. New York, 1963.
Traditions and Memories of American Yachting. Motor Boating, 1942.

Acknowledgments

Portions of *Racing* were written by Peter Swerdloff. For help given in the preparation of this book, the editors wish to thank the following: Harry Anderson, New York, New York; Bob Brown, Van Nuys, California; Mary Jane Danilek, Port Washington, New York; Phil and Althea Doolittle, Union Lake, Michigan; Larchmont Yacht Club Race Committee, Larchmont, New York; John Leavens, Chilmark, Massachusetts; David McComb, Greenwich, Connecticut; Atwood Manley, Canton, New York; Chuck and Cathy Millican, Pewaukee, Wisconsin; Virginia Moore, Pelham, New York; Mystic Seaport, Mystic, Connecticut; Mimi Neff, Seawanhaka Corinthian Yacht Club, Center Island, New York; Bob Nordskog, Van Nuys, California; C. Stanley Ogilvy, Mamaroneck, New York; Peabody Museum, Salem, Massachusetts; Rusty Rae, Westerville, Ohio; Stanley Rosenfeld, New York, New York; *Rudder* magazine, New York, New York; Mary Bruce Standley, Rowayton, Connecticut; Edward J. Steadman, Port Washington, New York; Roger Taylor, Camden, Maine.

Picture Credits

Credits from left to right are separated by semicolons, from top to bottom by dashes.

Cover—Christopher Cunningham. 6,7—Kenneth Wagner. 9—Robert N. Bavier Jr. 12—Michael Salas. 14—AMF—drawings by Roger Metcalf. 15—David Weiner—drawings by Roger Metcalf. 16—Drawings by Roger Metcalf—Tom Sawyer. 17—Chris Caswell—drawings by Roger Metcalf. 18—Dan Nerney—drawings by Roger Metcalf. 19—Drawings by Roger Metcalf—George Silk. 20—Chris Caswell; drawings by Roger Metcalf. 21—Drawings by Roger Metcalf—courtesy Coast Catamaran. 22—Diane Beeston; drawings by Roger Metcalf. 23—Drawing by Roger Metcalf—Stanley Rosenfeld. 24—Chris Caswell. 26,27—Drawings by Dale Gustafson. 28—Drawing by Dale Gustafson; drawings by John Sagan. 29—Drawings by Dale Gustafson; drawings by John Sagan. 30—Drawings by Dale Gustafson; drawings by John Sagan. 31,32,33—Drawings by Dale Gustafson. 34—Drawings by Roger Metcalf. 35—Drawings by Roger Metcalf and John Sagan—drawing by Roger Metcalf. 36—Drawings by Roger Metcalf—drawings by John Sagan. 37—Drawings by Roger Metcalf. 38,39—Drawings by William G. Teodecki. 40,41—Drawings by John Sagan. 42—Drawings by William G. Teodecki—drawings by John Sagan. 43—Drawings by William G. Teodecki—drawings by John Sagan. 44,45,46—Drawings by Dale Gustafson. 47—Drawing by John Sagan. 48,49—Drawings by Dale Gustafson. 50,51—From *The Catboat Book* by John M. Leavens, International Marine Publishing Co., Camden, Maine, courtesy Marshall Cook. 52—Morris Rosenfeld & Sons. 53—From Foster Collection, Hart Nautical Museum, M.I.T.—from *Scientific American* supplement, No. 42, October 14, 1876. 54,55—Courtesy Atwood Manley, except bottom left New York State Historical Association. 56—Reprinted with permission of *Rudder,* October 1895, ©Fawcett Publications Inc., copied by Frank Lerner—courtesy Seawanhaka Corinthian Yacht Club. 57—Courtesy Seawanhaka Corinthian Yacht Club. 58,59—Courtesy Mystic Seaport—courtesy Mrs. John David Lannon; Morris Rosenfeld & Sons. 60,61—Morris Rosenfeld & Sons. 62—Eric Schweikardt. 64—Courtesy Larchmont Yacht Club. 66—Drawings by John Sagan. 67,68,69—Eric Schweikardt. 70 through 79—Drawings by Dale Gustafson. 80—Eric Schweikardt. 81—John T. Hopf—drawing by John Sagan; courtesy United States Yacht Racing Union. 82—Dan Nerney. 84,85—Drawings by Whitman Studio, Inc. 86,87—Dan Nerney. 88 through 93—Drawings by Dale Gustafson. 94,95—Dan Nerney. 96 through 105—Drawings by Roger Metcalf. 106—Dan Nerney—Humphrey Sutton. 107—Drawing by Roger Metcalf. 108—Humphrey Sutton (2)—drawings by Nicholas Fasciano. 109—Humphrey Sutton. 110,111—Dan Nerney. 112,113—Drawings by Roger Metcalf. 114,115—Dan Nerney. 116—Drawings by Whitman Studio, Inc. 117—Dan Nerney. 118,119—Drawings by Whitman Studio, Inc. 120—Dan Nerney. 121, 122,123—Drawings by Whitman Studio, Inc. 124—Drawings by Walter Johnson. 125—Drawings by Whitman Studio, Inc. 126 through 130—Drawings by Fred L. Wolff. 131,132,133—Dan Nerney. 134 through 139—Drawings by John Sagan. 140—Stephen Green-Armytage. 142—Courtesy Huguenot Yacht Club—Stephen Green-Armytage. 143,144—Stephen Green-Armytage. 145—Chart by National Oceanic and Atmospheric Administration (NOAA), National Ocean Survey (NOS). 146—Chart and table by NOAA, NOS. 147—Courtesy Huguenot Yacht Club. 148, 149—Stephen Green-Armytage. 150,151—Stephen Green-Armytage, except bottom left courtesy Huguenot Yacht Club. 152 through 159—Morris Rosenfeld & Sons. 160,161—Eric Schweikardt for *Sports Illustrated.* 162,163—Al Freni (2)—Rusty Rae (2). 164—Rocky Weldon. 165—Eric Schweikardt for *Sports Illustrated.* 166,167—Stephen Green-Armytage for *Sports Illustrated.*

Index

Page numbers in italics indicate a photograph or drawing of the subject mentioned.

Printed in U.S.A.